D0436910

EDITORIAL RESEARCH REPORTS ON

THE Rights Revolution

Timely Reports to Keep
Journalists, Scholars and the Public
Abreast of Developing Issues, Events and Trends

Published by Congressional Quarterly Inc.
1414 22nd Street, N.W.
Washington, D.C. 20037

About the Cover

The cover was designed by Art Director Richard Pottern, who also provided many of the graphics in this book.

Editor, Hoyt Gimlin
Associate Editor, Sandra Stencel
Editorial Assistants, Diane Huffman, Patricia S. Ochs
Production Manager, I.D. Fuller
Assistant Production Manager, Maceo Mayo

Library of Congress Cataloging in Publication Data

Congressional Quarterly, Inc.
Editorial research reports on the rights revolution.

Bibliography: p.
Includes index.

1. Civil rights—United States. I. Title. II. Title: The rights revolution.
JC599.U5E36 323.4'0973 78-31931
ISBN 0-87187-144-0

Contents

Foreword

The once-vaunted vision of the American melting pot has been shattered in the last three decades by the emergence of countless minority groups demanding that their special needs be recognized and ministered to. Starting with the civil rights movement of the 1950s and 1960s, the demand for equal rights and for protection from discrimination spread to such diverse groups as women, the physically handicapped, Indians, homosexuals, the poor, and inmates of prisons, jails and mental institutions.

The list of those asserting their rights is practically endless. Children, for instance, are demanding the right to be recognized as legal "persons" capable of making decisions for themselves at home and at school. Welfare recipients argue that they have the right to more respect and better benefits. Terminally ill patients want the right to die with dignity. Non-smokers demand the right to ban smoking in public places, while smokers argue that they should have the right to light up whenever and wherever they want.

The rights movements have unquestionably bettered the lives of millions of Americans. But in recent years signs of a "rights backlash" have begun to appear. Voters in several cities have repealed ordinances barring discrimination against homosexuals. A group called the Interstate Congress for Equal Rights and Responsibilities is leading a nationwide protest against recent court decisions vastly expanding Indian rights. The Equal Rights Amendment, overwhelmingly passed by Congress in 1972, is stalled three states short of ratification. And growing numbers of white males, charging that they are victims of reverse discrimination, are going to court seeking redress.

Most observers believe that the emergence of a backlash movement is not likely to quiet demands for group rights. But the proliferating number and variety of discrimination complaints have raised serious questions about the limits of the rights revolution.

Sandra Stencel
Associate Editor

January 1979
Washington, D.C.

THE RIGHTS REVOLUTION

by

Sandra Stencel

June 23
1 9 7 8

Editor's Note: The pending Supreme Court ruling that is discussed in the box on page 5 was issued on June 28, 1978. The court ruled in favor of Allan Bakke, the white engineer who charged that reverse discrimination had blocked his efforts to get into medical school. But the court also held that it is constitutionally permissible for admissions officers to consider race as one of the complex of factors that determine which applicant is accepted and which is rejected.

On the question of the Equal Rights Amendment, discussed on page 9, Congress in October 1978 approved a resolution extending the deadline for ratification from March 22, 1979 to June 30, 1982.

THE RIGHTS REVOLUTION

OVER THE PAST three decades, Americans have witnessed a rights revolution. Starting with the civil rights movement of the 1950s and 1960s, the demand for equal rights and for protection from discrimination spread to such diverse groups as women, the physically handicapped, homosexuals, the poor and inmates of prisons, jails and mental institutions. "The result," wrote professor Milton R. Konvitz of Cornell University, "was an unprecedented period of progress toward equality within the nation."[1]

The rights movements have unquestionably bettered the social and economic positions of millions of Americans. At the same time, however, there is a growing fear that the demand for group rights has gone too far. The once-vaunted vision of the American melting pot is seen by some as being irreparably shattered by group demands for special treatment.

As these strains intensify, signs of a "rights backlash" are beginning to appear. In recent months, voters in Dade County, Fla., St. Paul, Minn., Wichita, Kan. and Eugene, Ore., have repealed ordinances barring discrimination against homosexuals. A group called the Interstate Congress for Equal Rights and Responsibilities is leading a nationwide protest against recent court decisions vastly expanding Indian rights. The Equal Rights Amendment, overwhelmingly passed by Congress in 1972, is stalled three states short of ratification. And growing numbers of white males, charging that they are victims of reverse discrimination, are going to court seeking redress.

The rights backlash, wrote Donald C. Bacon, associate editor of *U.S. News & World Report* magazine, "flows out of a broad concern on how far various groups can be accommodated without impairing not only national unity but standards of human character, individual and national achievement levels and the place of competition."[2] Much of the furor stems from the government's decade-old policy of requiring educators and employers to take "affirmative action" to prevent racial or sexual discrimination.

---

[1] Milton R. Konvitz, "The Flower and the Thorn," in *The Pulse of Freedom: American Liberties, 1920-1970s* (1975), edited by Alan Reitman, p. 218.

[2] Donald C. Bacon, "The 'Rights' Explosion Splintering America?" *U.S. News & World Report,* Oct. 31, 1977, p. 29.

To make up for alleged past discriminatory hiring practices, the government forced businesses and organizations holding federal contracts to set up goals and timetables for hiring women and minorities. "Once affirmative action programs were in place...," wrote Tom Bethell, the Washington editor of *Harper's* magazine, "it was foreseeable that the remainder of the population would soon devise ways of sectoring itself up into further minorities, so that they, too, could make a plausible claim upon the public conscience."[3]

The result has been a proliferating number and variety of discrimination complaints. In fiscal year 1970 the U.S. Equal Employment Opportunity Commission received 14,234 discrimination complaints. The number of complaints had reached 48,900 by 1973 and 79,311 by 1977. The commission estimates that this year it will process about 85,000.

Some observers maintain that claims of discrimination have gotten out of hand. In North Carolina, for example, two career marines charged that the Marine Corps unconstitutionally discriminated when it discharged them for being chronically overweight. In Kentucky, a left-handed postal clerk charged that the U.S. Postal Service discriminated against him by setting up its filing cases for the convenience of righthanded clerks. In Colorado, a 24-year-old man is suing his mother and father for "parental malpractice" and asking for $350,000 in damages *(see p. 459).* Cases such as these promoted one observer to write: "There must be some sensible bounds — no matter how elusive — to the claims that can be made in the name of non-discrimination....Too many excursions into absurdity...could make the whole cause of fair play seem silly."[4]

Repeal of Laws Protecting Homosexuals

"Too many excursions into absurdity" is one explanation given for the rights backlash. One of the first groups to feel the effects of the backlash has been homosexuals. The campaign against gay rights first gained national attention last year when singer Anita Bryant and her "Save Our Children" movement launched a drive to repeal a Dade County, Fla., ordinance that had been enacted in January 1977, banning discrimination in employment, housing and public accommodation based on a person's "affectional or sexual preferences." Bryant, a devout Baptist, argued that the statute condoned homosexuality, which she said was against God's law. She also claimed that the ordinance would force schools to hire homosexual teachers who could lead their students astray.

---

[3] Tom Bethell, "Anti-Discrimination Run Amuck," *Newsweek,* Jan. 17, 1977, p. 11. See also "Reverse Discrimination," *E.R.R.,* 1976 Vol. II, pp. 561-580.

[4] Frank Trippett, "The Sensible Limits of Non-Discrimination," *Time,* July 25, 1977, pp. 52-53.

The Bakke Case

The most publicized "reverse discrimination" lawsuit to grow out of the current rights backlash awaits a decision by the Supreme Court. The decision is expected before the Court's current term ends this month.

The case, *Regents of the University of California v. Allan Bakke,* is an attack on a government-decreed "affirmative action" program to place more blacks and other minorities in medical schools. Bakke, who is white, applied for admission to 13 medical schools in 1972 and 1973. He was turned down by all of them. He applied to the University of California at Davis for the second time in 1974 and was turned down again. On both occasions, 16 minority applicants were admitted to Davis under an affirmative action program.

Bakke sued the university, saying his grades and test scores were better than were those of most of the minority applicants who were admitted. The California Supreme Court agreed that he had been deprived of equal protection under the law. The university appealed the decision to the U.S. Supreme Court.

After an intense and often bitter campaign, the ordinance was overturned in June 1977 by a margin of more than two to one. The Miami vote was a catalyst for the repeal this year of similar ordinances in St. Paul (April 25), Wichita (May 9), and Eugene (May 23). There have been other signs of a backlash:

The day after the Miami vote, Florida Gov. Reubin Askew signed a law barring homosexuals from marrying members of the same sex or adopting children.

On Oct. 3, the Supreme Court refused to consider the case of a Tacoma, Wash., teacher who was fired after his school board discovered he was homosexual.

The Massachusetts legislature, on Oct. 13, defeated a bill that would have banned discrimination against homosexuals in public employment.

In May, the Supreme Court let stand a North Carolina law that makes it a crime for consenting adults, in private, to engage in homosexual acts.

Also in May, the General Assembly of the United Presbyterian Church voted overwhelmingly not to sanction the ordination of acknowledged, practicing homosexuals.

One of the next battles over homosexual rights will occur in California. An initiative to remove homosexual teachers from California public schools has qualified for the November general election ballot. The initiative, which was sponsored by State Sen. John V. Briggs, calls for firing teachers, teachers' aides, school administrators and counselors "for advocating, soliciting, imposing, encouraging or promoting private or public sexual acts defined in the penal code between persons of the same sex...."

The recent outpouring of anti-gay sentiment has surprised many homosexual leaders. Some admit that they underestimated the depth of public animosity. One reason for the hostility toward them may be that the public seems convinced that homosexuality is on the rise. Two of every three people, 66 per cent, interviewed by the Gallup polling organization in June 1977 said they believed homosexuality was more widespread than it was 25 years ago.[5]

Although a majority of those polled, 56 per cent, said that homosexuals should have "equal rights in terms of job opportunities," most would exclude gays from certain professions. For example, 65 per cent were against homosexuals as elementary school teachers, while 54 per cent were opposed to homosexuals as members of the clergy. When asked whether homosexual relations between consenting adults should be legal, 43 per cent said yes and 43 per cent said no; 14 per cent had no opinion.

Some gay activists welcome the publicity that the backlash movement is giving to the homosexual cause. "[Anita] Bryant is doing for us what we couldn't do ourselves — making gay rights a subject of household discussion," said Jean O'Leary, co-chairman of the National Gay Task Force in New York.[6] Others fear that all the publicity will provoke a further backlash. In either case, gay leaders have promised to continue the fight for homosexual rights.

Response to Indian Courtroom Victories

The debate over homosexual rights is taking place primarily at the local level. The battle over Indian rights, on the other hand, is being fought primarily in Congress and the federal courts.[7] At least 11 bills have been introduced in the 95th Congress which, if passed, would limit Indian rights, either directly or indirectly. The anti-Indian sentiment in Congress in part reflects constituent unhappiness with recent Indian court victories. "Of the last 12 'Indian cases' heard by the U.S. Supreme Court — in which tribes challenged one or another aspect of white tenure or authority — 11 were decided in favor of the Indians," according to free-lance writer Richard J. Margolis.[8] Lower court decisions also have tended to favor Native Americans in recent years.

Many of the cases involve Indian claims to huge tracts of land in several eastern states. The basis of the suits is the Non-

---

[5] "The Gallup Opinion Index: Homosexuals in America," October 1977, p. 10.

[6] Quoted in *The New Republic,* May 7, 1977, p. 15.

[7] See "Indian Rights," *E.R.R.,* 1977 Vol. I, pp. 265-288.

[8] Richard J. Margolis, "The New Indian Wars," *Foundation News,* May-June 1978, pp. 13-14.

Intercourse Act of 1790, which required that all land transactions between tribes and white settlers be authorized by Congress. Perhaps the most publicized suit was the one brought in 1972 by the Passamaquoddy and Penobscot tribes against the state of Maine. The Indians argued that the "sale" of their land in 1794 to Massachusetts — of which Maine was then still a part — was illegal since it was not ratified by Congress.

A U.S. District Court in Maine ruled in January 1975 that the Passamaquoddies and Penobscots were covered by the 1790 act and that the federal government was obligated to prosecute the Indians' claim. This decision was upheld by the U.S. Court of Appeals for the First Circuit in Boston in March 1976. Under court orders, the Justice Department entered the case on the side of the two tribes.

On Feb. 10, 1978, the Carter administration and the tribes announced that they had reached an agreement for an out-of-court settlement of the claim. The administration said it would seek passage of legislation which would provide the two tribes $25 million. In exchange, the Indians agreed to relinquish claims to all but about 3.3 million acres of land.[9] All claims against householders, small business, counties and municipalities would be dropped. According to the government, about 350,000 acres of the land still in dispute is held by the state; the remaining three million acres is held by approximately 14 large landowners. At this time it is not known whether the other parties to the suit will accept the agreement. Maine's Attorney General, Joseph Brennan, has called the proposal "irresponsible and indefensible."[10]

The suit in Maine has non-Indian landowners, real estate agents, bankers and state and city officials worried. There also is apprehension about claims in other parts of the country where treaties with the Indians were approved by Congress, but where the terms of the treaties were violated. Disputes also have arisen over Indian attempts to assert their rights to hunt, fish and use the water on or near their lands. In 1974, for example, a federal court in the state of Washington upheld an 1854 treaty which guaranteed Puget Sound Indian tribes 50 per cent of the "harvestable catch" of fish each year. The ruling created hostility between Indians and non-Indians in the area.

Another source of tension has been recent attempts by some tribes to get higher prices for the minerals and timber on their lands. The Indian reservations of the West are thought to contain between 25 and 40 per cent of all U.S. uranium, nearly one-third of all western coal and about 5 per cent of U.S. reserves of oil and

---

[9] In the original suit, the two tribes claimed 12.5 million acres.

[10] Quoted by Peter Kovler in "Native American Land Rights," *Inquiry,* May 15, 1978, p. 19.

natural gas. In 1976 over 20 western tribes set up the Council of Energy Resources Tribe (CERT) to determine mineral wealth on Indian lands and advise tribes on how to get higher prices for their resources. The chairman of the Navajo Tribal Council, Peter MacDonald, who led the move, explained the Indians' position. "We want to contribute to meeting America's goals of energy independence," he said, "but America will not be permitted to march to that goal as it marched to the Pacific — over the backs of this country's native peoples."[11]

The recent spate of Indian assertiveness has triggered substantial opposition in white communities. In 1975 a group called the Interstate Congress for Equal Rights and Responsibilities was set up in Winner, S.D., near the Rosebud Sioux reservation, to coordinate opposition to Indian legal victories. Today ICERR claims to have 10,000 members in 17 states who say they are victims of reverse discrimination. They complain that Indians vote and have a voice in local affairs but are not required to pay taxes. Moreover, they say that treaties setting out hunting and fishing rights give Indians a disproportionate share of the fish and game in their areas. The organization is supporting countersuits in 20 states contesting Indian claims to land, water and fishing rights, and its members are lobbying for passage of so-called "backlash" bills in Congress. The most extreme of these — H.R. 9054, introduced by Rep. John E. Cunningham (R Wash.) — would "abrogate all treaties entered into by the United States with Indian tribes."

Alarmed by such prospects, representatives of more than 120 tribes met in April at Window Rock, Ariz., on the Navajo reservation, to plan ways to counter the demonstrations and marches, call attention to their plight, and "educate" other Americans about the Indians' social and economic problems they still encounter. Suzan Harjo, a Cheyenne and the Washington representative of the Native American Rights Fund,[12] expressed the view of many Indian leaders: "When Indians tried to make their problems known by going outside the system — at Wounded Knee, for instance — everybody told us to work within the system. That is what we're doing. And if the government or anybody else is going to tell us — now that the system is working for us — that the system is wrong...well, I don't like to think of the consequences."

Working within the system, feminist leaders have discovered, does not always guarantee success. For six years, women's rights

---

[11] Quoted in *Newsweek,* March 20, 1978, pp. 62-63.

[12] NARF is based in Boulder, Colo. It was set up in 1971 with a grant from the Ford Foundation as a non-profit organization to protect Indian Rights. The group is controlled by Indian leaders and staffed largely by Indian attorneys.

advocates have been lobbying for approval of the Equal Rights Amendment. With the deadline for ratification only months away (March 1979), the drive appears to be stalled. Ratification has been won in 35 states — three short of the number needed to make the amendment part of the Constitution. Opponents of the amendment argue that its passage would end alimony and child support, would require military conscription of women, would ban separate washrooms for men and women, and permit homosexual marriages. Feminists dismiss such arguments as ridiculous, and accuse opponents of deliberately misinterpreting the effects of the amendment.

Conflict Over Equal Rights Amendment

Angered by what they consider unfair tactics on the part of opponents, ERA advocates are fighting back. More than 50 national organizations have agreed not to hold their conventions in states that have not ratified the amendment. The ERA boycott was organized in February 1977 by the National Organization for Women (NOW). Some persons worry that the boycott could intensify opposition to the Equal Rights Amendment. The tactic has been criticized even by some ERA supporters. Morris B. Abram, a New York lawyer and civil liberties advocate, called the boycott unjustified. Abram wrote last December: "As long as the equal protection clause of the Constitution stands, as long as free speech lasts, as long as women have the right to vote...there is no dire emergency that requires or justifies the holding of the people of whole states hostages in a campaign to enact a constitutional amendment."[13] Despite such criticism, ERA proponents are pressing ahead with the boycott. In fact, some are convinced that the amendment would be law if the boycott had been initiated sooner.

A resolution that would extend the ratification deadline from March 1979 to 1986 was approved by the Civil and Constitutional Rights Subcommittee of the House Judiciary Committee on June 5. The resolution is now before the full committee, where its future is uncertain; a similar measure was introduced in the Senate May 17 by Sen. Birch Bayh (D Ind.). Phyllis Schlafly, leader of the anti-ERA forces, called the extension effort "an act of desperation" and said she would fight it through lobbying and in court. "It's illegal and unfair," she said. "It's like a losing football team demanding that a fifth quarter be played. You can't change the rules in the middle of the game just because you're losing."[14] The extension was defended by Liz Carpenter of ERA-merica, an alliance of 200 pro-ERA organizations. "There must be no arbitrary barrier to ultimate justice in America," she told the House subcommittee May 17.

[13] Writing in *The New York Times,* Dec. 29, 1977.

[14] Quoted in the *Los Angeles Times,* Oct. 24, 1977.

Feminists believe that the struggle to ratify the Equal Rights Amendment provides further evidence that Americans remain deeply divided over the role of women in society. Over 56 per cent of the American women aged 20 to 64 work outside the home. Yet a nationwide survey conducted in 1976[15] found that the overwhelming majority of American parents — including three-fourths of the working mothers interviewed — believe that women with small children should not work unless the money is really needed. Nearly 70 per cent of the parents said that children were better off when their mothers did not work.

The public's ambivalence about the women's movement was made clear by the results of an April 1977 Louis Harris poll. On the one hand, the poll indicated that between 1970 and 1977 the number of Americans favoring "efforts to strengthen and change women's status in society" grew from 42 to 64 per cent. On the other hand, the poll indicated that between 1976 and 1977 the number of Americans favoring passage of the Equal Rights Amendment dropped from 65 to 56 per cent. By February 1978, according to another Harris poll, the number supporting the amendment had dropped to 51 per cent.

Changing Tenor of Protest

THE RIGHTS REVOLUTION began with the black civil rights movement of the 1950s and 1960s. The decade following the Supreme Court's landmark Brown decision in 1954,[16] which overturned the "separate but equal" doctrine for public education, was a period of demonstrations in which blacks and their sympathizers took to the streets, facing up to heckling, intimidation, attack, arrest and reprisal. The demonstrations focused public attention on the grievances of American Negroes and instilled in them the confidence that they had the power to force change in a system that disabled and humiliated them. The demonstrations had specific objectives as well, and the record shows that by taking to the streets blacks scored significant victories for their cause.

The heightened militance of the Negro protest movement was evident in the demonstrations which broke out in Birmingham, Ala., in the spring of 1963. The Birmingham demonstrations created an atmosphere of crisis that led to new local and federal

---

[15] By Yankelovich, Skelly and White for the General Mills Consumer Center. Results published in "The General Mills American Family Report 1976-77: Raising Children in a Changing Society," 1977.

[16] *Brown v. Board of Education,* 347 U.S. 483 (1954).

action for protection of Negro rights. Intensive news coverage of the Birmingham events, including police attacks on demonstrators, stirred sympathy for the Negro both at home and abroad and inspired demonstrations in other communities. In the spring and summer of 1963 there were sit-ins, boycotts, rallies, kneel-ins, wade-ins, picketing and other demonstrations involving hundreds of thousands of persons. "The summer of 1963 was a revolution...," wrote Dr. Martin Luther King Jr. "Its fever boiled in nearly 1,000 cities, and by the time it had passed its peak, many thousands of lunch counters, hotels, parks and other places...had become integrated."[17]

The Birmingham situation precipitated action on national civil rights legislation. The measure President Kennedy proposed on June 19, 1963, and which was finally signed into law by President Johnson on July 2, 1964, gave the strongest boost to Negro rights since Reconstruction. The Civil Rights Act of 1964 barred racial discrimination (1) in public accommodations, (2) in employment practices of most businesses and (3) in any program or activity receiving federal assistance.

An important gap in federal legislation on civil rights was a measure that would actually prevent the denial of a Negro's right to vote in localities where that right was systematically withheld from him. Previous civil rights amendments had created legal machinery to protect the right to vote in federal elections, but blacks complained that it was ineffective and cumbersome.

Dr. King once more took action to bring on a crisis situation to force government action. His voting rights campaign in Selma, Ala., in the winter of 1965, like the earlier demonstrations in Birmingham, was marked by violence. It led to conflicts with local authorities and provoked sympathy demonstrations in many other places. The last act of the drama was a four-day, five-mile march from Selma to Montgomery, carried out by thousands of black demonstrators and white sympathizers under the protection of federalized National Guard troops.

The Voting Rights Act of 1965, signed into law on Aug. 6, provided for direct federal action to enable blacks to register and vote. Its passage led to the enfranchisement of hundreds of thousands of new black voters and helped elect blacks to public office in the South and throughout the nation.

Urban Riots, Black Power, White Backlash

Five days after President Johnson signed the Voting Rights Act of 1965, a riot broke out in the Watts section of Los Angeles. In terms of death and destruction, the Watts riot was the worst racial disorder in the nation's history. Six days of terrorism left

[17] Martin Luther King Jr., *Why We Can't Wait* (1963), p. 127.

34 dead, 856 wounded and damage approaching $200 million. In succeeding summers Negro neighborhoods in city after city erupted in violent outbursts. The urban riots, Bayard Rustin wrote, "brought out in the open, as no other aspect of the Negro protest [had] done, the despair and hatred that continued to brew in the northern ghettos despite the civil rights legislation of recent years and the...war on poverty."[18]

The deep, underlying cause of urban riots was "the racial attitudes and behavior of white Americans toward black Americans," the National Advisory Commission on Civil Disorders reported to President Johnson in 1968. In one of the most controversial statements written during the 1960s, the commission held that the persistence of "white racism" was moving the nation "toward two societies, one black, one white — separate and unequal."

Although the country remained essentially sympathetic toward black aspirations for equality, there was a discernible stiffening of resistance to rapid change. A Louis Harris public-opinion survey taken in the fall of 1966 showed that 75 per cent of the whites interviewed thought blacks were moving too fast. Only 50 per cent felt that way two years before. In the South resentment built up against the efforts of the Department of Health, Education and Welfare to enforce the 1964 Civil Rights Act by requiring schools and hospitals to desegregate. In the North a "white backlash" was directed against efforts of civil rights leaders to bus school children and break down the pattern of segregated housing. The emotional impact of the housing issue was reflected by the refusal of Congress in 1966 and 1967 to pass new civil rights legislation containing "open housing" provisions.[19]

The shift in public attitudes and congressional inaction on civil rights in 1966 and 1967 gave impetus to the emerging "black power" movement.[20] The phrase was introduced by Stokley Carmichael, chairman of the Student Nonviolent Coordinating Committee, during the "March Against Fear" through Mississippi in June 1966, but it expressed tendencies that had long been present in the black community. Blacks were angry and bitter over the increasing attacks on civil rights workers in the South and the failure of the Justice Department to protect them. The murders of Michael Schwerner, Andrew Goodman and James Chaney near Philadelphia, Miss., during the summer of

---

[18] Bayard Rustin, *Down the Line* (1971), p. 140.

[19] Congress passed the Fair Housing Act of 1968 on April 10, six days after Dr. King's assassination. When fully implemented in 1970, the act prohibited discrimination in the sale or rental of 80 per cent of all housing, including single-family residences. For details, see Congressional Quarterly's *Congress and the Nation, Vol. II* (1969), pp. 378-388.

[20] See "Negro Power Struggle," *E.R.R.*, 1968 Vol. I, pp. 123-140 and "Black Pride," *E.R.R.*, 1968 Vol. II, pp. 663-680.

1964 fueled the growing belief in the necessity of armed self-defense. Disillusionment with non-violent protest grew with the recognition that success often came only after some social disorder or even violence occurred. By the mid-1960s "the distinction between direct action and violence began to disappear both in the mind of the general public and among many activists."[21]

Emergence of 'Gay Lib' and 'Red Power'

This observation was not lost on other minority groups which, spurred by the success of the civil rights movement, had begun to organize and demonstrate for their rights. All of the emerging minorities, including homosexuals, American Indians and women, faced the problem of attracting the nation's attention. The fewer the people affected, the more difficult was this task. Mass demonstrations, marches and violent protests helped generate interest among the press, legislators and the public. This, in turn, frequently led to legislative and judicial victories.

The emergence of the "Gay Liberation Movement" as a full-fledged social-protest movement is traced to June 27, 1969, when New York City policemen raided the Stonewall Inn, a bar in Greenwich Village catering to homosexuals. The bar patrons resisted arrest and brawled with the police for several hours that night, to the apparent surprise of both groups. This turn of events — homosexuals openingly fighting for their claim to civil rights — imparted a new sense of boldness to many other homosexuals. Within a month, the first Gay Liberation Front group was organized in New York City. By the second anniversary of the "Stonewall Rebellion" other militant homosexual organizations, including the Gay Activist Alliance, had sprung up all across the country. Gay Pride Week, commemorating the Stonewall incident, became an annual event and homosexual-sponsored protest demonstrations were a frequent sight.[22]

The late 1960s also was a time of growing, and often violent, Indian assertiveness. Indian militants were not mollified by Title II of the Civil Rights Act of 1968 — the Indian Bill of Rights — which (1) said that the states could not assume civil or criminal jurisdiction over Indian areas without tribal consent and (2) prohibited Indian tribal governments from depriving members of specified constitutional rights. White liberals applauded the law for finally recognizing that Native Americans had the same rights as other citizens. Many Indians reacted differently, criticizing the law as another example of the old assimilationist policies which sought to destroy tribal customs and undermine the Indians' communal way of life.

---

[21] August Meir and Elliott Rudwick, *Core: A Study in the Civil Rights Movement 1942-1968* (1973), p. 299.

[22] See Homosexual Legal Rights," *E.R.R.*, 1974 Vol. I, pp. 181-200.

Indian grievances against the government fueled a Red Power movement and led to numerous demonstrations and confrontations, many of them organized by the militant American Indian Movement (AIM). In 1965, Indian groups banded together to stage a series of "fish-ins" in defense of Indian fishing rights in Washington state. Four years later, in November 1969, Indians gained national attention by seizing Alcatraz Island in San Francisco Bay. Since that time, militant Native Americans have occupied, or attempted to occupy, other public sites, including a Coast Guard station in Milwaukee, Ellis Island in New York harbor, the deactivated Army post of Ft. Lawton in Seattle, offices of the Bureau of Indian Affairs in Washington, D.C., the hamlet of Wounded Knee on the Pine Ridge Reservation in South Dakota, and part of Adirondack State Park in New York.

Probably the most publicized of these incidents was AIM's occupation of Wounded Knee, which began on Feb. 27, 1973, and lasted 71 days. The lengthy confrontation resulted in two Indian deaths, the wounding of several Indians and law-enforcement officers, $240,000 in damages and 300 arrests of persons trying to enter or leave the village. The occupation was intended to dramatize the government's violation of the Ft. Laramie Treaty of 1868, which stated: "No white person or persons shall be permitted to settle upon or occupy any portion of the territory or without the consent of the Indians to pass through the same."

Conscious Raising in Women's Movement

The climate of protest that pervaded the 1960s was ideal for the emergence of militant feminism in the manner and shape it took. Disillusionment with reform played its part among women righters as it had with other aggrieved groups. Civil rights and welfare legislation had not remade the world for the blacks and for the poor, and gains in women's rights had not lessened the feeling women had of being at a disadvantage because of their sex.

A major contribution to the development of the women's liberation movement was the publication of *The Feminine Mystique,* written in 1963 by Betty Friedan. She called on women to escape from what she considered the deadening enclosure of suburban domesticity and to seek a more fulfilling life as human beings. Interest stirred by her book led Friedan and others to found the National Organization for Women (NOW) in 1966 to serve as an activist group for bringing pressure on government and industry to end sex discrimination.

Another factor in the emergence of militant feminism was the experiences of women in other protest movements, including the civil rights movement and the protest against the Vietnam War. Though these movements generally were dedicated to an egalitarian ideal and opposed the prevailing "power structure," the women found that they were no less victims of sexist oppression in their groups than they were in the larger society. Realizing that men in the liberal and radical movements were not ready to accept women as equals, the women decided to strike out on a feminist struggle of their own.

In their battle to eliminate sexism, feminists employed a variety of tactics, including "consciousness raising" sessions.[23] By talking together in small groups women began to recognize their shared disabilities and thus discover the relevance of the liberation movement to their own situation. Numerous demonstrations served to widen the range of recognition of the movement beyond the immediately affected circle. Some of these actions — picketing and sit-ins — had a specific objective, as when the women protested a particular form of sex discrimination. But many of the actions were taken primarily to "raise women's consciousness of their social oppression and reveal men to themselves as oppressors."[24]

Much of what seemed silliest or most outrageous in women's lib activism was a form of "street theater," a tactic borrowed from other protest movements for gaining attention to the cause. The so-called bra-burning episode, for example, did as much as anything in liberation activism to push the movement to the forefront of national consciousness. In fact, bras were not burned. The occasion was a protest on Sept. 7, 1968, against the Miss America beauty pageant in Atlantic City, which the protestors denounced as one of many ways society demeans women. A group of women threw undergarments, hair rollers, and high-heeled shoes into a trash can — discarding symbols of the male ideal of feminine allure.

Purported Ethnic Resentment of Blacks

In the late 1960s and early 1970s another voice was added to the swelling chorus of American protestors. It was the voice of ethnic Americans.[25] Much criticized as bigots and racists, ethnics viewed themselves as forgotten people, trapped between poor blacks and Spanish-speaking Americans who were eligible for public assistance, and the WASPS (white Anglo-Saxon Protestants) who controlled the power structure.

Hostility between white ethnics and the black community, many observers said, was triggered by the implementation of President Johnson's "Great Society" programs. "Blacks were increasingly seen as the major beneficiaries of these programs and quickly became the targets of other groups frustrated by their in-

[23] See "Women's Consciousness Raising," *E.R.R.*, 1973 Vol. II, pp. 497-516.
[24] Cellestine Ware, *Woman Power: The Movement for Women's Liberation* (1970), p. 130.
[25] See "Ethnic America," *E.R.R.*, 1971 Vol. I, pp. 45-64.

ability to receive what they perceived to be their fair share," wrote Fred Barbaro in 1974. "As the [Vietnam] War effort consumed more and more resources...anti-black sentiments increased. Non-black minority groups reasoned that there would be only one pie, that it was being baked for and consumed by blacks, and that they must more aggressively stake their claims if they wished to receive a slice of that pie."[26]

The estrangement between white ethnics and blacks was noted as early as 1965 by sociologist Nathan Glazer, who attributed it to "conflicts over the adoption and administration of fair employment laws, fair housing laws and measures to combat *de facto* school segregation."[27]

A recent study by the National Opinion Research Center at the University of Chicago indicates that the extent of "white backlash" in the early 1970s may have been exaggerated. "The facts do not support the common assumption that the pace of liberalization in racial matters has been slowed by a white backlash," the study concluded. "Instead the rate of change toward a more integrationist attitude has been rather constant since 1963, with a short period of faster change in the early 1970s."[28] The authors of the study found this pattern to be true even among white ethnic groups, with the greatest increases in racial tolerance among ethnics being registered by Irish, Italian and Slavic Catholics.

Future of the Rights Struggle

MOST OBSERVERS BELIEVE that the emergence of a backlash movement is not likely to quiet demands for group rights. Harvard sociologist David Riesman, for example, predicts that there will be more questioning of rights in the future. "The growth of grievance groups leads to an increase in the number of individuals who feel they are aggrieved," he said earlier this year.[29]

The list of those asserting their rights is practically endless. Children, for instance, are demanding the right to be recognized as legal "persons" capable of making decisions for themselves at home and in school *(see p. 18).* Welfare recipients argue that

[26] Fred Barbaro, "Ethnic Resentment," *Society,* March-April 1974, p. 67.

[27] Nathan Glazer, "The Peoples of America," *The Nation,* Sept. 20, 1965, reprinted in *The Annals of America, Vol. II,* pp. 261-267. See also Nathan Glazer and Daniel Patrick Moynihan, *Beyond the Melting Pot* (1963).

[28] D. Garth Taylor, Paul B. Sheatsley and Andrew M. Greeley, "Attitudes Toward Racial Integration," *Scientific American,* June 1978, p. 45.

[29] Quoted in *U.S. News & World Report,* March 27, 1978, p. 40.

they have a right to more respect and better benefits. Tenants are demanding the right to decent housing. Terminally ill patients want the right to die with dignity.[30] Non-smokers demand the right to ban smoking in public places, while smokers argue that they should have the right to light up whenever and wherever they want.[31]

For years older people have been lobbying for the right to work as long as they are physically able. Under pressure from such groups as the Gray Panthers, the National Council on Aging and the National Council of Senior Citizens, Congress, on March 23, 1978, cleared legislation which raised the mandatory retirement age from 65 to 70 in private industry and removed it altogether for federal employees.[32]

The government also has intervened on behalf of the nation's alcoholics and drug addicts. Earlier this year, Attorney General Griffin B. Bell ruled that the Rehabilitation Act of 1973 — which prohibits discrimination against handicapped individuals in federally assisted programs — covers persons who are alcoholics or drug addicts "so long as their addiction does not prevent effective job performance." As a result of the ruling, the Justice Department, in May 1978, filed a "friend-of-the-court" brief on behalf of a Brooklyn College professor who said that he was denied tenure because of a drinking problem.

Rights for Handicapped, Institutionalized

The Rehabilitation Act was an important victory in the struggle for equal rights for the handicapped.[33] The act was twice vetoed by President Nixon before its final enactment in 1973, and some disabled persons say that the battle over this legislation was the catalyst which helped unify the handicapped activist movement. Among other things, the act required that any company or organization with a federal contract amounting to more than $2,500 must take "affirmative action" to employ and promote the handicapped. In addition, the measure provided that any handicapped individuals who felt they were being discriminated against in employment could file complaints with the Department of Labor.

The act also stated, in what is often called a landmark provision, that "no otherwise qualified handicapped individual in the United States...shall, solely by reason of his handicap, be excluded from participation in, be denied the benefits of, or be subject to discrimination under any program or activity receiving federal financial assistance."

[30] See "Right to Death," *E.R.R.*, 1978 Vol. I, pp. 61-80.
[31] See "Anti-Smoking Campaign," *E.R.R.*, 1977 Vol. I, pp. 41-60.
[32] For details see *Congressional Quarterly Weekly Report*, April 1, 1978, pp. 807-808, and "Mandatory Retirement," *E.R.R.*, 1977 Vol. II, pp. 849-868.
[33] See "Rights of the Handicapped," *E.R.R.*, 1974 Vol. II, pp. 885-904.

A major aim of the movement has been elimination of architectural barriers which impede the mobility of handicapped people, especially the wheelchair-bound. The Rehabilitation Act established a board to supervise compliance with the Architectural Barriers Act of 1968, which required that all buildings financed with federal funds must be designed, constructed or remodeled in order to be accessible to the physically handicapped. Another concern of the handicapped has been the right to education. It is estimated that six million school-age children in the United States have mental, physical, emotional or learning handicaps. In recent years school districts around the country have taken steps to implement the provisions of a 1975 law which granted all disabled children the right to a free public education.

The Education for All Handicapped Children Act, as the law is known, requires that specifically designed instruction to meet the unique needs of the child be provided at no cost to parents or guardians. Moreover, special education must be provided in the "least restricted" environment. That means that to the maximum extent possible, handicapped children must be educated with children who are not handicapped. The placement of handicapped with non-handicapped children — which is known as "mainstreaming" — is the most controversial element of the 1975 law. Some educators contend that teachers in regular classrooms are not equipped to deal on a regular basis with handicapped students.

Congress now is considering a bill, sponsored by Rep. Robert W. Kastenmeier (D Wis.), to authorize the Justice Department to initiate or intervene in lawsuits to safeguard the rights of persons confined to state-operated prisons, mental institutions, nursing homes, juvenile centers and facilities for the chronically ill. The bill, approved by the House Judiciary Committee on April 18, 1978, would allow the federal government to bring suits against state-operated or funded-institutions where (1) the Justice Department finds a "pattern or practice" of violations of the constitutional rights of persons in an institution and (2) where the Attorney General certifies that federal intervention is of "general public importance" and will lead to the vindication of the rights of the institutionalized.[34]

Attempt to Improve Child's Legal Status

Historically, legal rights and responsibilities have been reserved for adults. Children have been treated paternally, their conduct controlled by parents or others in authority. Such control has been justified by the notion that children need to be protected from the harshness of the outside world until they become strong and clever enough to cope with it. But it has

[34] For details see *Congressional Quarterly Weekly Report,* April 29, 1978, pp. 1071-1078.

become clear that the interests of children do not always coincide with those of their parents or of the state, and in recent years there have been attempts to change the legal status of children.

"By and large, the legal profession considers children — when it considers them at all — as objects of domestic relations and inheritance laws or as victims of the cycle of neglect, abuse and delinquency," wrote an Arkansas attorney and child advocate, Hillary Rodham, in the *Yale Law Journal* in June 1977. "Yet the law's treatment of children is undergoing great challenge and change. Presumptions about children's capacities are being rebutted; the legal rights of children are being expanded."

The movement for children's rights is being led by a handful of legal centers specializing in law for children. They include the Youth Law Center in San Francisco, the Children's Defense Fund in Washington, D.C., and the National Coalition for Children's Justice in Princeton, N.J. At present, the movement for children's rights is focusing on two general themes: extending more adult rights to children and seeking legally enforceable recognition of children's special needs and interests.

The first approach is exemplified by proposals for (1) extending all the rights of adult criminal defendants to accused delinquents, (2) empowering children to request medical care without parental consent and (3) providing a child with legal representation in any situation where his or her interests are affected. The second approach to children's rights begins with the belief that even if all adult rights were granted to children and were strictly enforced, this would not guarantee that certain needs unique to children would be met. This line of reasoning finds expression in various bills of rights which have been proposed for children, including the rights to adequate nutrition, a healthy environment, continuous loving care, and intellectual and emotional stimulation.[35]

Many lawmakers and lawyers are reluctant to change laws to enlarge the rights of children because they say it would lead to discord in the family. Expanding children's rights, they argue, would only encourage more suits like the one filed in May 1978 by Tom Hansen, 24, of Boulder, Colo. Institutionalized twice in mental hospitals since he was 17, Hansen is demanding $250,000 in compensatory damages and $100,000 in punitive damages because, he claims, his parents neglected his needs for "food, clothing, shelter and psychological support." Most legal scholars doubt that Hansen's suit will survive. But it has raised questions about the limits of the rights revolution.

---

[35] For background information see *Trial* magazine, May-June 1974, pp. 11-40, and *Harvard Educational Review*, November 1973 and February 1974.

Books

Berger, Morroe, *Equality By Statute: The Revolution in Civil Rights,* Doubleday, 1967.
Fraenkel, Osmond K., *The Rights We Have: A Handbook of Civil Liberties,* Thomas Y. Crowell, 1971.
Humphrey, Hubert H., *Beyond Civil Rights: A New Day of Equality,* Random House, 1968.
Konvitz, Milton R., *Expanding Liberties: Freedom's Gains in Postwar America,* Viking, 1966.
Reitman, Alan, ed., *The Pulse of Freedom: American Liberties, 1920-1970s,* W. W. Norton, 1975.

Articles

Bacon, Donald C., "The 'Rights' Explosion Splintering America?" *U.S. News & World Report,* Oct. 31, 1977.
Berlow, Alan, "Rights of Institutionalized: Whose Problem?" *Congressional Quarterly Weekly Report,* April 29, 1978.
Chapman, William, "Native Americans' New Clout," *The Progressive,* August 1977.
"Fat People's Fight Against Job Bias," *U.S. News & World Report,* Dec. 5, 1977.
Ferleger, David, "The Battle Over Children's Rights," *Psychology Today,* July 7, 1977.
Kleinfield, Sonny, "The Handicapped: Hidden No Longer," *The Atlantic Monthly,* December 1977.
Kovler, Peter, "Native American Land Rights," *Inquiry,* May 15, 1978.
Margolies, Richard J., "The New Indian Wars," *Foundation News,* May-June 1978.
Mathews, Tom, "Battle Over Gay Rights," *Newsweek,* June 6, 1977.
"Reverse Discrimination: Has It Gone Too Far?" *U.S. News & World Report,* March 29, 1976.
Ross, Ken, "Gay Rights: The Coming Struggle," *The Nation,* Nov. 19, 1977.
Stein, Howard F. and Robert F. Hill, "The Limits of Ethnicity," *The American Scholar,* spring 1977.
Taylor, D. Garth *et al.,* "Toward Racial Integration," *Scientific American,* June 1978.
Williams, Roger M., "Women Against Women: The Clamor Over Equal Rights," *Saturday Review,* June 25, 1977.

Reports and Studies

Editorial Research Reports, "Black Americans, 1963-73," 1973 Vol. II, p. 623; "Homosexual Legal Rights," 1974 Vol. I, p. 181; "Indian Rights," 1977 Vol. I, p. 265; "Reverse Discrimination," 1976 Vol. II, p. 562; "Rights of the Handicapped," 1973 Vol. II, p. 623; "Women's Consciousness Raising," 1973 Vol. II, p. 499.
U.S. Commission on Civil Rights, "The State of Civil Rights: 1977," February 1978.

EQUAL RIGHTS FIGHT

by

Sandra Stencel

Dec. 15
1 9 7 8

Editor's Note: At least three state legislatures took action on the Equal Rights Amendment early in their 1979 sessions. The Wyoming Senate narrowly defeated a resolution to retract the Wyoming legislature's 1973 approval of the amendment. In Nevada, ERA met defeat for the fourth straight session. And in Virginia, the Senate Privileges and Elections Committee for the seventh time in as many years blocked a proposal to ratify the amendment.

EQUAL RIGHTS FIGHT

THE STRUGGLE to ratify the Equal Rights Amendment (ERA) is beginning to resemble the ordeal of Tantalus — the mythical Greek king who was condemned to perpetual hunger and thirst, with food and water lying just beyond reach. So far, 35 state legislatures have ratified the proposed amendment to prohibit discrimination on the basis of sex *(see box, p. 25)*. Only three more must do so before it becomes part of the Constitution. But it is entirely possible that the ERA will die inches short of its goal. Organized resistance remains strong in all 15 of the remaining states — some of which have defeated the amendment over and over — and no consensus exists on which three states, if any, might raise the total to the required 38.

Congress in October approved a resolution extending the deadline for ratification from March 22, 1979, to June 30, 1982. Passage of the resolution capped a year-long lobbying effort by backers of the amendment and marked the first time Congress had extended the ratification period for a constitutional amendment since it began setting time limits in 1917. Women's rights advocates hope the extension will give momentum to the stalled equal rights drive.

The last state to ratify the ERA was Indiana, which did so in January 1977. Since then the amendment has suffered a string of defeats. In the last two years resolutions to approve the amendment were defeated in Alabama, Arizona, Florida, Illinois, Missouri, Nevada, North Carolina, South Carolina and Virginia. In the other eight unratified states *(see map)*, ERA resolutions did not come up for a vote in 1977 or 1978. Furthermore, legislatures in three states — Tennessee, Nebraska and Idaho — voted to rescind earlier ratifications, although there is a legal question as to whether the rescissions will be permitted to stand *(see p. 38)*.

ERA supporters received a double setback in the November elections when voters in Florida and Nevada — two key states in the ratification drive — decisively rejected proposals which were viewed as test votes on the amendment. Florida voters rejected an amendment to the state Bill of Rights that would have forbidden discrimination against women. In Nevada, an advisory referendum asked voters if they favored passage of the amendment; over half of those going to the polls said no.

ERA proponents are by no means resigned to defeat. They point to public opinion polls which have consistently shown widespread support for the amendment. A poll conducted by the Gallup organization in June 1978 indicated that 58 percent of the respondents favored ratification. A Louis Harris poll conducted the same month found 55 percent in favor of the amendment. Support appears to have increased in the past year after a two-year period of decline. Earlier Harris polls indicated that between 1976 and 1977 the number of Americans favoring passage had dropped from 65 to 56 percent. By February 1978 the number supporting the ERA had dropped to 51 percent.

ERA supporters contend that the results of last month's elections bolstered their chances for winning approval of the amendment. "We are very, very pleased at the strong showing by candidates who support ratification," Mildred Jeffrey, head of the National Women's Political Caucus, said Nov. 9. She said that candidates which the caucus endorsed won 35 of 47 state senate races and 71 of 96 state house races. But opponents of the amendment also saw cause for optimism in the election results. "We feel we gained in every legislature," said Phyllis Schlafly, a leader of the anti-ERA forces.

Growing Resistance to Women's Movement

The extent of the opposition to the Equal Rights Amendment surprised many feminists. When Congress finally passed the amendment on March 22, 1972 — after a 50-year struggle *(see p. 30)* — it seemed like an idea whose time had come. Supporters predicted that it would be ratified well before the original 1979 deadline. Early reaction seemed to promise quick ratification. In the first two years after Congress approved it, 32 states ratified the amendment. But only three more have done so in the four years since then. "Success came too easily and we were not prepared," Dr. Jo Freeman, a political scientist, said recently. "There's always a backlash to social movements, and we were caught sleeping."[1]

Feminists believe that the struggle to ratify the Equal Rights Amendment provides further evidence that Americans remain deeply divided over the role of women in society. Over 50 percent of all adult American women now are in the labor force.[2] Yet a nationwide survey conducted in 1976[3] found that the overwhelming majority of American parents — including three-fourths of the working mothers interviewed — believed that

[1] Quoted in *The Christian Science Monitor,* Oct. 19, 1978.

[2] Figures, released by the Department of Labor in October 1978, include women looking for work as well as those actually working.

[3] By Yankelovich, Skelly and White for the General Mills Consumer Center. Results published in "The General Mills American Family Report 1976-77: Raising Children in a Changing Society," 1977.

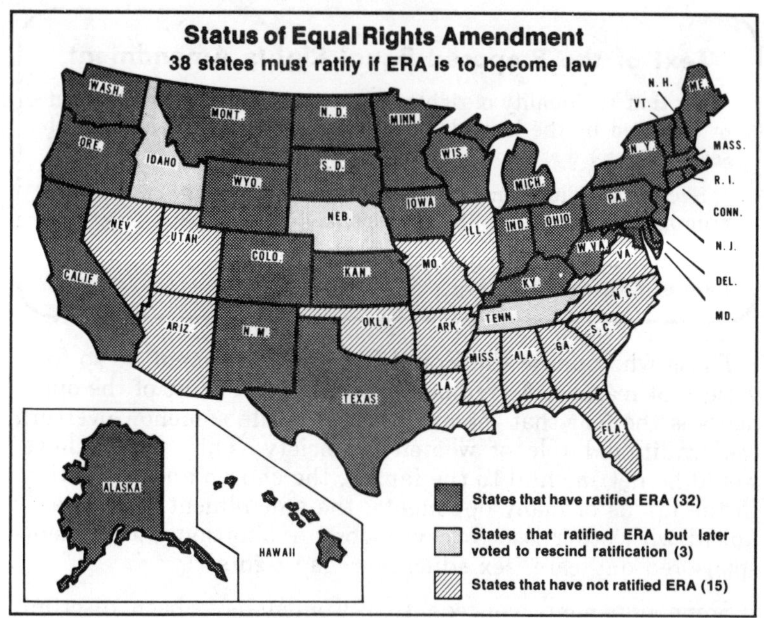

women with small children should not work outside the home unless the money is really needed. Nearly 70 percent of the parents said that children were better off when their mothers did not work.

Women's rights groups generally acknowledge that divisions within their ranks over tactics and priorities hampered the ratification effort. They also admit that at first they tended to underestimate the determination and political savvy of the opposition. But most believe that the chief obstacle to ratification has been what they consider unfair tactics on the part of ERA opponents. Legislators in unratified states have been flooded with literature linking the Equal Rights Amendment with lesbianism and the disruption of family life.

Anti-ERA groups argue that the amendment's passage would end alimony and child support, require military conscription of mothers, ban separate washrooms for men and women, and permit homosexual marriages. Feminists dismiss such arguments as ridiculous and charge opponents with deliberately misinterpreting the effects of the amendment. But they concede that such charges have put them on the defensive. "We've found ourselves arguing about women being drafted and losing custody of their children, instead of discussing discrimination in housing, insurance and credit," said New York lawyer Brenda Feigen Fasteau. "We cannot spend all our time telling our opponents how wrong they are and not go after the votes of grass-roots politicians."[4]

[4] Quoted in *Newsweek*, July 25, 1977, p. 35.

Text of the Proposed Equal Rights Amendment

Section 1. Equality of rights under the law shall not be denied or abridged by the United States or by any State on account of sex.

Section 2. The Congress shall have the power to enforce, by appropriate legislation, the provisions of this article.

Section 3. This amendment shall take effect two years after the date of ratification.

Those who oppose the Equal Rights Amendment do so for a variety of reasons. A common thread linking most of the opponents is the fear that the amendment would somehow overturn the traditional role of women in society. This, they believe, would be detrimental to the family, the church and the nation. In the minds of many opponents, the amendment is invariably linked with other issues they oppose — abortion, government-sponsored day care, sex education, gay rights.

Some opponents concede that women have been discriminated against. But they argue that specific legislation, such as equal-pay and equal-credit laws, are a better remedy than a sweeping constitutional amendment. Some admit that they personally have benefitted from improved opportunities for women in recent years. But they do not want to be associated with the "militant women-libbers" who, they say, are pushing the Equal Rights Amendment.

In most states conservative political groups and fundamentalist churches have led the opposition. Mormons, for example, have been instrumental in preventing ratification in Utah, Nevada and Arizona. The hierarchy of the Catholic Church has shown strong opposition to the amendment. A major committee of the National Conference of Catholic Bishops last May refused to endorse the amendment on the ground that it would, as one spokesman said, "pave the way for more abortions." On the other hand, many priests, nuns and lay members of the Church have indicated support for the amendment.

The nation's leading foe of the Equal Rights Amendment is Phyllis Schlafly of Alton, Ill. Long active in conservative Republican politics and a three-time unsuccessful candidate for Congress, Mrs. Schlafly publishes a monthly newsletter called the *Phyllis Schlafly Report* and has written eight books, the best known of which is *A Choice Not an Echo,* which boosted the 1964 presidential candidacy of Barry M. Goldwater. It was in the February 1972 issue of the *Phyllis Schlafly Report* that Mrs. Schlafly first publicly attacked the Equal Rights Amendment, then pending in Congress. To help in her anti-ERA campaign, she set up an organization called Stop-ERA, and it has chapters across the country. Later she established a second group, the Eagle Forum, which she called her answer to "women's lib" and it, too, joined the fight against the proposed amendment.

Since 1972 Schlafly has campaigned tirelessly against the ERA, which she calls the "extra responsibility amendment." In her view it would give women no new rights and it would take away some old ones while adding new responsibilities. "The claim that American women are downtrodden and unfairly treated is the fraud of the century," she once said. "The truth is that American women have never had it so good. Why should we lower ourselves to 'equal rights' when we already have the status of special privilege."[5]

Mrs. Schlafly has concentrated her opposition to the Equal Rights Amendment primarily around the issues of military service and financial support laws. In her latest book, *The Power of the Positive Woman* (1977), she contends that the amendment would "require mothers to be drafted" and "invalidate all the state laws that require the husband to support his wife and family and provide them with a home."[6]

Reaction of Supporters to Recent Setbacks

Women's rights activists have reacted to the backlash with a mixture of rage and frustration. But the success of the opposition has forced them to reassess their strategies. "ERA proponents, armed with what they regarded as the righteousness of their cause . . . neglected the political tactics by which any cause must be advanced," Roger M. Williams observed in 1977.[7] Williams also criticized ERA proponents for placing most of their state campaigns in the hands of feminist activists and female legislators.

"While [these women] may 'deserve' to direct the battle," he wrote, "they are seldom the best people for the job — the former because their ideological commitment is ill-suited to a political arena, the latter because they are vastly outnumbered, relatively inexperienced and, on this issue, seldom willing to make the routine trade-offs that would improve the chances of success." While some feminists might regard Williams' remarks as sexist, few could deny that in many of the unratified states ERA supporters were outmaneuvered by opponents who skillfully lobbied state legislators.

Feminists have made a concerted effort in recent years to broaden their appeal. The National Organization for Women, the largest of the women's rights groups, has doubled its mem-

[5] Quoted by Lisa Cronin Wohl in "Phyllis Schlafly: The Sweetheart of the Silent Majority," *Ms.*, March 1974, pp. 55-56.

[6] Phyllis Schlafly, *The Power of the Positive Woman* (1977), pp. 72, 99.

[7] Roger M. Williams, "Women Against Women," *Saturday Review*, June 25, 1977, p. 13.

bership in the past 18 months. Much of the credit is given to NOW's president, Eleanor Smeal, who identifies herself as a Pittsbugh housewife. "By assuring women that the movement is not trying to force them out of their homes, she has projected a new image of the organization and expanded its constituency," a recent article in the *Christian Science Monitor* noted.[8]

Concentration of Lobbying in Four States

Amendment backers are concentrating their lobbying efforts in four states — Florida, Illinois, North Carolina and Oklahoma. Florida long has been considered a must-win state by the amendment's supporters. They were stunned when the Florida Senate narrowly defeated the amendment in April 1977. State Sen. Lori Wilson, who sponsored the resolution, attributed that defeat to the "good ole boy" tradition in southern life.

So far this year the ERA resolution has not been brought up in the Florida legislature. The legislature is not scheduled to convene again until April 2, 1979. Gov. Reubin Askew, who is leaving office in January, had indicated that he might take up the issue at a special session of the legislature in December. But because proponents could not assure him that they had the votes for ratification, ERA was left off the agenda. ERA's prospects in Florida also were hurt when the state's voters in November rejected an amendment to the state's constitution that would have banned discrimination on the basis of sex.

Illinois, the only northern industrial state that has not ratified the amendment, has been a special source of frustration for ERA proponents. To pass in Illinois, the amendment must be approved by a three-fifths vote of each house. Last June the Illinois House of Representatives twice rejected the amendment, despite a personal appeal from President Carter, the support of Republican Gov. James R. Thompson and a massive lobbying effort by the League of Women Voters.[9]

ERA has been the subject of repeated votes in the Illinois legislature during the past six years. Before the two June ballots, the House had voted on the amendment six times and the Senate five times. In 1975 the amendment passed with 113 votes in the House, only to be bottled up in a Senate committee. ERA supporters still insist they can win in Illinois, but a spokesman for ERA-America, a coalition of some 200 groups supporting the amendment, recently said that the outlook was "quite iffy." In North Carolina, the amendment appears to have lost ground, ac-

[8] *Christian Science Monitor,* Oct. 19, 1978. At its annual meeting in Washington, D.C., on Oct. 8, NOW voted to focus most of its resources during the next year on the ERA ratification drive.

[9] The second vote, on June 22, was 105 to 71, just two votes short of the number needed for approval. The first vote, on June 7, fell six short of ratification; five black legislators who had been considered supporters of the amendment abstained because of a dispute with the House leadership.

cording to an analysis of the November election results by *The New York Times.*[10]

Supporters believe that there now are just 21 solid "yes" votes in the state Senate, five short of the 26 needed for ratification. They are afraid that anti-ERA forces will seek a Senate vote on the amendment shortly after the legislature convenes Jan. 10, in the hope that it will fail. ERA backers also face an uphill battle in Oklahoma, where the amendment has failed three times in the House but passed once in the Senate. The amendment has the support of Oklahoma Gov.-elect George Nigh.

Prospects for the amendment in the other 11 unratified states are not good, at least not next year. Many of the remaining states are in the South *(see map),* where support for the amendment is lowest. Supporters thought they had a chance last year in Virginia, where the amendment had the support of the state's labor unions. But their efforts failed when the House Privilege and Elections Committee refused to bring the question to the floor for a vote.

Debate Over Impact of Economic Boycott

Virginia and the 14 other ERA holdouts are paying a price for their opposition. Over 50 business, political and professional associations have agreed not to hold their conventions in states that have not ratified the amendment. The list includes the Democratic National Committee, the League of Women Voters, the National Council of Churches, the National Education Association, the American Psychological Association and the United Auto Workers union.

The boycott, which is backed by the National Organization for Women, has had considerable impact on such big convention cities as Atlanta, New Orleans, Chicago and Miami Beach. There are no exact figures on overall losses incurred in these and other cities, but estimates run into the millions. The Chicago Convention and Tourism Bureau estimated that as of September 1977 the city had lost $15 million. As a result, the bureau passed a resolution supporting the ERA and urging state legislators to ratify it.

Missouri officials have estimated that the ERA boycott has caused the loss of at least $1.1 million in convention business in the Kansas City area alone. The estimate was included in an antitrust suit filed by the state against the National Organization for Women last February. The suit alleges that the boycott constitutes an illegal restraint of trade. Representatives of several national organizations testified in U.S. District Court in Kansas City Nov. 7 that NOW did not influence their decisions

[10] *The New York Times,* Nov. 27, 1978.

to move their conventions out of unratified states. U.S. District Court Judge Elmo B. Hunter indicated that he will not issue a ruling in the case until early next year.

Some persons worry that the boycott could intensify opposition to the amendment. The tactic has been criticized even by some ERA supporters. Morris B. Abram, a New York lawyer, wrote last year: "As long as the equal protection clause of the Constitution stands, as long as free speech lasts, as long as women have the right to vote...there is no dire emergency that requires or justifies the holding of the people of whole states hostages on a campaign to enact a constitutional amendment."[11] Despite such criticism, ERA proponents are pressing ahead with the boycott. In fact, some are convinced that the amendment already would be law if the boycott had been initiated sooner.

Long Struggle for ERA Passage

THE EQUAL RIGHTS AMENDMENT has been a source of controversy since it first was proposed in the early 1920s. Endorsed by one wing of the suffrage movement and opposed by the other, the amendment "embroiled the woman's movement in bitter strife and as much as anything else prevented the development of a united feminist appeal," William Henry Chafe wrote in 1972.[12]

The conflict over the Equal Rights Amendment can be traced back to the split between the more militant and conservative suffragettes. The militants, led by Alice Paul, founder of the National Woman's Party, turned to picketing, hunger strikes and other radical tactics when their lobbying efforts failed to persuade more congressmen to give woman the vote. The more conservative suffragettes, led by the National American Woman Suffrage Association (NAWSA), thought such actions would antagonize the people who would be needed for the suffrage movement to succeed.

The split between the two wings of the suffrage movement widened after the Nineteenth Amendment was ratified in 1920, giving women the right to vote. The conservatives felt their mission was accomplished, and turned their attention to an array of social reforms, including wage-hour laws, child-labor bans, social security and welfare measures, provisions for maternal-child health and other public health programs.

[11] Writing in *The New York Times*, Dec. 29, 1977.

[12] William Henry Chafe, *The American Woman: Her Changing Social, Economic and Political Roles, 1920-1970* (1972), p. 113.

The more radical suffragettes, on the other hand, viewed the vote as only an intermediate step on the road to full sexual equality. Only by inscribing the principle of female equality in the basic law of the land, they maintained, could women achieve true parity with men. The National Woman's Party in 1921 embarked on a campaign for an Equal Rights Amendment. Such a proposal first was introduced in Congress in 1923 by two Kansas Republicans, Sen. Charles Curtis and Rep. Daniel R. Anthony Jr. "The Woman's Party wished to eliminate in one blow all remaining laws which distinguished between men and women," William Henry Chafe wrote. "To campaign in each state for piecemeal reform, the feminists reasoned, would take years of effort. Consequently they relied on a blanket amendment which would outlaw all discriminatory legislation throughout the country."[13]

Continued Opposition to ERA During 1940s

Congress showed little interest in the Equal Rights Amendment from 1923 to 1940, safely burying the measure in committee year after year. The Woman's Party, the National Federation of Business and Professional Women and other early supporters continued to lobby for it, arguing that only a constitutional guarantee could eliminate continuing discrimination against women. In 1940, 11 states provided that a wife could not hold her own earnings without her husband's consent; 16 states denied a married woman the right to make contracts; seven states favored the father in custody cases; over 20 states prohibited women from serving on juries. Early supporters of the Equal Rights Amendment were particularly concerned about laws fixing the conditions under which women could be employed. In the mid-1940s, 43 states limited the daily and weekly hours a woman could work outside the home; 15 states prohibited night work for women.

Many states in the 1940s restricted the types of jobs women could hold. In Pennsylvania, for example, women were prohibited from working as crane operators, welders, truckers, meter readers, or on railroad tracks or in boiler rooms. At least 17 states prohibited women from working in the mines. Ohio had the longest list of occupational restrictions. Women were banned from bowling alleys, pool rooms and shoe-shine parlors; they could not handle freight or baggage, operate freight elevators, guard railroad crossings, or operate vehicles for hire.[14]

Opposition to the Equal Rights Amendment remained strong during the 1940s. Among the organizations which were prominent in the campaign against the amendment were the National

---

[13] *Ibid.*, p. 116.

[14] "Summary of State Labor Laws for Women," Women's Bureau, Department of Labor, August 1944.

League of Women Voters, the National Women's Trade Union League, and the American Association of University Women. In 1944 a "National Committee to Defeat the Un-Equal Rights Amendment" was organized. It included representatives from 42 organizations, among them the American Federation of Labor (AFL), the Congress of Industrial Organizations (CIO), American Civil Liberties Union, National Farmers Union, American Federation of Teachers, Young Women's Christian Association, and the National Councils of Catholic Women, of Jewish Women and of Negro Women.

The amendment was opposed by Frances Perkins, President Roosevelt's Secretary of Labor, and by the director of the Labor Department's Women's Bureau, Mary Anderson. Anderson denounced the amendment as "vicious," "doctrinaire"and "a kind of hysterial feminism with a slogan for a program." She also said it would be meaningless "because most of the real discriminations against women were a matter of custom and prejudice and would not be affected by a constitutional amendment."[15]

Attempt to Preserve Protective Legislation

What bothered Anderson and the other opponents of the amendment the most, especially organized labor, was its potentially destructive effect on protective legislation for women. The amendment, they feared, would endanger wage and hour laws for women, undermine support laws for wives and children, and terminate special penalties in the law for rape and sexual offenses against women. Secretary Perkins, testifying before the Senate Judiciary Committee in 1945, said that special labor laws for women represented a realistic recognition of biological differences which no constitutional amendment could alter. Their effect, she said, had been to lessen inequalities between men and women in industry.

ERA supporters argued that the position of working women could be improved by the removal of protective legislation based on sex. Many of the conditions originally cited to justify special laws, they pointed out, had improved by the 1940s. The only purpose of protective legislation, Maud Younger wrote in 1934, was "to lower women's economic status, keep them in the ranks with little chance for advancement...and perpetuate the psychology that they are cheap labor and inferior to other adult workers."[16]

Most ERA supporters insisted that they were not advocating the removal of all protective legislation, but merely the removal

[15] Mary Anderson, *Women at Work* (1951), pp. 163, 168.

[16] Maud Younger, "The NRA and Protective Laws for Women," *Literary Digest,* June 2, 1934, p. 27.

of the sex basis in most protective laws. "Protective legislation," said Alice Paul of the National Woman's Party, "should be made to apply to everyone alike so that industrial conditions may be definitely improved."[17]

Public and Congressional Support in 1970s

While women's groups argued among themselves about the ramifications of an Equal Rights Amendment, the fight for approval continued in Congress. From the late 1940s to 1970 the proposed amendment remained buried in the House, but it was favorably reported out of Senate committees or subcommittees at least ten times.[18] The first time the amendment was voted on by the full Senate was 1946 and it was defeated. The Senate in 1950 and 1953 passed resolutions to place the amendment before the states for ratification, but both times with a rider which supporters of the amendment said would have made it meaningless. The rider, introduced by Sen. Carl Hayden, D-Ariz., stated that the amendment "shall not be construed to impair any rights, benefits or exemptions now or hereafter conferred by law upon members of the female sex."

Support for the amendment picked up in the 1960s and early 1970s. Among its staunchest advocates during this period was the National Organization for Women, founded in 1966 by Betty Friedan, author of *The Feminine Mystique.*[19] Interest in the amendment also spread to civil libertarian groups, such as the American Civil Liberties Union (ACLU), and to government agencies. The Department of Labor, which for decades had opposed the ERA, switched its position in 1969 when Elizabeth Duncan Koontz became director of the department's Women's Bureau. The Citizens Advisory Council on the Status of Women[20] endorsed the amendment for the first time in February 1972. The council's Feb. 12 bulletin stated that "ratification. . . is the most effective and expeditous method of securing equal protection of the laws for women, who lag 40 years behind minority groups in achieving constitutional protection."

Among those who changed their position on the amendment during this period was Rep. Edith Green, D-Ore. She told her House colleagues on Oct. 12, 1971: "In the past I rejected the idea of an Equal Rights Amendment, arguing . . . that wrongs

---

[17] Quoted by June Sochen in *Movers and Shakers: American Women Thinkers and Activists, 1900-1970* (1973), pp. 118-119.

[18] See Mary A. Delsman, *Everything You Need to Know about ERA* (1975), p. 30, and "Equal Rights Amendment," *E.R.R.*, 1946 Vol. I, pp. 217-236.

[19] In *The Feminine Mystique* (1963), often referred to as the bible of feminism, Friedan denounced the forces in society that depicted women as sexpots or idealized them as perfect housewives and mothers.

[20] The council was established by executive order of the president in 1963 to advise government agencies on the status of women.

could be righted, and more quickly, through the legislative process and through the courts. But through the years I have watched the legislative actions on both the national and state levels and I have come to the conclusion that I was wrong . . . and that the groups who supported the Equal Rights Amendment were correct."

Increased public support for the amendment was translated into increased support in Congress. In July 1970, Rep. Martha W. Griffiths, D-Mich., succeeded in extracting the proposal from the House Judiciary Committee, a burial ground for the measure in years past, by getting the required 218 signatures of members on a discharge petition. The measure then went to the floor for debate. Less than a month later, on Aug. 10, 1970, the House approved the equal rights measure by a 350-15 vote.

The House-passed measure was placed directly on the Senate calendar, without approval by the Senate Judiciary Committee. After three days of debate in October, senators added two amendments to the ERA resolution — one upholding existing laws exempting women from the military draft and another guaranteeing the right of non-denominational prayers in public schools. Passage of the amendments was tantamount to defeat of the bill because it meant that a House-Senate conference would have been required to resolve differences between the two versions. The leader of the House conferees would have been Emanuel Celler, D-N.Y., chairman of the House Judiciary Committee, who for 20 years had refused to hold hearings on the Equal Rights Amendment in the House. The Senate adjourned without taking a final vote on the ERA resolution and the measure died at the end of the 91st Congress.[21]

The House approved the measure again in October 1971, after stripping it of a provision which the House Judiciary Committee had added, stating: "This article shall not impair the validity of any law of the United States which exempts a person from compulsory military service or any other law of the United States or of any state which reasonably promotes the health and safety of the people." Women's rights advocates argued that the effect of the additional language would be to undermine ERA's usefulness. In the Senate, a companion measure was introduced by Birch Bayh, D-Ind. But Senate action was postponed until 1972, partly due to the illness of Bayh's wife, Marvella, who was recovering from a cancer operation.

The chief Senate opponent of the Equal Rights Amendment was Sam J. Ervin Jr., D-N.C. Ervin asserted that the amendment, which he called the unisex amendment, would "have a

[21] See *1970 CQ Almanac*, p. 706.

most serious impact upon the social structure of America and for that reason, in my opinion, would constitute evil."[22] He said if the amendment were ratified, women would be conscripted into the armed services "and sent into battle to have their fair forms blasted into fragments by the bombs and shells of the enemy." He agreed that the "traditional customs and usages of society undoubtedly subject women to many discriminations." But he went on to say that since these discriminations "are not created by law, they cannot be abolished by law. They can be altered only by changed attitudes in the society which imposes them." Amending the Constituton to correct harm done by outmoded state laws, Ervin concluded, "would be about as wise as using an atomic bomb to exterminate a few mice."

Despite Ervin's opposition, the Senate finally approved the Equal Rights Amendment on March 22, 1972, and sent it to the states for ratification. Less than two hours later, Hawaii became the first state to ratify it. By the end of 1972, 21 other states had followed suit. But the problems which were to plague the ratification drive quickly became apparent. By January 1973, *The New York Times* was reporting that ratification of the Equal Rights Amendment no longer looked like a sure thing.

Future of the Ratification Drive

HAVING STRUGGLED so long and so hard to get the Equal Rights Amendment through Congress, many feminists find it difficult to accept the possibility that the amendment might not be ratified by the requisite 38 states. If the ERA is blocked, Betty Friedan said last spring, "it will be politically disastrous . . . . We will be set back 50 years." NOW President Eleanor Smeal concurred. Defeat of the amendment, she said, "might give a false message to the courts and state legislatures that the country does not want to have a policy against sex discrimination. The unthinkable risk is that we might go backward in the gains for women."[23]

Some feminists worry about the effect that defeat would have on the morale of the women's movement. But Gloria Steinem, the founder of *Ms.* magazine, insists that the feminist drive will persist even if the amendment fails to be ratified. "Some people would be very discouraged and bitter for six months, and I'm sure a few would never come back," she said. "But there's no

[22] Senate floor debate March 20, 1972.

[23] Both Friedan and Smeal were quoted in *The New York Times,* May 31, 1978.

turning back. No matter how discouraged we get, looking at where we've come from is more than enough to keep us moving ahead."[24]

Since The Equal Rights Amendment resolution was passed by Congress in 1972, new federal and state legislation and court decisions have provided women equal credit, educational and employment opportunities and moved to eliminate inequities in Social Security benefits.[25] But Steinem and other women's rights advocates stress that there still are thousands of laws on the books that discriminate against women. In a title by title review of the U.S. Code released in April 1977, the U.S. Commission on Civil Rights found hundreds of federal statutes that contained "unwarranted sex-based differentials."[26]

The cumulative effect of the sex-bias in the U.S. Code, the commission stated in a later report, "was to assign to women, solely on the basis of their sex, a subordinate or dependent role."[27] A report on the employment prospects of professional women and minorities released in November 1978 by the Department of Labor found that women with college degrees earned substantially less in 1976 than white male high school dropouts. According to Betty M. Vetter, co-author of the report, white men who dropped out of high school earned an average of $9,379 in 1976; white women with college degrees averaged $7,176.

Attempts to Determine Amendment's Effects

Whether or not the Equal Rights Amendment is ratified, there undoubtedly will be plenty of lawsuits over sex discrimination for years to come. If the amendment is adopted, the lack of specifics in its language leaves lots of room for interpretation by the courts. "The language of the ERA is written in the same grand manner in which many constitutional guarantees have been written," UCLA Law Professor Kenneth L. Karst said last year. "That's an advantage to courts in the long run. But in the near future . . . lots of litigation will be required."[28]

If the courts are called on to interpret the Equal Rights Amendment, they will rely to a large degree on its legislative history as contained in the Senate Judiciary Committee's 1972 report recommending its approval.[29] The report states, in part:

---

[24] Quoted in *The New York Times,* May 31, 1978.

[25] See "Reverse Discrimination," *E.R.R.,* 1976, Vol. II, pp. 561-580; "Women in the Work Force," *E.R.R.,* 1977 Vol. I, pp. 121-142; and "Burger Court's Tenth Year," *E.R.R.,* 1978 Vol. II, pp. 681-700.

[26] "Sex Bias in the U.S. Code," U.S. Commission on Civil Rights, April 1977.

[27] "The State of Civil Rights: 1977," U.S. Commission on Civil Rights, February 1978, p. 23.

[28] Quoted in the *Los Angeles Times,* Nov. 21, 1977.

[29] "Equal Rights for Men and Women," Senate Judiciary Committee, 92nd Congress, 2nd session (1972).

Essentially, the amendment requires that the federal government and all state and local governments treat each person, male and female, as an individual. It does not require that any level of government establish quotas for men or for women in any of its activities; rather, it simply prohibits discrimination on the basis of a person's sex. The amendment applies only to government action; it does not affect private action or the purely social relationships between men and women.

Most experts agree that the amendment would require that qualified women, as well as men, be subject to the draft and that the full range of military activities, including combat duty, be open to women. It would ban sexually segregated public schools and require that the obligations of spouses toward one another and of parents toward their children be defined in sexually neutral terms. But as the legislative history makes clear, there would be some key limitations to the general rule of sexual equality under the law. These exceptions occur for (1) situations which relate to the individual's constitutional right to personal privacy and (2) situations which relate to a unique physical characteristic of one sex. Thus the Equal Rights Amendment would not require both sexes to share restrooms or that colleges, prisons and the military services put men and women in the same barracks or dormitories.

Perhaps the best evidence of what the Equal Rights Amendment would mean comes from the 16 states that have written equal rights amendments into their own constitutions.[30] "The general trend, both in terms of common-law doctrines and statutory law, has been for courts in ERA jurisdictions to strike down outdated or unreasonable restrictions on one sex and to extend important rights, benefits and obligations to members of both sexes."[31] In Illinois, for example, a court ruled that under the state's equal rights amendment, a mother may not automatically be preferred over the father in deciding child custody after divorce. A state university in Texas was told that the state amendment required it to provide on-campus housing for men as well as women and to allow women as well as men to live off campus.

The state Supreme Court in Washington ruled that husbands as well as wives should not be denied unemployment benefits for leaving work to follow their spouses to a new location under

---

[30] In nine of the states — Colorado, Hawaii, Maryland, Massachusetts, New Hampshire, New Mexico, Pennsylvania, Texas and Washington —— the equal rights provisions closely resemble the federal amendment. In the other seven states — Alaska, Connecticut, Illinois, Montana, Utah, Virginia and Wyoming — the state provisions vary, but most are less inclusive than the federal proposal.

[31] Barbara A. Brown, Ann E. Freedman, Harriet N. Katz and Alice M. Price, *Women's Rights and the Law: The Impact of the ERA on State Laws* (1977), p. 32.

appropriate circumstances. The Pennsylvania Supreme Court ruled that a husband may no longer be presumed to be the sole owner of property acquired during the marriage, even if he paid for most of it.

Expected Challenges to Rescission Attempts

The future of the Equal Rights Amendment is clouded by several unresolved issues. Opponents of the measure, led by Phyllis Schlafly, have promised to challenge in the courts the resolution extending the ratification deadline to 1982. The courts will be asked to decide whether Congress had the power to extend the deadline and whether an extension would require a simple majority vote of the House and Senate, as was the case, or whether it would require a two-thirds vote.

Although Article V of the Constitution specifies how many states must ratify an amendment before it becomes law, it is silent on the question of how long the process may take. The Supreme Court ruled in 1921 *(Dillon v. Gloss)* that ratification should come "within some reasonable time after the proposal." On the question of what constitutes a "reasonable limit of time for ratification," the court held in 1939 *(Coleman v. Miller)* that it is a political matter which Congress is empowered to determine.

Until 1919 Congress set no time limits on the passage of constitutional amendments. The Eighteenth Amendment (Prohibition) was the first to specify a deadline for ratification. Three subsequent amendments contained a deadline in their texts. Since 1951, the time limitation has been included in resolutions proposing amendments rather than in the amendments. Traditionally, seven years has been the maximum time allowed.

Another unanswered question in ERA's future is whether the states can rescind ratification. In recent years the legislatures of four states — Nebraska, Tennessee, Idaho and Kentucky — have voted to rescind earlier approval of the Equal Rights Amendment. But in Kentucky, the rescission bill was vetoed by Lt. Gov. Thelma Stovall who was acting governor while Gov. Julian Carroll was out of the state. During the debate over extension of the ratification deadline, opponents argued that it would be unfair to allow the states more time to approve the Equal Rights Amendment without giving those states that had ratified it a chance to change their minds. In approving the extension bill, however, the Senate rejected a rescission amendment sponsored by Jake Garn, R-Utah.

The constitutionality of rescission never has been tested. The Department of Justice takes the position that once a state has

Amending the Constitution

Article V of the U.S. Constitution provides two methods for amending the Constitution — (1) via a convention called by Congress at the request of the legislatures of two-thirds of the states or (2) by a two-thirds majority vote of each house of Congress. Of the two methods only the latter has been used. An amendment that is proposed by Congress or by a Constitutional convention does not become part of the Constitution until after it is approved, or ratified, by the legislatures of three-fourths of the states or by constitutional conventions in three-fourths of the states. Congress determines which form of ratification will be employed. The president has no formal authority over constitutional amendments (his veto power does not extend to them); nor can governors veto legislative approval of amendments.

ratified a proposed amendment it cannot reverse the decision. Assistant Attorney General John M. Harmon told the House Judiciary Subcommittee on Civil and Constitutional Rights in November 1977 that Article V of the Constitution "gives the states the power to ratify a proposed amendment, but not the power to reject." ERA opponents disagree. They point out that although the Constitution only gives Congress the power to make laws, no one questions the authority of Congress to repeal laws.

Many legal experts, including Harvard Law Professor Laurence H. Tribe, contend that the final determination on rescission will rest with Congress. Before the amendment becomes law, Congress must certify that 38 states properly ratified it. At that time Congress will decide whether a state that rescinded its ratification should be included among the 38 ratifiers. The only historical precedent for this occurred when Congress ignored rescission attempts by Ohio and New Jersey in the ratification of the Fourteenth Amendment. Although the courts are likely to defer to Congress' judgment on rescission, Tribe added that "in a very close case, the courts might agree to review the congressional decision."[32]

Whatever the fate of the Equal Rights Amendment, the battle over ratification has had important side effects. It has prompted legislative reform aimed at eliminating sex discrimination from state and federal statutes. It has been at least partly responsible for the dramatic shift in judicial treatment of sex discrimination cases. And, according to Robert O'Leary of Common Cause, it "has served to pump people into the political process in the states more than any other issue."[33] But these achievements will be small comfort to women's rights advocates if the Equal Rights Amendment is not ratified.

[32] Quoted by Robert Shrum in "ERA Extension: All's Fair," *New Times*, Nov. 13, 1978, p. 7.

[33] Quoted by Jeff Mullican in "ERA: Beginning of the End?" *State Legislatures*, March-April 1978, p. 6.

Books

Alexander, Shana, *State-By-State Guide to Women's Legal Rights,* Wollstonecraft, Inc., 1975.

Brown, Barbara A., Ann E. Freedman, Harriet N. Katz, and Alice M. Price, *Women's Rights and the Law: The Impact of the ERA on State Laws,* Praeger, 1977.

Chafe, William Henry, *The American Woman: Her Changing Social, Economic, and Political Roles, 1920-1970,* Oxford University Press, 1972.

Delsman, Mary A., *Everything You Need to Know About ERA,* Meranza Press, 1975.

O'Neill, William L., *Everyone Was Brave: The Rise and Fall of Feminism in America,* Quadrangle Books, 1969.

Ross, Susan C., *The Rights of Women: The Basic ACLU Guide to a Woman's Rights,* Avon, 1973.

Schlafly, Phyllis, *The Power of the Positive Woman,* Arlington House, 1977.

Sochen, June, *Movers and Shakers: American Women Thinkers and Activists, 1900-1970,* Quadrangle, 1973.

Stimpson, Catherine, ed., *Women and the "Equal Rights" Amendment: Senate Subcommittee Hearings on the Constitutional Amendment, 91st Congress,* R.R. Bowker Co., 1972.

Articles

Congressional Digest, June-July 1977.

Ginsburg, Ruth Bader, "From No Rights, to Half Rights, to Confusing Rights," *Human Rights,* May 1978.

Miller, Judith, "ERA in Trouble," *The Progressive,* May 1977.

Mullican, Jeff, "ERA: Beginning of the End?" *State Legislatures,* March-April 1978.

O'Reilly, Jane, "The Bogus Fear of ERA," *The Nation,* July 8-15, 1978.

"The Unmaking of an Amendment," *Time,* April 25, 1977.

"What's Your ERA IQ?" *National Business Woman,* October 1978.

"Why Woman's Lib is in Trouble," *U.S. News & World Report,* Nov. 28, 1977.

Williams, Roger M., "Women Against Women: The Clamor Over Equal Rights," *Saturday Review,* June 25, 1977.

Wohl, Lisa Cronin, "Phyllis Schlafly: The Sweetheart of the Silent Majority," *Ms.,* March 1974.

Reports and Studies

Editorial Research Reports, "Equal Rights Amendment," 1946 Vol. I, p. 217; "Status of Women," 1970 Vol. II, p. 563; "Women's Consciousness Raising," 1973 Vol. II, p. 497; "Reverse Discrimination," 1976 Vol. II, p. 561; "Women in the Work Force," 1977 Vol. I, p. 121; "The Rights Revolution," 1978 Vol. I, p. 441.

United States Commission on Civil Rights, "Sex Bias in the U.S. Code," April 1977.

——"Social Indicators of Equality for Minorities and Women," August 1978.

——"The Federal Civil Rights Enforcement Effort-1977," December 1977.

——"The State of Civil Rights-1977," February 1978.

INDIAN RIGHTS

by

Mary Costello

Apr. 15
1977

Editor's Note: Since this report was first published the battle over Indian rights has intensified in Congress and the federal courts. For an updated discussion of the issue, see pages 6-9 in the Report on "The Rights Revolution."

INDIAN RIGHTS

AMERICAN INDIANS have embarked on a campaign to seek restitution for what they charge has been more than two centuries of exploitation, fraud and double-dealing by the government and the white majority. In contrast to past campaigns that sought redress through often-violent confrontations, the country's most impoverished minority is now working within the political system to settle its grievances. The Indians are taking their case to court, and their suits—the most publicized of which is a claim by two tribes to a large part of the state of Maine—are being taken very seriously.

At the heart of the legal battle is the issue of tribal sovereignty that was acknowledged in almost 400 treaties between the government and Indian tribes from the late 18th century until 1868. But tribal sovereignty is not an absolute concept, the 8th U.S. Circuit Court of Appeals held in 1956.[1] The court said: "It would seem clear that the Constitution as construed by the Supreme Court, acknowledges the paramount authority of the United States with regard to Indian tribes but recognizes the existence of Indian tribes as quasi-sovereign entities possessing all the inherent rights of sovereignty except where restrictions have been placed thereon by the United States."

A two-year congressional review of federal policy toward the Indians tended to support Indian claims that the government, particularly the Department of the Interior's Bureau of Indian Affairs (BIA), has placed too many restrictions on tribal sovereignty and that some of these restrictions violate the government's treaties with the Indians. The American Indian Policy Review Commission, under the chairmanship of Sen. James Abourezk (D S.D.), made more than 100 recommendations for revising federal Indian policies. These include the replacement of BIA with an agency independent of Interior, tribal control over mineral, water, fishing, hunting and agricultural resources in Indian territory, and full jurisdiction over taxation and the trial of offenders in tribal courts. The report will be submitted to Congress on May 18.

The commission's proposals are likely to strengthen the backlash that Indian legal assertiveness has produced. More

[1] *Iron Crow v. Oglala Sioux Tribe of Pine Tree Reservation*, 231 F. 2d 89 (1956).

than a year ago, non-Indians from a dozen states set up the Interstate Congress for Equal Rights and Responsibilities to oppose Indian claims to land, water and minerals and jurisdiction over non-Indians on Indian lands. The group, supported by businessmen, ranchers and fishermen, has grown to over 10,000 members in 17 states and has become more vocal in demanding that the rights of non-Indians be considered.

According to the Bureau of Indian Affairs, there are 487 federally recognized Indian tribes in the United States. The recent spate of court cases involves two types of tribal challenge against the government. In some of the eastern states, where only three of more than 70 tribes are recognized by the federal government, there is a question of whether treaties ceding land to the white settlers were valid. For the more than 500,000 Indians living west of the Mississippi River, most of them on reservations, the issue is the violation of the treaty rights they were granted and the compensation they should be given for these violations.

Court cases, brought primarily by the Native American Rights Fund (NARF), include land claims, hunting, fishing and water rights, taxation, government jurisdiction on reservations, mineral development on Indian lands and regulation of air quality and water pollution.[2] During the past year, Indians have won several important cases in state and federal courts. In some of these suits, including the highly publicized Indian claim to millions of acres of land in Maine, the tribes were supported by the Department of Justice.

Suits to Recover Land; The Case in Maine

"Land is the basis of all things Indian," the Citizens Advisory Center in Washington, D.C., wrote almost a decade ago. "The relationship of a tribe to its land defines that tribe: its identity, its culture, its way of life, its fundamental rights, its methods of adaptation, its pattern of survival...Indian land is synonomous with Indian existence."[3] For Native Americans, land has been a dwindling asset. Of the 1.9 billion acres roamed by the tribes 500 years ago, a mere 140 million acres were left in Indian hands by the end of the 19th century Indian wars. Today, only about 50 million acres remain.

It is hardly surprising that the Indians, with this reverence for their ancestral lands, want them back. Since 1946, various

---

[2] NARF is based in Boulder, Colo. It was set up in 1971, with a grant from the Ford Foundation, as a non-profit organization to protect Indian rights. The federal government now provides $446,000 a year, about one-third of the fund's $1.2-million budget. The group is controlled by Indian leaders and staffed largely by Indian attorneys.

[3] Edgar S. Cahn (ed.), *Our Brother's Keeper: The Indian in White America* (1969), p. 68. The report was based on an investigation by the Center on the condition of American Indians.

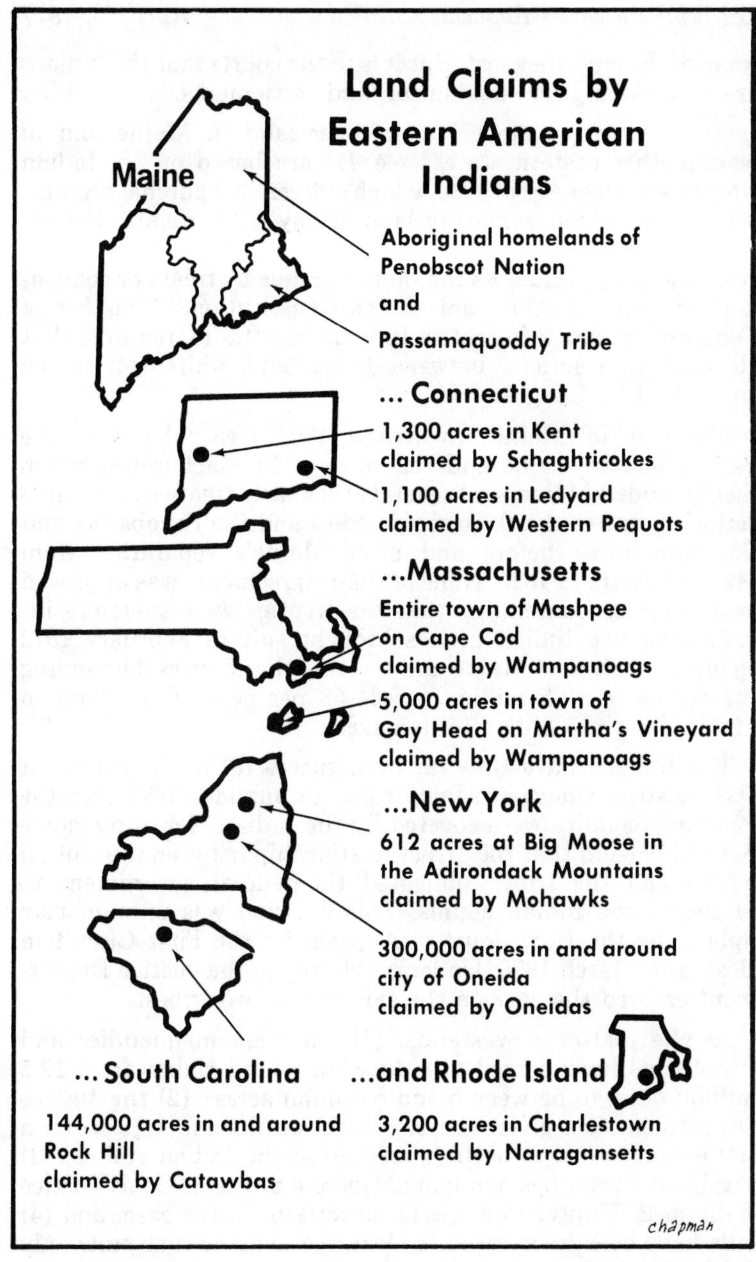

tribes have received over $500-million from the Indian Claims Commission for lands taken from them. On rare occasions—through congressional action, presidential decree or outright gifts from well-wishers [4]—they have actually recovered

[4] For instance, actor Marlon Brando's donation of 40 acres of his property in California to the 23-tribe Redwind Association of West Coast Indians in late 1974.

some of the land they lost. But it is to the courts that the Indians are now looking for substantial land settlements.

Indian court challenges to recover land in Maine and in several other eastern states *(see 45)* are based on the Indian Non-Intercourse Act of 1790, which states: "No purchase, grant, lease or other conveyance of land or any title or claim thereto from any Indian nation or tribe of Indians shall be of any validity in law or equity unless the same be made by treaty or convention entered into pursuant to the Constitution." This act of Congress, intended to protect Indians from fraud, required that all land transactions between tribes and white settlers be authorized by Congress.

The suit in Maine involves a 1794 treaty between the Passamaquoddy tribe and the state of Massachusetts, which then included Maine, and several other early treaties and transactions between the Passamaquoddies and the Penobscots and the two states before and after Maine's separation from Massachusetts in 1820. None of these agreements was approved by Congress. Contending that the treaties were therefore invalid, the two Indian groups brought suit in February 1972 against the state of Maine and several other parties demanding the return of 12.5 million acres—58 per cent of the land in Maine—and $25-billion in damages.

The Indians have thus far been successful in the courts. A U.S. District Court in Maine ruled in January 1975 that the Passamaquoddies were covered by the Indian Non-Intercourse Act of 1790 and that the "trust relationship between the United States and the tribe" obligated the federal government to prosecute the Indian claims. This decision was unanimously upheld by the U.S. Court of Appeals for the First Circuit in Boston in March 1976. Under court orders, the Justice Department entered the case on the side of the two tribes.

As the matter now stands, (1) the Passamaquoddies and Penobscots have agreed to reduce their land claims from 12.5 million acres to between 5 and 8 million acres,[5] (2) the Justice Department has given the two sides until June 1 to reach a settlement before it begins prosecuting the Indian claims, (3) President Carter has nominated Georgia Supreme Court Justice William B. Gunter as a special negotiator in the case, and (4) bills have been introduced in Congress to allow such suits only for monetary damages—not to reclaim land.

The suit in Maine has non-Indian landowners, real estate agents, bankers, and state and city officials worried. It has been

[5] Under the agreement, the Maine Indians agreed to withdraw their claims to lands along the Atlantic Coast, which is the most populous part of the claimed area, and not to press claims to land held by homeowners and small businesses within the remaining area of disputed lands.

difficult for municipalities in the disputed area to sell bonds and mortgage lending has all but ceased. There is also apprehension about suits in other parts of the country, particularly the West, where treaties were approved by Congress but where the terms of those treaties have been violated. A writer observed recently that the Fort Laramie Treaty of 1868 between the seven bands of the Teton Sioux and the U.S. government "recognized the sovereignty of the Native Americans over the present-day lands of Wyoming, Montana, the Dakotas and Nebraska." The treaty was ratified by Congress and has never been rescinded. But it has been violated many times and, as a result, the tribal area "has shrunk to 3 million acres—and of that acreage, one-half million is owned by whites who live on reservation lands. The people there have been reduced to a condition of poverty, apathy and despair."[6]

Efforts to Extend Control Over Resources

Indian activists have focused on several remedies for overcoming the "poverty, apathy and despair" that beset Native Americans. The most dramatic of the current lawsuits seek to recover land that was lost through invalid or violated treaties. In instances where large-scale recovery of land was impossible, some tribes have accepted a financial settlement. Other tribes are concentrating on getting a higher price for the minerals and timber on their lands, while still others are asserting their rights to hunt, fish and use the water on or near their lands.

Last year, 22 western tribes set up the Council of Energy Resources Tribes to determine mineral wealth on Indian lands and advise the tribes on how to get higher prices for their resources. These tribes control millions of acres containing most of the country's known reserves of uranium and large amounts of coal, oil and natural gas. The 151,000-member Navajo tribe, the nation's largest, owns 15 million acres in Arizona, New Mexico, Colorado and Utah, an area as big as all of West Virginia. There is estimated to be some 100 million barrels of oil, 25 trillion cubic feet of natural gas, 80 million pounds of uranium and 50 million tons of coal on Navajo land.

For decades, western Indians tended to approve unquestioningly the agreements that the Bureau of Indian Affairs negotiated for them with coal, oil and power companies. But in recent years, as the value of their resources rose, Indians have been demanding that the leases be renegotiated or voided. Some tribes, including the Navajo, Blackfeet, Chippewa-Cree and Fort Belknap Indians, have signed "joint-venture contracts" in

---

[6] John A. Sullivan, "Native Americans' Right to Be Different," *The Christian Century*, Nov. 3, 1976, p. 960.

Ten Largest Indian Tribes*

Tribe	Location	Membership
Navajo	Arizona, New Mexico, Utah, Colorado	151,000
Creek	Oklahoma	26,000
Cherokee	Oklahoma	23,000
Papaga	Arizona	15,000
Choctaw	Oklahoma	12,000
Oglala Sioux	South Dakota	12,000
Osage	Oklahoma	10,000
Gila River	Arizona	9,000
Rosebud	South Dakota	8,000
White Mountain Apache	Arizona	8,000

Source: Bureau of Indian Affairs, Office of Statistics, 1976.

**The Bureau of Indian Affairs defines an Indian as an individual enrolled in a tribe, living on or near a reservation and being of at least one-quarter Indian blood.*

partnership with oil and gas companies in the production of minerals on tribal lands. And in Montana, the Northern Cheyenne and the Crow have succeeded in persuading the Department of the Interior to overturn a series of strip-mining agreements on the ground that the BIA failed to protect Indian interests when the leases were negotiated.[7]

A federal court in the state of Washington upheld Indian claims based on an 1854 treaty that Puget Sound Indian tribes are entitled to 50 per cent of the "harvestable catch" of fish each year. And in late 1976, the Michigan Supreme Court upheld the Chippewa tribe's right to fish in Lake Superior without having to conform to most state restrictions. A few months earlier, the same tribe won a case in the U.S. Supreme Court exempting reservation Indians from state and local taxes.

Indian tribes are also asserting rights to the water that flows through their reservations and the timber on their lands. In 1908, the Supreme Court ruled in *Winters v. U.S.* that federal treaties creating reservations for the Indians entitled the tribes to the use of all the water necessary to make these lands "adequate and valuable." The court further held that the right of the Indians to water on their reservations could not be denied by state law. But the "court did not decide the precise standard for measuring the quantity of water reserved and subsequent courts have not been able to agree on such a standard." [8] In one case,

---

[7] For a view of the Northern Cheyenne and Crow cases, see "An Unfinished Drama" in Native American Rights Fund *Announcements*, April-June 1975, pp. 9-35.

[8] Monroe E. Price and Gary D. Weatherford, "Indian Water Rights in Theory and Practice," *Law and Contemporary Problems*, winter 1976, p. 102.

the Gila Indian Community is claiming more than 70 per cent of Colorado River waters that the Central Arizona Project is expected to divert to the Phoenix and Tucson areas.

Because of its abundance and renewability, timber is one of the most valuable resources that Indian tribes possess. Some 13 million acres, a quarter of all Indian lands, are forested; this timber is a major source of income for about half of all the reservations. The timber on Indian lands is certain to appreciate in value in the years ahead, according to a study issued by the General Accounting Office, Aug. 18, 1975, entitled "Indian Natural Resources: Opportunities for Improving Management." "Demands for lumber and plywood are increasing more rapidly than sawtimber supplies can be made available," the report said.

Tribal Relations With Federal Agencies

Shortly after the completion of the American Indian Policy Review Commission's study, Chairman James Abourezk wrote in the *Washington Post* on March 21, 1977: "Each time a tribal right seems to conflict with the ambitions of an often politically more powerful non-Indian group—such as irrigators—the federal government yields to the political pressures of non-Indians. Vast quantities of Indian land and water rights have been unjustly taken in this manner. The commission recommends that this practice stop and that the U.S. government live up to what is left of its treaty obligations."

The report said the Bureau of Indian Affairs and its parent organization, the Department of the Interior, were responsible for a major share of the treaty violations. The bureau has been neither "accountable nor responsible" to the tribes it was charged with protecting while the department was accused of showing more interest in fostering the aims of the large corporations that seek to develop Indian lands than in the Indians' welfare. The commission recommended, and the Carter administration has been considering, abolishing the BIA and establishing a new Indian agency independent of Interior.

Steve Nickeson of the National Indian Youth Council in Albuquerque, N.M., argues that far more than structural change is needed in government agencies concerned with Indian affairs. He wrote: "In the long run it will make little difference whether the bureau takes on the form of Amtrak and the TVA, or dissolves into the total federal network. If the elements of policy and power remain unchanged, the bureau will still be the bureau. Such has always been the case. Despite the six structural changes that the bureau has undergone in the past six years—despite all past changes—the bureau has remained essentially unchanged since 1824, because Indian policy and the powers that implement it have changed only in their complexity since John Cabot put Britain's Christian claim on North America in 1497."[9]

It can be argued, however, that there have been substantive changes in the way the executive branch, Congress and the states have dealt with the Indians. For two centuries, federal policy toward Native Americans has vacillated between allowing them a large measure of self-government and encouraging them to assimilate. The latest policy, as announced by President Nixon in 1970, is to foster Indian self-government. To implement it, a special Office of Indian Rights was set up in the Justice Department in 1973, federal money was increased to more than $3-billion a year, and the government began to support tribal claims to land and resources in the courts.[10]

Indian treaty rights can be given and taken away by Congress, so it is hardly surprising that Congress has been subjected to strong criticism for its treatment of Native Americans. What is often forgotten is that it was the legislative branch that approved the establishment of the Indian Claims Commission in 1946 to facilitate the processing of Indian claims against the United States;[11] passed the Civil Rights Act of 1968, Title II of which contains an Indian Bill of Rights to remedy the "continued denial of constitutional guarantees" to Native Americans; enacted legislation returning land to Alaskan Indians and Eskimos; and, in 1975, set up the American Indian Policy Review Commission to study federal policy toward the Indians.

It is the special relationship between Indian tribes and the federal government, as outlined in the Constitution, provided for in acts of Congress and upheld by the courts, that excludes Indian lands from most state laws and jurisdiction. This has led to considerable confusion over issues like taxation, the status of whites living on Indian reservations, and the applicability of state and local laws and ordinances. Nevertheless, the tribes possess what the late Felix Cohen calls the "inherent powers of a limited dependent sovereignty which had not been extinguished by federal action. What is not expressly limited often remains within the domain of tribal sovereignty simply because state jurisdiction is federally excluded."[12]

[9] Steve Nickeson, "The Structure of the Bureau of Indian Affairs," *Law and Contemporary Problems*, winter 1976, p. 76.

[10] At a meeting with Indian leaders at the White House on July 16, 1976, Thomas S. Kleppe, who was then Secretary of the Interior, summed up the government's attitude. "We are committed to Indian self-determination," he said. "This means encouraging the tribes to make their own decisions, and not only abiding by those decisions but helping to implement these decisions where there is no legal barrier."

[11] The Indian Claims Commission, which receives about $1.5-million a year to resolve pre-1946 Indian claims against the government, will terminate on Sept. 30, 1978. All unresolved cases before it will be transferred to the U.S. Court of Claims.

[12] Felix Cohen, *Handbook of Federal Indian Law* (1940 edition), p. 396.

Evolving U.S. Policy on Indians

THE CONSTITUTION gives Congress major jurisdiction over Indian affairs. Article I, Section 8, specifies that "the Congress shall have the power to regulate commerce with foreign nations and among the several states and with Indian tribes." The special relationship between the federal government and Indian tribes has been the subject of confusion and litigation ever since the Constitution was written. Probably the two most important decisions dealing with this special relationship were handed down by the Supreme Court in the early 1830s: *Cherokee Nation v. Georgia* (1831) and *Worcester v. Georgia* (1832).

In the first case, Chief Justice John Marshall asserted on behalf of the court that "Indian territory is...a part of the United States" and that the Indians "are in a state of pupilage. Their relation to the United States resembles that of a ward to his guardian." Indian tribes may thus "be denominated domestic dependent nations." In the second case, the court held that a state, in this instance Georgia, had no right to execute its laws on Indian lands. Indian tribes or nations, Marshall declared, "had always been considered as distinct, independent, political communities, retaining their original natural rights.... The Cherokee nation, then, is a distinct community occupying its own territory...in which the laws of Georgia can have no force."

The decisions were based not on some abstract idea of tribal sovereignty but on treaties between the government and the Indians. However, the decisions encountered harsh political reality. President Jackson, Marshall's bitter foe, wanted southern lands cleared of Indian inhabitants and made available to white settlers. Jackson responded to Marshall's decisions by ignoring them. The President's attitude was expressed in the famous, though perhaps apocryphal, remark after the *Worcester* ruling: "John Marshall has made his decision; let him enforce it." Indian treaty rights were ignored and the Cherokees were driven from their homelands.

Treaty-making with the Indians had been going on since the first English settlers arrived in the New World. The practice seemed to be sanctioned under Article III, Section 2, of the Constitution which gave the President the "Power, by and with the Advice and Consent of the Senate, to make Treaties...." But the government's treaties with the Indians implied tribal sovereignty, and by the mid-19th century there was growing opposition to dealing with Indian tribes in the same manner that the United States dealt with sovereign nations.

The Indian's Land Mystique

"Our land is more valuable than your money. It will last forever. It will not even perish by the flames of fire. As long as the sun shines and the waters flow, this land will be here to give life to man and animals. We cannot sell the lives of men and animals; therefore we cannot sell this land. It was put here for us by the Great Spirit and we cannot sell it because it does not belong to us. You can count your money and burn it within the nod of a buffalo's head, but only the Great Spirit can count the grains of sand and the blades of grass of these plains. As a present to you, we will give you anything we have that you can take with you; but the land, never."

Blackfeet Chief in 19th-century treaty council
Quoted by National Indian Youth Council

Congress reacted in 1871 by passing a law which declared that "hereafter no Indian nation or tribe within the territory of the United States shall be acknowledged or recognized as an independent nation, tribe or power with whom the United States may contract by treaty." Between 1778, when the first treaty was signed between the Indians and the U.S. government, and 1868, when the last was concluded, the Senate had ratified 370 treaties and the Indians had ceded almost a billion acres of land to the new nation.

The prevailing view of these treaties is that they made possible the forcible removal of tribes from their lands, with small compensation, to make way for white settlements. This view is not entirely accurate. The 1778 Fort Pitt Treaty with the Delaware Indians, the first between a tribe and the U.S. government, was a model of enlightenment. It provided that friendly Indian tribes might, at a time of their own choosing, send representatives to Congress and might join the Union in a state of their own. A treaty with the Cherokees in 1785 stipulated: "The Indians may have full confidence in the justice of the United States respecting their interests; they shall have the right to send a deputy of their choice to Congress."

The first major declaration of the government's Indian policy was made in the Northwest Territory Ordinance of July 13, 1787: "The utmost good faith shall always be observed towards the Indians; their land and property shall never be taken from them without their consent; and in their property, rights and liberty, they shall never be invaded or disturbed.... Laws founded in justice and humanity shall from time to time be made, for preventing wrongs being done to them and for preserving peace and friendship with them."

By 1830, "good faith" had been discarded as excess baggage. Congress passed the Indian Removal Act that year giving President Jackson and his successors authority to resettle the eastern tribes on uninhabited land west of the Mississippi to which they would be given perpetual title. In enacting that law, "Congress paved the way for white society to satisfy its craving for rich Indian territory. Whites began to force Indians from their traditional homes as relentlessly as they had earlier replaced Indian traditions with their own values."[13]

The territory west of the Mississippi, expected to be of little interest to white settlers, turned out otherwise. Discovery of gold in California in 1848 put heavy pressure on the government to renegotiate treaties that gave Indians title to lands that lay astride the routes of travel and trade. For four decades, beginning in 1850, whites and Indians fought a series of pitched battles and intermittent skirmishes. Federal policy was summed up in 1872 by Francis A. Walker, commissioner of Indian Affairs, in his annual report to Congress: "There is no question of national dignity, be it remembered, involved in the treatment of savages by a civilized power. With wild men, as with beasts, the question whether in a given situation one shall fight, coax or run is a question merely of what is easiest and safest."[14]

Indians as Victims of Westward Expansion

The Indian wars that began in the mid-19th century ended in 1890 with the slaying of nearly 300 Sioux at Wounded Knee, S.D. These wars are widely viewed today as a dark chapter in American history, a time when greedy white settlers, backed by the government and the military, murdered, robbed and enslaved the noble savages.[15] But during these years there was savagery on both sides. There was also considerable sympathy in the white community for the plight of the Indians. Gen. Philip H. Sheridan, the Civil War hero who later fought against the Indians and allegedly said "the only good Indians I ever saw were dead," also expressed compassion for Native Americans. He wrote: "We took away their country and their means of support, broke up their mode of living, their habits of life, introduced disease and decay among them and it was for this and against this they made war. Could anyone expect less?"[16]

Until the treaty-making system was abandoned in 1871, the government entered into treaties with the survivors of Indian tribes, setting aside tracts of land for them. The treaties often

---

[13] Kirke Kickingbird, " 'In Our Image...After Our Likeness:' The Drive for the Assimilation of Indian Court Systems," *American Criminal Law Review*, spring 1976, p. 676. Kickingbird served as general counsel for the American Indian Policy Review Commission.

[14] Quoted by D'Arcy McNickle in *Indian Man: The Life of Oliver LaFarge* (1971), p. 71.

[15] See, for example, Dee Brown's *Bury My Heart at Wounded Knee* (1970).

[16] Quoted by Thomas C. Leonard, "The Reluctant Conquerors," *American Heritage*, August 1976, p. 36.

Allotment Act Paternalism

The General Allotment Act of 1887 "had the backing of those who wished the Indian well and of those who wished him ill. About the only group which was not enthusiastic for the bill was the group it was designed to help: the Indians. White reformers...thought that the Indian would become integrated into white society if he could be taught to value private property and individual welfare above the interests of his tribe.... [This] condescension [was] more reprehensible than the greed of the white land grabbers...."

Wilcomb E. Washburn
Red Man's Land/White Man's Law (1971)

relegated the tribes to relatively large reservations and guaranteed that they could remain on these lands "forever," without interference by non-Indians or other Indians. But in the years that followed, Indians "were forced to relinquish most of the land in their large reservations because the government considered those early reserves to contain far more land than the Indians required.... The government had the services of expert surveyors; the Indians had only the vaguest notion of what they were granting. Less often, but not unusual, outright fraud and duress were practiced to obtain Indian lands on the most favorable terms."[17]

In 1887, Congress passed the General Allotment Act, often called the Dawes Act for its sponsor, Sen. Henry L. Dawes (R Mass.). It resulted in the relinquishment of millions of acres of Indian land to white settlers. The act authorized the President to divide reservations into individual parcels of land—a policy known as "severalty"—and to give each Indian, whether he wanted it or not, a particular piece of tribally owned land. To avoid making the transition from Indian custom too abrupt, the land would be held in trust for 25 years. Reservation land remaining after all living members of the tribes had been provided with allotments was to be declared surplus and made available to non-Indian homesteaders.

The Allotment Act ushered in the ascendancy of the Bureau of Indian Affairs which had been set up in 1824 in the War Department and transferred to the new Department of the Interior in 1849. After 1887, the bureau became the guardian of all Indians, as individuals and as tribes, assuming responsibility for the most minute decisions. The bureau's policy, like the philosophy behind the Allotment Act, was to speed the assimilation of Indians into white society.

Largely as a result of the Allotment Act, tribal landholdings fell from 138 million acres in 1887 to 48 million acres in 1934.

[17] Margaret Hunter Pierce, "The Work of the Indian Claims Commission," *American Bar Association Journal*, February 1977, p. 231. Pierce is a member of the commission.

The results of the government's assimilation policy were summed up in a study conducted for the Coolidge administration by Lewis Meriam of the Brookings Institution. The report, in 1928, found most Indians "extremely poor," in bad health, without education and not adjusted to the dominant culture around them. The study, entitled "The Problems of Indian Administration" and often referred to as the Meriam Report, said:

> It almost seems [the report said] as if the government assumed that some magic in individual ownership of property would in itself prove an educational civilizing factor, but unfortunately this policy for the most part operated in the opposite direction. Many Indians were not ready to make effective use of their individual allotments. Some of the allotments were of such a character that they could not be used by anyone in small units.
>
> The solution was to permit the Indians through the government to lease their lands to the whites. In some instances government officers encouraged leasing, as the whites were anxious for the use of the land and it was far easier to administer property leased to whites than to educate and stimulate Indians to use their own property.

Arguments Over Autonomy or Assimilation

With notable exceptions, such as Jackson's policy of Indian removal, the assimilationism of the Allotment Act had expressed the dominant attitude toward Indians for more than a century. An early expression of assimilation is found in a message President Jefferson sent to Congress on Jan. 18, 1803. Jefferson spoke of leading Indians "to agriculture, to manufactures and civilization, in bringing together their and our sentiments, and in preparing them ultimately to participate in the benefits of our government."

The Jacksonian notion of dealing with Indians—the antithesis of Jefferson's thought—had run its course by late in the 19th century. The census of 1890 declared that the frontier had vanished; there was simply no room left in which to isolate the Indians. For their own "greatest good" or because others wanted their land, they would have to be assimilated. Under the more benign approach, Indians who had not become citizens under the Allotment Act, gained citizenship and the right to vote in 1924.[18]

The impact of paternalism or desire for land that the government's assimilation policies had inflicted on the Indians was brought to public attention by the 1928 Meriam Report. Spurred by the commission's findings, Congress passed the Indian Reorganization Act of 1934. That law endorsed greater responsibility for Indians. It (1) prohibited allotment of tribal

[18] Arizona and New Mexico continued to deny Indians the franchise until 1948 and Indians living on state reservations in Maine were not allowed to vote until 1953.

lands in the future but allowed the tribes to assign use rights to individuals, (2) authorized return to the tribes of surplus lands not preempted by homesteaders, (3) authorized tribes to adopt written constitutions and charters of incorporation embodying their management of internal affairs, (4) established a revolving credit program for land purchases, and (5) allowed any tribe to repudiate provisions of the act in a referendum of eligible tribal voters..

Probably the most important provisions of the act were those for tribal self-government. About 160 tribes, bands and Alaskan villages adopted written constitutions, some of which combined traditional practices with modern parliamentary methods. In addition, the revolving-credit fund helped Indians to improve their economic position. Land purchase funds were used to buy 395,000 acres and tribes used their own money to acquire an additional 390,000 acres. Restoration of unsettled land and the transfer of public domain property added a million acres to Indian holdings.

Alvin M. Josephy Jr., an authority on Indian affairs, argues that the 1934 act was not a radical departure from past assimilationist policies. "The Indian Reorganization Act was an admission that assimilation was still far off, but though it halted allotments as a self-defeating and disastrous policy, it substituted slower-moving and more considerate methods that were still designed, ultimately, to achieve the national goal of Indian assimilation. At the same time, it attempted to confer on the tribes greater freedom to proceed toward assimilation at a rate of speed and under conditions of their own choosing. In confirming Indian self-government—although in the image of the way white men did things—it tried to return to the Indians the right to organize their own institutions and manage their own affairs."[19]

The gains achieved under the Reorganization Act were short-lived. Sentiment began to grow in Congress for the termination of all federal Indian programs. The 1947 Hoover Commission report on reorganizing the federal government recommended a "policy of rapid integration into American life" for the Indians. Under the Eisenhower administration, termination became a reality. A concurrent resolution adopted by the House and Senate in the summer of 1953 declared it to be the "policy of Congress, as rapidly as possible, to make the Indians...subject to the same laws and entitled to the same privileges and responsibilities as are applicable to other citizens." The resolution

[19] Alvin M. Josephy Jr., "Toward Freedom: The American Indian in the Twentieth Century," a lecture given on April 24, 1971, to the Indiana History Workshop and included in the Indiana Historical Society's *Lectures, 1970-71* (1971), p. 51.

further proposed that specific Indian groups "be freed from federal supervision and control" as soon as possible.

The termination policy drew protests from many Indians. They feared that it would result in the final breakup of reservations and the creation of a pauper class in the white man's society. Nevertheless, in the next five years, several tribes were terminated, all with disastrous results.[20] The impact of termination soon became apparent and in 1958 the government announced that no tribe would be subject to termination without its consent.

Growth of Indian Consciousness in 1960s

It was President Nixon, however, who in a message to Congress on Indian affairs, July 13, 1970, asked for a formal repeal of the termination policy. "Because termination is morally and legally unacceptable, because it produces bad practical results and because the mere threat of termination tends to discourage greater self-sufficiency among Indian groups, I am asking the Congress to pass a new concurrent resolution which would expressly renounce, repudiate and repeal the termination policy."

Congress never approved the resolution that Nixon requested, but the President pushed ahead with the new policy of self-determination without termination. A thorough "shaking up" of the Bureau of Indian Affairs was ordered, Native Americans were hired at top-level positions at the bureau, an Office of Indian Rights in the Justice Department and a National Council on Indian Opportunity were set up, Indians were given access to the highest levels of the government, and federal funds for the tribes were increased.

The Nixon policy came at a time of growing and, often, violent Indian assertiveness. This activism, spurred by the black civil rights protests, began to erupt on a nationwide scale in the mid-1960s. Militants were not mollified by Title II of the Civil Rights Act of 1968—the Indian Bill of Rights—which they viewed as paternalistic and assimilationist. That law prohibited tribal governments from making or enforcing laws that violated such constitutional guarantees as freedom of religion, speech and the press, protection from unreasonable search and seizure and from self-incrimination, and it mandated the rights to counsel and trial by jury.

The act also directed the Secretary of the Interior to recommend to Congress a model code governing Indian tribal courts. White liberals applauded the Indian Bill of Rights for finally

[20] See "American Indians: Using the System," a study by the League of Women Voters, March 1973, p. 3.

recognizing that Native Americans had the same rights as other citizens. Many Indians reacted differently, criticizing the law as another example of the old assimilationist policies which sought to destroy tribal customs and undermine the Indians' communal way of life.[21]

By the late 1960s, Indian grievances against the government fueled a Red Power movement and led to numerous demonstrations and confrontations, many of them organized by the militant American Indian Movement (AIM). In 1965, Indian groups banded together to stage a series of "fish-ins" in defense of Indian fishing rights in Washington state. Four years later, in November 1969, Indians gained national attention by seizing Alcatraz Island in San Francisco Bay. Since that time, militant Native Americans have occupied, or attempted to occupy, other public sites, including a Coast Guard station in Milwaukee, Ellis Island in New York harbor, the deactivated Army post of Fort Lawton at Seattle, offices of the Bureau of Indian Affairs in Washington, D.C., the hamlet of Wounded Knee on the Pine Ridge Reservation in South Dakota, and part of Adirondack State Park in New York.

Probably the most publicized of these incidents was AIM's occupation of Wounded Knee. A siege by law-enforcement officers began on Feb. 27, 1973, and lasted 71 days; when it ended, two Indians were dead and several Indians and law-enforcement officers had been wounded. The occupation was intended to dramatize the government's violation of the Fort Laramie Treaty of 1868, which stated: "No white person or persons shall be permitted to settle upon or occupy any portion of the territory or without the consent of the Indians to pass through the same." The Wounded Knee incident led Senator Abourezk to propose the establishment of the American Indian Policy Review Commission "to determine the nature and scope of necessary revisions" in U.S. Indian policy. Abourezk's sympathies with the Indians date from his childhood; he was reared on the Rosebud Indian Reservation in South Dakota.

The most important aspect of Indian activism occurred not in militant demonstrations or in Congress but in the courts. Vine Deloria Jr., a Sioux, foresaw the legal battle in his book *Custer Died for Your Sins* (1969). "As I sat there listening," he wrote, "I could visualize a legal program for the Indian people.... I could see us piling case upon case, precedent upon precedent, until we had forged out a new definition of Indian rights by which our Indian communities could live in peace from encroachment from any source."

---

[21] For background on the 1968 Indian Civil Rights Act, see United States Commission on Civil Rights, "American Indian Civil Rights Handbook," March 1972.

Legal and Moral Issues Involved

A QUESTION that is likely to receive increasing attention in the months ahead is whether the report of the American Indian Policy Review Commission will have an impact similar to that of the 1928 Meriam Report. The commission studied 11 areas [22] and tended to be concerned more with righting alleged wrongs that have been and are being done to Indians than with the effect of its recommendations on the rest of society. In the introduction to its report, the commission said: "The question goes far beyond that of 'restitution' for past wrongs. From the misdirected present, can the U.S. government redirect its relations with American Indians to enable them to determine their own lives now and in the future?" The report attempted to answer this question affirmatively with over 100 recommendations for improving federal policy.

Most of the recommendations favor greater autonomy for the Indians. These include the right to try non-Indians in tribal courts, levy taxes and impose business licenses on non-Indians living or working on or near reservations, exert control over waterways, fishing and hunting on reservations, have all federal funds channeled directly to the tribes rather than through the state governments, and replace the Bureau of Indian Affairs with an agency or department more sympathetic to the Indians. While the report will not be presented to Congress until May 18, there have been numerous complaints about its pro-Indian bias.

Many of these criticisms are based on the argument that while wrongs have been done to the Indians in the past, it is unfair to make the rest of the country now pay for inequities committed over 100 years ago. There are two rights in conflict, critics contend, and any attempt to right a historical wrong done to the Indians must not inflict a new injustice on non-Indians.[23] There is likely to be a stronger backlash to the commission's proposals once the report is made public. And there is likely to be a far more adverse reaction to Indian assertiveness if Native Americans win many of the court cases now pending and continue to press their demands for land, money, reopening of the

[22] (1) Trust responsibility and federal Indian relationship, (2) tribal government, (3) federal administration and structure of Indian affairs, (4) federal, state and tribal jurisdiction, (5) Indian education, (6) Indian health, (7) reservation development, (8) urban and rural non-reservation, (9) Indian law revision, consolidation and codification, (10) terminated and non-federally recognized Indians, and (11) alcoholism and drug abuse.

[23] Rep. Lloyd Meeds (D Wash.), a member of the commission, declares himself "violently opposed" to giving tribes the right to tax non-Indians on reservations since they "don't have any participation in the decision-making" on the reservations.

treaty-making process, renegotiation of old treaties and a separate state or even a separate nation.

The idea of a separate Indian nation is hardly new. Proposals for an Indian nation date from the 18th century and were popular during the westward expansion in the 19th century. More recently, Mohawks in New York proclaimed an independent North American state upon briefly seizing some land in the Adirondack Mountains in May 1974. The Oglala Sioux in the Northwest have joined with almost 100 other tribes to establish an International Treaty Council to seek recognition as sovereign entities by the United Nations.

Carole E. Goldberg, a professor of law at the University of California at Los Angeles, points out that tribal taxing powers may hasten the development of a distinct Indian entity. "There are few direct federal restraints on the exercise" of tribal taxing power over non-Indians, he wrote. "Federal restraints may be increased through the mechanism of the Indian Civil Rights Act, especially in the direction of homogenizing tribal governments with state and local counterparts. Freedom from state taxation may be available only if the tribes take on functions traditionally performed by the state. Significantly, both of these developments propel a strong tribe like the Navajo in the direction of becoming a state itself, a subordinate entity within a state, or a commonwealth such as Puerto Rico."[24]

Question of Tradition and Current Needs

Something like a separate state or commonwealth might eventually emerge if the American Indian Policy Review Commission's recommendations for revitalizing traditional Indian values and tribal self-government are acted upon. But there is some debate about whether it is possible or desirable to allow the tribes the degree of cultural autonomy and self-government that the commission proposes. The desire of Indian traditionalists and their supporters for criminal and civil jurisdiction in tribal courts[25] is one example of the dilemma facing both the Indians and the federal government. The number of tribal courts has increased from 75 to more than 120 in the last six years. But these courts do not hear major cases and cannot impose sentences greater than six months in jail and $500 in fines for any offense.

Indian law tends to be less procedural than English and

---

[24] Carole E. Goldberg, "A Dynamic View of Tribal Jurisdiction to Tax Non-Indians," *Law and Contemporary Problems*, winter 1976, p. 189.

[25] This argument was presented by Kirke Kickingbird in the spring 1976 issue of *American Criminal Law Review*. Because of "the differences between the cultural values of Indians and whites," he wrote, "Indians living under a legal system reflecting Indian values and administered by Indians will maintain a more orderly society."

American Indian Population*

State	Population	State	Population
TOTAL	792,730	Mo.	5,405
Ala.	2,443	Mont.	27,130
Alaska	16,276	Neb.	6,624
Ariz.	95,812	Nev.	7,933
Ark.	2,014	N.H.	361
Calif.	91,018	N.J.	4,706
Colo.	8,836	N.M.	72,788
Conn.	2,222	N.Y.	28,355
Del.	656	N.C.	44,406
D.C.	956	N.D.	14,369
Fla.	6,677	Ohio	6,654
Ga.	2,347	Okla.	98,468
Hawaii	1,126	Ore.	13,510
Idaho	6,687	Pa.	5,533
Ill.	11,413	R.I.	1,390
Ind.	3,887	S.C.	2,241
Iowa	2,992	S.D.	32,365
Kan.	8,672	Tenn.	2,276
Ky.	1,531	Texas	17,957
La.	5,294	Utah	11,273
Maine	2,195	Vermont	229
Md.	4,239	Va.	4,853
Mass.	4,475	Wash.	33,386
Mich.	16,854	W.Va.	751
Minn.	23,128	Wis.	18,924
Miss.	4,113	Wyo.	4,980

*Based on the number of persons who identified themselves in the 1970 census as American Indians.

American law and more concerned with what Indian attorneys call "fundamental fairness." A criminal is a person out of harmony with the community; in order to reestablish that harmony, Indian law focuses more on rehabilitation than on retribution. Traditionalists want their unique judicial system preserved and extended. But, David F. Salisbury pointed out in *The Christian Science Monitor* on Jan. 28, 1977, the requirements of the Indian Civil Rights Act of 1968 that tribal courts afford due process and enforce other constitutional guarantees have meant that "an increasing number of Indian courts are modeling themselves along Anglo lines."

The proposal for greater jurisdiction for tribal courts raises the question of whether "separate reservation existence for Indians as a permanent phenomenon is realistic, desirable and desired by the Indian people, as opposed to some of their more vocal spokesmen," Samuel J. Brakel wrote in the *American Bar Association Journal.* "Although it is fashionable to support the 'sovereignty' of Indian tribes, the separateness of Indian existence and the legitimacy of autonomously Indian institutions, including tribal courts, it is rarely explained whether and why these should be taken for granted. A key factor should be what people on the reservations want." When they are questioned, he said, it is found that "the romance of abstract self-sufficiency and self-determination often fades...in practice."[26]

The situation in Alaska indicates that many Indians will forsake "the romance of abstract self-sufficiency" and work within the system when given the opportunity. The Alaska Native Claims Settlement Act of 1971 gave the state's approximately 60,000 Eskimos, Indians and Aleuts 40 million acres of land and $960.5-million payable over several years. The land is being apportioned by a complex formula that established 12 regional corporations, divided geographically on roughly ethnic lines, and about 220 village corporations. To the surprise of many, the native corporations have turned out to be remarkably aggressive and successful experiments in minority capitalism.

They have invested in nearly every segment of the Alaskan economy—banking, mineral and oil exploration, construction, real estate, logging, hotel management, fishing and reindeer herding. One of the largest regional corporations, Doyon, Ltd., has about 9,200 stockholders, mostly Athabascan Indians, and formed a partnership with the Louisiana Land & Exploration Co. to drill for oil along the Yukon River. Another, Koniag, Inc., has joined with the oil companies in supporting Outer Continental Shelf petroleum sales.[27]

Judicial Limitations; Congress as Arbiter

The experience in Alaska tentatively suggests that by giving the Indians back some portion of their aboriginal lands and the means to develop them, Native Americans will react in much

---

[26] Samuel J. Brakel, "American Indian Tribal Courts: Separate? 'Yes,' Equal? 'Probably Not,' " *American Bar Association Journal,* August 1976, p. 1006. Brakel directed the American Bar Foundation's study on Indian tribal courts.

[27] See Peter Gruenstein, 'Alaska's Natives, Inc.," *The Progressive,* March 1977. Gruenstein is writing a book about Alaska. For background, see "Alaskan Development," *E.R.R.,* 1976 Vol. II, pp. 936-938.

the same way as the white entrepreneurs they previously condemned. This view is at the opposite extreme from the theories of those who believe that the return of large tracts of land to the Indians and the institution of full tribal sovereignty will enable Indians to show other Americans how to live in harmony with nature and with their fellow human beings.

Many observers are convinced that neither of these views is likely to be tested to any great extent. *Time* magazine summed up the most probable outcome of Indian land claims on April 11: "It is impossible to imagine either the courts or Congress actually returning long-populated lands to the Indians. This would entail the dispossession of thousands of innocent owners and the unthinkable unraveling of large segments of ongoing society. At the same time, it is likely that the Indians will receive money for damages, and fair enough. It might even be feasible to award them some symbolic parcels of unpopulated lands."

The *Boston Sunday Globe,* in editorial commentary on the claims of the Passamaquoddies and Penobscots in Maine, took note of the limits of a purely judicial solution: "It would be impossible to simply return the land to Indian hands, regardless of the merits of their legal case. Such an outcome would heap injustice upon apparent injustice...."[28]

Earlier this year, legislation was introduced in Congress by members from Maine to prevent the Passamaquoddies and Penobscots from suing to recover land but allow them to seek monetary damages. While Congress has the power to abrogate treaties and take tribal lands, the Supreme Court held in 1942, in *Sioux Tribe of Indians v. United States,* that the Constitution requires compensation to be paid.

Robert McLaughlin, an authority on Indian legal matters, considered what the Passamaquoddies and Penobscots could do if Congress ignores "the painstaking accumulation of judicial opinion" and strips the tribes "of aboriginal title and thus their direct route to recovering land." Their only alternative, McLaughlin contends, "will be to press their monetary damage claims of $25-billion with no mercy, focusing on the smaller landowners who are unable to pay the amounts involved, and foreclosing on their property."[29] Indian leaders in Maine and elsewhere have said repeatedly that they have no wish to dispossess individual property owners. But they have also made it clear that they intend to press their claims to rights they believe they have been denied.

---

[28] The *Boston Sunday Globe,* Feb. 6, 1977.

[29] Robert McLaughlin, "Giving It Back to the Indians," *The Atlantic,* February 1977, p. 85.

Selected Bibliography

Books

Brown, Dee, *Bury My Heart at Wounded Knee,* Holt, Rinehart & Winston, 1970.

Cohen, Felix S., *Handbook of Federal Indian Law,* U.S. Government Printing Office, 1940.

Deloria, Vine, *Behind the Trail of Broken Treaties,* Delacorte, 1974.

Jacobs, Wilbur R., *Dispossessing the American Indian,* Charles Scribner's Sons, 1972.

McNickle, D'Arcy, *Native American Tribalism,* Oxford University Press, 1973.

Price, Monroe E., *Law and the American Indian,* Bobbs-Merrill, 1973.

Sutton, Imre, *Indian Land Tenure,* Clearwater Publishers, 1975.

Washburn, Wilcomb E., *Red Man's Land/White Man's Law,* Charles Scribner's Sons, 1971.

Articles

Allis, Samuel, "This Land Is Your Land, This Land Is My Land," *The New Englander,* January 1977.

Civil Rights Digest, selected issues.

Gibson, Michael M., "Indian Claims in the Beds of Oklahoma Watercourses," *American Indian Law Review,* summer 1976.

Gruenstein, Peter, "Alaska's Natives, Inc.," *The Progressive,* March 1977.

The Indian Historian, selected issues.

Kickingbird, Kirke, " 'In Our Image...After Our Likeness:' The Drive for the Assimilation of Indian Court Systems," *American Criminal Law Review,* spring 1976.

Martone, Frederick J., "American Indian Tribal Self-Government in the Federal System: Inherent Right or Congressional License?" *Notre Dame Lawyer,* April 1976.

McLaughlin, Robert, "Giving It Back to the Indians," *The Atlantic,* February 1977.

Meeds, Lloyd, "The Indian Policy Review Commission," *Law and Contemporary Problems,* winter 1976.

Native American Rights Fund, *Announcements,* selected issues.

Pierce, Margaret Hunter, "The Work of the Indian Claims Commission," *American Bar Association Journal,* February 1977.

Ruffing, Lorraine Turner, "Navajo Economic Development Subject to Cultural Constraints," *Economic Development and Cultural Change,* April 1976.

Reports and Studies

Bureau of the Census, Department of Commerce, "American Indians," June 1973.

Bureau of Indian Affairs, Department of the Interior, selected reports and studies.

Editorial Research Reports, "American Indians: Neglected Minority," 1966 Vol. II, p. 623; "Changing Status of American Indians," 1954 Vol. I, p. 381; "Preservation of Indian Culture," 1972 Vol. II, p. 847.

Indian Claims Commission, "Annual Report to Congress, 1976," 1976.

United States Commission on Civil Rights, "American Indian Civil Rights Handbook," March 1972.

ACCESS TO LEGAL SERVICES

by

Sandra Stencel

July 22
1977

ACCESS TO LEGAL SERVICES

ACCORDING TO the basic laws of economics, excess supply usually results in lower prices and greater accessibility to a product. Conversely, high prices along with growing difficulty in obtaining the product should indicate an inadequate supply. But the law of supply and demand does not always function smoothly, as the current state of legal services in the United States demonstrates.

In the past 10 years, law has become the country's fastest growing profession. There are now approximately 445,000 lawyers in the United States. The nation has one lawyer for every 484 persons—a higher ratio than in any other country except Israel. Despite the number of attorneys, there appears to be a significant demand for legal services that has not been met. The problem, according to a *Trial* magazine editor, Barbara A. Stein, revolves around two factors: (1) the public's ignorance of how to find an attorney as well as the kind of services lawyers provide, and (2) an apparent inability of the legal profession to deliver services at prices that are reasonable.[1]

A recent survey by the American Bar Association and the American Bar Foundation underscored the magnitude of the problem. Only about one-third (35.8 per cent) of the adults who were surveyed had ever consulted a lawyer, and only about a quarter (27.9 per cent) had actually retained a lawyer. One reason so many people appear to avoid lawyers is the perceived cost of their services. Over 60 per cent of the respondents to the survey agreed to the statement: "Most lawyers charge more for their services than they are worth."

In addition, more than a quarter of the respondents said that "lawyers needlessly complicate clients' problems." The survey indicated that many people do not know where to turn for legal advice or how to determine a lawyer's competence. Nearly half of the people questioned said that if they needed to choose a lawyer they would ask friends, relatives or neighbors to recommend one. The telephone book was the next most frequently mentioned source.[2]

---

[1] Barbara A. Stein, "Legal Economics," *Trial,* June 1976, p. 12. *Trial* is published by The Association of Trial Lawyers of America.

[2] Survey results published in *alternatives: legal services & the public,* Vol. 3, No. 1, January 1976. *alternatives* is a bimonthly newsletter of the ABA Consortium on Legal Services and the Public. Research for the survey was conducted by the ABA's Special Committee to Survey Legal Needs in collaboration with the American Bar Foundation.

In the past, discussions of access to legal services generally centered on the problems of people too poor to pay any legal fees at all—people who constitute about 20 per cent of the population. Although much more needs to be done before a truly effective or comprehensive legal services program is available to persons in the lowest economic brackets, legal aid programs financed by the government and private sources have begun to meet the legal needs of the poor. At the other extreme, people in the upper 10 per cent of the economic spectrum have sufficient funds to take care of even very high legal costs.

Caught in the middle are perhaps 140 million Americans who do not qualify for free legal aid and who cannot afford standard legal fees, which now average $40 to $50 an hour in urban areas. The legal needs of the middle class "have been greatly overlooked," said a Philadelphia lawyer, Robert T. Richards.[3] In recent years the legal profession has begun to rectify this oversight. Programs designed to improve the availability of legal services to people of moderate means have sprung up across the nation.

Introduction of Pre-Paid Legal Insurance

One answer to the problem of providing low-cost legal services is pre-paid legal insurance. Under such plans, which are similar to Blue Cross and other health insurance programs, individuals or someone acting on their behalf contribute regularly to a fund for legal services that the individuals may need or use in the future. By spreading the cost of services over a large number of people over a period of time, the expense to the individual client is kept relatively low. Pre-paid plans are "probably the best way for the majority of Americans to be able to assure themselves of legal assistance when they need it," according to James Fellers, a former president of the American Bar Association.[4]

In addition to providing reasonably priced legal services, pre-paid plans encourage members to practice "preventive law"—to seek legal advice before they get into trouble, not just afterward. The ABA survey indicated that in only three situations—(1) the making of wills, (2) serious difficulty with a former spouse about alimony and child support, and (3) difficulties with custody of children[5]—did the majority of Americans consult with lawyers. When faced with other legal problems—such as the acquisition of property, personal injuries, landlord-tenant disputes, serious problems with a creditor, or denial of constitutional rights—most people either consulted a non-legal resource, handled the problem themselves, or did nothing about it.

[3] Quoted in *The New York Times,* May 2, 1977.

[4] Quoted in "Pre-paid Legal Services," a pamphlet published by the Resource Center for Consumers of Legal Services.

[5] Inexplicably, divorce itself was not among the situations listed.

Lawyer Surplus

Current problems with the delivery of legal services exist side by side with a growing surplus of lawyers. Since 1968, enrollment in the nation's law schools has doubled to approximately 125,000 students. Women have accounted for much of this increase. Today about 23 per cent of all law students in the United States are women, up from 8.5 per cent in 1971.

Nearly 30,000 students graduate from law school each year, but according to the latest figures from the Bureau of Labor Statistics, there are only about 21,000 jobs awaiting them in the legal profession. Nearly one-third of all law school graduates must seek jobs in other fields. By 1985, the Bureau of Labor Statistics estimates, there may be as many as 100,000 surplus lawyers.

Some of the graduates who do find jobs are prospering as never before. Starting salaries at top New York law firms average $25,000 a year. Outside of New York, starting salaries at top firms run about $5,000 less. The median income for lawyers in private practice is slightly under $30,000—considerably less than the median income of the nation's doctors, which is above $50,000.

According to the ABA there are now about 150 full-scale prepaid legal insurance plans operating in the United States, covering approximately two million people. Lillian Deitch and David Weinstein estimate that such plans may cover 10 million to 20 million subscribers by 1985.[6] Prepaid plans vary widely according to how they are run, how much they cost, who operates them and what benefits they provide. Most plans now operating in the United States are sponsored by labor unions and are funded through collective bargaining agreements or from union dues. Other plans are administered by state and local bar associations, credit unions, insurance companies and other private businesses. One of the newest providers is Blue Cross, the nation's biggest health insurer. Its western Pennsylvania unit started writing legal insurance policies in May, selling to individuals as well as groups—a major innovation, according to Sandy DeMent, executive director of the Resource Center for Consumers of Legal Services.[7]

The cost of pre-paid legal insurance ranges from $25 to $300 a year, typically falling between $40 and $90. Benefits vary greatly, from fairly modest amounts of advice, office work and litigation services to coverage of almost every legal need that might arise. Some plans even provide for "major legal" expenses

[6] Lillian Deitch and David Weinstein, *Prepaid Legal Services: Socioeconomic Impacts* (1976), p. 6. Deitch is an economist and Secretary of the Futures Group. Weinstein is an independent consultant in matters concerning the administration of justice and protection of personal property.

[7] The Resource Center for Consumers of Legal Services is a tax-exempt, nonprofit organization that was established in 1975 in Washington, D.C., to analyze, produce and promote the most effective techniques for developing legal services plans.

just as health plans cover "major medical" problems. Most plans, however, do not provide coverage when lawsuits are initiated by the insured, an exclusion designed to discourage trigger-happy litigants.

Pre-paid legal insurance dates only from the early 1970s, and it has spread considerably in the last four years. A 1973 amendment to the Taft-Hartley Act allowed legal services to be a subject for collective bargaining. At its 1973 convention, the AFL-CIO recommended that pre-paid plans be incorporated into the collective bargaining programs of all affiliated national and international unions. The pre-paid movement achieved an important breakthrough in February 1975, when the ABA, after intense debate, adopted rules for the establishment, operation and promotion of pre-paid plans. Such plans also received a boost from last year's tax reform law, which put legal insurance on a par with health insurance, granting tax exemptions both for employers' premium payments and for the dollar value of services provided under insurance coverage.

Critics of legal insurance say such programs could lead to higher, not lower, legal costs. They cite the tendency of health care costs to rise under health insurance programs such as Blue Cross and Blue Shield. If legal insurance becomes widespread, the critics say, lawyers will feel free to raise prices, as doctors have done, confident that the insurance companies will pay whatever they charge.

Legal Clinics for Middle-Income Americans

Another alternative to traditional methods of providing legal services is the legal clinic. Patterned after low-cost medical clinics, legal clinics provide basic legal services for substantially lower prices than those charged by most lawyers. Most clinics also let clients pay in installments or with credit cards. Legal clinics are able to keep prices down by handling a high volume of cases and by making use of "paralegals" *(see box, p. 72)*, standardized forms and procedures, and other money-saving efficiencies.

Persons who oppose legal clinics argue that they provide unfair competition that will drive out individual lawyers and small law practices. Clinic advocates say that competition is healthy for any business. They add that clinics do not take potential clients away from existing lawyers, but instead draw people who otherwise would not seek legal advice. Legal clinics were never intended as a panacea for every legal problem, Denver lawyer Karen Metzger wrote in *Trial* magazine. Rather, they were viewed as a means of handling routine matters such as uncontested divorces, individual bankruptcies, consumer problems, traffic questions, landlord-tenant disputes, wills, and real estate transactions.[8] Generally, legal clinics are not prepared to pursue big cases pushed by consumer, environmental or other public interest groups—most of these are handled by "public interest" law firms financed through foundation grants.[9]

The country's first legal clinic was set up in Los Angeles in 1972 by two young lawyers, Stephen Z. Meyers and Leonard D. Jacoby. Today, Meyers and Jacoby have four offices in the Los Angeles area which serve about 350 clients a month. Despite their success only about 10 other legal clinics are known to be operating around the country. The slow growth of legal clinics, according to Meyers and Jacoby, is due to the opposition of the organized bar, which, they say, feels "economically threatened by such a successful attempt at delivering high-quality, low-cost legal services."[10] On the other hand, the ABA itself is sponsoring an experimental legal clinic in Philadelphia. Fees at the eight-month-old clinic range from $10 for the initial visit to $350 for an uncontested divorce.

Supreme Court's Decision on Advertising

The number of legal clinics in the United States is expected to increase significantly now that the Supreme Court has lifted restrictions on advertising legal fees and services. The court ruled June 27 that state laws and bar association rules against advertising by lawyers violated the First Amendment right to free speech. Supporters of legal clinics had long maintained that the clinics needed to advertise to attract enough business to offer low rates.

The ruling reversed a decision by the Arizona Supreme Court. The Arizona court last year upheld the public censure of two young attorneys, John Bates and Van O'Steen, who had placed an ad in a Phoenix newspaper, the *Arizona Republic,* to publicize their legal clinic. The censure was rooted in an advertising ban originated by the ABA in 1908 and subsequently adopted in all of the states, either by statute or court-imposed regulation. Defenders of the ban said it helped protect consumers from unscrupulous lawyers, discouraged needless lawsuits, and preserved the dignity and standards of the legal profession.

But the Supreme Court rejected these arguments. Justice Harry A. Blackmun, writing for the majority, said: "It is at least somewhat incongruous for the opponents of advertising to extol

---

[8] Karen Metzger, "Legal Clinics: Getting into the Routine," *Trial,* June 1976, p. 32.

[9] Public interest law generally is defined as legal representation for persons and groups that have been unrepresented or underrepresented. *(See p. 565.)*

[10] Quoted in "Legal Clinics: Lawyers in Storefronts," *Consumer Reports,* May 1977, p. 287.

Use of Paralegals

Some traditional law firms, as well as legal clinics and public interest law firms, have turned to non-lawyers—paralegals—to help them with their work. Lay persons have been involved in the practice of law since colonial times, when no special training was required to assume the role of attorney or judge. But according to Constance D. Capistrant, executive director of the National Alliance of Paralegal and Consumer Interests, it was not until the 1960s that paralegals were employed extensively to perform "lawyer tasks."

Today paralegals perform a wide variety of tasks. They may interview clients and witnesses; prepare case histories and do legal research; assist in preparing depositions, motions and pleadings; preparing wills and materials for divorce, custody and adoption proceedings, real estate transfer closings and incorporation filings.

Training of paralegals is almost as varied as the types of work they do. Some paralegals are trained on the job—some through experience as legal secretaries. Others hold degrees in paralegal studies from two- or four-year colleges. Still others are trained in special paralegal institutes, some of whose programs accept persons with only a high school diploma.

the virtues and altruism of the legal profession at one point, and, at another, to assert that its members will seize the opportunity to mislead and distort." Blackmun went on to say: "Bankers and engineers advertise, and yet these professions are not regarded as undignified. In fact, it has been suggested that the failure of lawyers to advertise creates public disillusionment with the profession. The absence of advertising may be seen to reflect the profession's failure to reach out and serve the community."

In a dissenting opinion, Justice Lewis F. Powell[11] said he was "apprehensive" that the decision "will be viewed by tens of thousands of lawyers as an invitation to engage in competitive advertising on an escalating basis." Powell did not oppose all advertising by attorneys, but decried price advertising: "It has long been thought that price advertising of legal services inevitably will be misleading because such services are individualized...and because the lay consumer of legal services usually does not know in advance the precise nature and scope of the services he requires.... The type of advertisement before us will inescapably mislead many who respond to it. In the end it will promote distrust of lawyers and disrespect for our own system of justice."

---

[11] Others dissenting were Chief Justice Warren E. Burger, Justices Potter Stewart and William H. Rehnquist. Joining Justice Blackmun in the majority opinion were Justices William J. Brennan Jr., Byron R. White, Thurgood Marshall and John Paul Stevens.

The majority opinion made clear that the decision was a narrow one concerning the newspaper advertising of routine services and fees, and that there remained a large area in which such attorney advertising could be curtailed or regulated. "There may be reasonable restrictions on the time, place and manner of advertising," Blackmun wrote. Advertising that was false, deceptive or misleading was subject to restraint, as well as advertising focusing on the claimed quality of service or involving in-person soliciting of clients. The decision left unclear whether television and radio ads would be acceptable.

It is too early to assess the impact of the Supreme Court ruling. Most observers say that it will principally benefit young attorneys just starting out in the business, smaller firms and legal clinics. For the moment, most big law firms appear to be adopting a wait-and-see attitude. There is much disagreement as to how legal costs will be affected by advertising. In the majority opinion, Blackmun wrote: "It is entirely possible that advertising will serve to reduce...the cost of legal services to the consumers." But others contend that the added expense of advertising will be shifted to clients, thus diluting whatever consumer savings might result from increased competition.

There also has been some concern expressed that the expense of advertising will bear hardest on the new members of the profession rather than on established law firms. James G. Reardon, president of the Massachusetts Academy of Trial Lawyers, said last year: "[Advertising] would be most unfair to those least able to afford it—the young practitioner just launching his career who has no allowance in his budget for an expensive campaign. Those firms whose volume of cases makes it possible for them to absorb such cost would have no need to hype an already successful office."[12]

Public Interest Law Movement

NEBRASKA LAWYER Roscoe Pound, who later would become America's foremost legal educator, delivered an address entitled "The Causes of Popular Dissatisfaction with the Administration of Justice" to the House of Delegates of the American Bar Association at its 1906 meeting in St. Paul, Minn. Pound told his fellow jurists: "The law does not respond quickly to new conditions. It does not change until ill effects are felt; often not until they are felt acutely." Those familiar with the

[12] Quoted by Barbara A. Stein, "Is Professional Advertising Unprofessional?" *Trial*, June 1976, p. 37.

history of public interest law have little reason to question Pound's words. A study undertaken in the 1970s by F. Raymond Marks for the American Bar Foundation concluded that the organized bar was "slow to recognize the consequences of the inequality of access to legal representation." Marks wrote:

> Although early views of a lawyer's responsibility to represent all who sought representation did include reference to the unpopular cause or client, they failed to include any recognition of a duty to represent those who lacked the lawyer's price.[13]

To a great extent, the legal profession was simply reflecting the attitudes of the broader community where, before the beginning of the 20th century, little formal attention was directed to the needs of the poor.

The access of the poor to legal services was further restricted by the emergence of a minimum fee concept which prevented lawyers from basing their charges on the client's ability to pay. Paradoxically, however, the adoption of minimum fee schedules forced the legal profession to face up to the problems of the poor. "If attention had not been paid to those who could not afford minimum fees," Marks wrote, "the bar would have been open to community charges and to self-admission that law and justice were for the rich and not the poor."

This new concern led to the establishment of legal aid societies to assist those who could not pay for legal advice. Legal aid services were available in New York City as early as 1876, and by 1916 there were 41 legal aid organizations in the United States, according to Emery Brownell.[14] The following year, the first national conference of state and local bar associations adopted a resolution urging the associations to help in forming and administering "Legal Aid societies for...the worthy poor." In 1922, the American Bar Association recommended that every state and local bar association appoint "a Standing Committee on Legal Aid Work."

One reason for the organized bar's growing interest in legal aid work was the publication in 1924 of Reginald Heber Smith's classic work, *Justice and the Poor.* Smith wrote that legal aid societies were "relieving the bar of a heavy burden by performing for the bar its legal and ethical obligation to see that no one shall suffer injustices through inability, because of poverty, to obtain needed legal advice and assistance." For Smith, legal aid work was a professional duty and not a charitable option. Most lawyers, however, did not share Smith's outlook. To them, Marks observed, "legal aid work was something that was out-

---

[13] F. Raymond Marks, *The Lawyer, The Public, and Professional Responsibility* (1972), pp. 15-16.

[14] Emery Brownell, *Legal Aid in the United States* (1951), p. 11.

side of professional pursuits—in fact, as organized, it was done by others, by staff lawyers considered marginal by the bar generally...." He added: "This is not to say that individual lawyers did not contribute money to legal aid, or, as a matter of charity, render assistance to 'deserving poor' on a no-fee or a reduced fee basis; they did. It is simply to say that the bar as a whole did not assume this responsibility."[15]

Court-Required Counsel; Poverty Programs

One aspect of poverty law did command growing attention—the problem of the indigent criminal defendant. One explanation for this, according to Marks, is that since relatively few lawyers made their living as defense attorneys, "the notion of professional responsibility to include free legal counsel in that area would bring little threat to the economic self-interest of the bar as a whole." But even more significant "was the awareness that the Sixth Amendment of the Constitution provides that a person accused of a crime shall be entitled to the assistance of counsel." Gradually the courts adopted the position that when defendants could not afford a lawyer, the courts would appoint one to represent him without charge.

In 1932, the Supreme Court extended the right to counsel to indigent defendants in state cases involving the death penalty.[16] This right was applied in 1938 to all federal felony cases and in 1963 to indigents in all felony cases.[17] The Supreme Court in 1966 established the suspect's right to counsel during police questioning, and in 1967 it ruled that juvenile courts must provide youths with counsel, even though these court proceedings are considered civil rather than criminal.[18]

Legal aid came into its own in the mid-1960s during the civil rights movement. *Fortune* magazine writer Peter Vanderwicken traced the legal activism of the 1960s to the summer of 1964 when some 400 law students and young lawyers went to Mississippi to defend civil rights workers who were registering blacks to vote. "They discovered there," Vanderwicken wrote, "that the blacks' problems were compounded by their inability to get legal advice and protection."[19]

President Johnson made access to legal services an important part of his war on poverty. When the Office of Economic Opportunity was established in 1965, it included legal services in the Community Action Program. The inadequacies of privately funded legal aid programs had been described the previous year

[15] Marks, *op. cit.*, pp. 18-19.
[16] *Powell v. Alabama,* 287 U.S. 45 (1932).
[17] *Johnson v. Zerbst,* 304 U.S. 458 (1938) and *Gideon v. Wainwright,* 372 U.S. 335 (1963). For a discussion of events leading to the *Gideon* decision, see *Gideon's Trumpet* (1964) by Anthony Lewis.
[18] *Miranda v. Arizona,* 384 U.S. 436 (1966) and *In re Gault,* 387 U.S. 1 (1967).
[19] Peter Vanderwicken, "The Angry Young Lawyers," *Fortune,* September 1971, p. 77.

by the president of the National Legal Aid and Defender Association. In the organization's 1964 annual report, he said: "Too often troubled people find that legal aid does not really exist in their communities or that it is fenced off from them by too stringent eligibility rules, anachronistic policy on the type of cases handled, lack of publicity, insufficient staff personnel or unconscionable delay in services."

Within a year of OEO's establishment, its budget for legal services ($20-million) was nearly double that of the legal aid societies affiliated with the National Legal Aid and Defender Association ($11.7-million). During fiscal year 1967, the anti-poverty agency boosted the funds allocated to legal services projects by $5-million. By the end of 1967, according to Sar A. Levitan, the legal services program was funding 250 projects, providing legal assistance in 48 states, employing nearly 2,000 lawyers in 800 neighborhood law offices, and devoting 49 other projects to research, training and technical assistance. OEO lawyers helped poor people fight creditors and landlords in court, obtain divorces and declare bankruptcy.[20] The 1968 *Report of the National Advisory Commission on Civil Disorders* commended the legal services program for making "a good beginning in providing legal assistance to the poor."[21]

The legal services program became mired in controversy in succeeding years. Conservative critics charged that its interests were social activism rather than helping poor people. The Nixon administration, opposed to much of Johnson's anti-poverty program, sought to dismantle the Office of Economic Opportunity and its legal services program. Supporters of legal services for the poor sought to preserve the program by placing it in an independent, quasi-private corporation. Nixon, in 1971, vetoed one bill to create a legal services corporation and threatened to veto another the following year, thereby effectively killing the measure.[22] A Senate filibuster blocked a similar bill in 1973. Legal services legislation in 1974 became embroiled in Watergate pressures, but was passed and signed by Nixon a few days before his resignation.

The Legal Services Corporation Act established an 11-member board to govern the corporation, with the members appointed by the President and subject to Senate confirmation. The law restricted the activities of legal services lawyers in several ways. For example, they were prohibited from handling cases involving such controversial matters as school

[20] Sar A. Levitan, *The Great Society's Poor Law: A New Approach to Poverty* (1969), p. 179.

[21] The commission was set up by President Johnson on July 27, 1967, after riots erupted in Newark, Detroit and several other cities. The commission was instructed to find the underlying causes of the riots and to recommend courses of action.

[22] See Congressional Quarterly, *Congress and the Nation,* Vol. III, p. 608.

desegregation, abortion and draft evasion. The act also contained a provision intended to eliminate "back-up centers"—outside "poverty law" research centers doing work for legal services programs.

Bills to lift some of these restrictions were approved in May 1977 by the House Judiciary Committee and the Senate Human Resources Committee but have not received floor action.[23] The president of the Legal Services Corporation, Thomas Ehrlich, testified in favor of removing all restrictions on legal services attorneys, a position supported by the American Bar Association. "Poor people should not be prevented from vindicating their rights through lawful means simply because a given issue may be politically unpopular," Ehrlich told the Senate Subcommittee on Employment, Poverty and Migrant Labor on April 25.

Ralph Nader and the Citizen Law Movement

While legal services lawyers concentrated on individual cases and client needs, other public interest lawyers litigated issues affecting broad segments of the public, such as consumer and environmental protection. Nearly 100 public interest law centers now operate in the United States, according to a recent study conducted by the Council for Public Interest Law.[24] Mitchell Rogovin, co-chairman of the council, wrote recently in the *American Bar Association Journal:*

> These centers were established in response to the problem that policy formulation in our society is too often a one-sided affair, a process in which only the voices of the economically or politically powerful are heard.... Ordinary citizens, because they are poorly organized and without financing, are unable to purchase the legal representation necessary to make their interests known, too.... Public interest law centers, by giving voice to citizen views in public policy deliberations, have made great strides in correcting this imbalance and assuring that government works for everyone, not just the rich and powerful.[25]

Ralph Nader is probably the country's best-known public interest lawyer. His career in consumer advocacy drew national attention with the publication of his book *Unsafe at any Speed* in November 1965 and General Motors' mishandled attempt to investigate his private life.[26] Although Nader attacked the entire U.S. automobile industry for emphasizing profits and styl-

[23] See *CQ Weekly Report,* June 4, 1977, p. 1104.

[24] Council for Public Interest Law, *Balancing the Scales of Justice: Financing Public Interest Law in America* (1976). The Council for Public Interest Law was set up in January 1975 under the sponsorship of the American Bar Association and the Edna McConnell Clark Foundation, the Ford Foundation and the Rockefeller Brothers Fund.

[25] Mitchell Rogovin, "Public Interest Law: The Next Horizon," *American Bar Association Journal,* March 1977, p. 336.

[26] The GM-sponsored investigation by private detectives drew a public apology from the corporation's president, James M. Roche, at televised hearings before the Senate Subcommittee on Executive Reorganization, March 22, 1966. Roche acknowledged that the investigation entailed some "harassment" of Nader.

ing rather than safety, he concentrated his fire on the Chevrolet Corvair. Chevrolet's subsequent decision to stop making the car and Congress's passage of the National Traffic and Motor Vehicle Safety Act of 1966 were both attributable to the book's influence.

Having won his initial victory on auto safety, Nader turned his attention to other areas where he felt the public interest was threatened. These included health hazards in mining, safety standards for natural-gas pipelines, the lot of American Indians, and indiscriminate use of X-rays in dental examinations. In the past decade Nader has greatly expanded the scope of his activities on behalf of consumers. To this end he has set up a number of organizations staffed largely by idealistic young people who receive small salaries and work exceptionally long hours—as does Nader himself.

The parent Nader organization is the Center for the Study of Responsive Law, based in Washington, D.C. Other important Nader groups are the Public Interest Research Group and the Corporate Accountability Research Group. Under the umbrella of a group called Public Citizen Inc., Nader sponsors seven public interest groups: Congress Watch, Critical Mass (an environmental group), Health Research Group, Freedom of Information Act Clearinghouse, Litigation Group, Tax Reform Research Group and the Public Citizen Visitors Center.

One of the earliest public interest law firms in the nation is not connected with the Nader organization. It is the Washington-based Center for Law and Social Policy, which engages in consumer affairs, environmental issues, health care, foreign affairs, women's rights, occupational safety and health, mine safety and media access. The Mental Health Law Project, an offshoot of the center, is devoted entirely to protecting the rights of mental patients. Some public interest groups, such as the Natural Resources Defense Council and the Sierra Club Legal Defense Fund are devoted to environmental issues.

Although the practice of public interest law is centered in Washington, such firms are now operating across the nation. Public Advocates, a San Francisco firm, is involved in education, employment, women's rights and the environment. The Women's Law Fund in Cleveland specializes in sex discrimination issues. Others are found elsewhere.

Problem of Funding Public Interest Firms

Over the years, public interest law has had a continuing problem: the lack of adequate and stable sources of funding. The principal source of funding has been foundation grants. But some persons fear this source may soon dry up. This fear was in-

Legal Conduct and Competence

Responding to a growing number of malpractice suits against lawyers, the American legal community has mounted a campaign to rid the profession of dishonest and incompetent members. In the past four years, there has been a 172 per cent increase in disciplinary actions taken against lawyers by professional legal groups. More than $8-million a year now is being spent on lawyer discipline—most of it by the legal profession itself.

Not everyone is satisfied with lawyers' efforts to police themselves. A recent report commissioned by Public Citizen, a Ralph Nader group, concluded that lawyers' self-regulation attempts had failed to provide adequate disciplining either of lawyers or judges. Although clients filed more than 37,000 complaints against lawyers in 1976, only 1,757 lawyers were disciplined, according to the American Bar Association.

In recent years the public has begun to take a more active role in judging legal competency. Herbert S. Denenberg, a former Pennsylvania insurance commissioner, has written "The Shoppers' Guide to Lawyers," a pamphlet now included in the *Shoppers' Guide Book.* The ABA advises the public not to hesitate to discuss fees with a lawyer. A good lawyer, the association said, should be able to provide a reasonably exact estimate of the costs for his services.

creased by the economic recession of 1973-74, which reduced the assets of most private foundations, inducing them to cut back on their grants. The Ford Foundation, for example, announced a 20 per cent across-the-board decrease in its support for public interest law.[27] Foundation funding presents other problems as well. Along with the money comes an Internal Revenue Service prohibition on lobbying by tax-exempt organizations.

The funding problems of public interest law firms were aggravated by a 1975 Supreme Court decision, *Alyeska Pipeline Service Co. v. Wilderness Society,*[28] which brought a halt to the widespread practice of awarding attorney's fees to the winning side in public interest cases. Striking down an award of attorney's fees to environmental groups which had challenged construction of the Alaska oil pipeline, the Supreme Court held that federal judges could not make such awards unless Congress expressly authorized them to do so.[29]

The congressional response to the *Alyeska* decision was the Civil Rights Attorney's Fees Awards Act of 1976. This act authorized fee awards, in the discretion of the courts, to victorious parties in cases brought under federal civil rights laws;

[27] See Carlyle W. Hall Jr., "In the Public Interest," *The Center Magazine,* January-February 1977, p. 31.

[28] 421 U.S. 240 (1975).

[29] A number of environmental and civil rights statutes provide for fee awards and were not affected by the *Alyeska* decision.

fee awards already available under other laws were left intact. Although most public interest advocates applauded the new law, Howard Lesnick, a law professor at the University of Pennsylvania, expressed concern that the foundations might seize on it to justify a further decrease in their support of public interest law firms.[30]

One funding proposal is to increase the contributions of the organized bar—perhaps through a system of voluntary checkoffs from annual bar association dues. A checkoff system for the benefit of legal aid has been in effect for many years in Chicago, and recently the Arizona State Bar established a dues checkoff for public interest firms in that state. The Council for Public Interest Law has proposed creation of a National Fund for Public Interest Law, to help finance public interest law efforts nationwide, especially in localities where resources are not readily available. The council has proposed that the ABA develop a voluntary dues checkoff system for this national fund, a plan supported by Supreme Court Justice Thurgood Marshall, among others.[31]

Another proposal is to let the government provide citizen advocates. They are already provided in a number of state attorneys general offices, and New Jersey is now operating a public advocate office as a separate state agency. "Placing the representation of the public in the hands of the state gives the public interest lawyer a secure base he or she has never enjoyed before," wrote Barbara Stein.[32] However, such plans pose problems. "Because public interest law centers are so heavily involved in the monitoring of government," argued Mitchell Rogovin of the Council for Public Interest Law, "it is crucial that their major support continue to come from nongovernmental sources."

Resolution of 'Minor Disputes'

PERSONS CONCERNED with improving the quality and broadening the scope of citizen access to legal help have found themselves in the middle of a complex debate over the role of the courts in resolving the conflicts and problems of American society. Among those who argue that the resolution of so-called "minor disputes" should be removed as much as

[30] Howard Lesnick, "What Next for Public Interest Law," *Judicature*, May 1977, p. 467.

[31] See Thurgood Marshall, "Financing Public Interest Law Practice: The Role of the Organized Bar," *American Bar Association Journal*, December 1975, p. 1488.

[32] Barbara A. Stein, "Public Interest Law: A Balancing Act," *Trial*, February 1976, p. 14. See also Arthur Penn, "Advocate from Within," *Trial*, February 1976, p. 20.

possible from the traditional legal framework is Chief Justice Warren E. Burger. "The notion that most people want black-robed judges, well-dressed lawyers and fine-paneled courtrooms as the setting to resolve their disputes is not correct," Burger said in a speech May 27. "People with problems, people with pains, want relief, and they want it as quickly and inexpensively as possible." If we do not devise substitutes for the courtroom processes, Burger continued, "we may well be on our way to a society overrun by hordes of lawyers hungry as locusts...."[33]

Burger has long spoken in favor of reducing federal court workloads. Under Burger's direction, the Supreme Court in recent years has handed down a number of decisions that have limited the types of cases that the federal courts may hear.[34] This has been done in some cases simply by stating that federal courts must use great discretion in intervening in state court proceedings. It has been done in other cases either by a stricter interpretation of the standards that a person must meet to get into court or by procedural obstacles to class action suits.

In his campaign to reduce the court's workload and to develop alternatives to litigation, Burger has recently been joined by a powerful ally—Attorney General Griffin B. Bell, a former federal appellate court judge. Bell generally endorses Burger's position that the court system is overcrowded, and he has said that one of his main priorities as Attorney General will be to provide better access to justice without putting an additional strain on the resources of the courts. To help achieve this goal, Bell has set up a new Office for Improvements in the Administration of Justice, headed by a former University of Virginia Law professor, Daniel J. Meador.

Proposed Substitutes for the Judicial Process

The Department of Justice announced recently that it was sponsoring an experimental program to give the public a speedy and inexpensive way to resolve minor disputes through neighborhood justice centers that would serve as alternatives to the courts. Bell said that three experimental centers, all funded with federal money but under local control, would be in operation by the fall. The centers would attempt, through mediation, to settle the sort of disputes—domestic spats, claims by customers against merchants, arguments between landlord and tenants—that clog the dockets of the lower courts in American cities.

---

[33] Burger made his remarks at a conference on the resolution of minor disputes sponsored by the American Bar Association at Columbia University in New York. The conference was a follow-up of an April 1976 conference convened by the Chief Justice in St. Paul, Minn., to commemorate the 70th anniversary of Roscoe Pound's address on "The Causes of Popular Dissatisfaction with the Administration of Justice."

[34] See "Politics and the Federal Courts," *E.R.R.*, 1977 Vol. I, pp. 473-496. See also *CQ Weekly Report*, June 18, 1977, pp. 1229-1234.

Other alternatives to litigation currently being explored include wider use of arbitration, mediation and conciliation; decriminalization of victimless crimes; expansion of the no-fault concept; and promoting the use of ombudsmen and newspaper and radio "action lines." Provisions requiring compulsory arbitration already are in effect in Pennsylvania, Ohio and New York, and in some cases apply to virtually all lawsuits involving claims for damages up to $10,000. Disputes between parties that have a continuing relationship, such as those between landlord and tenants, employer and employees, and certain disagreements over sales of consumer goods, are particularly suitable for resolution by arbitration, according to Junius L. Allison, a professor of law at Vanderbilt University.[35]

There has been much discussion recently of expanding the small claims court system. An ABA task force concluded that "revitalization and expanded use of small claims courts offers substantial promise of assuring the delivery of justice to all citizens in a manner which is both speedy and efficient."[36] Experiments with small claims courts in the United States began about 1913, after Roscoe Pound suggested there was a need to "make adequate provision for petty litigation." In 1924, Reginald Heber Smith, the legal aid pioneer, called for an alternative forum in which the poor litigant could seek relief in matters involving difficulties with landlords, creditors and employers. Early experiments with small claims courts in Oregon, Kansas and Cleveland, Ohio, were based on these suggestions.

The main advantage to the small claims courts, often hailed as "the people's court" or "consumer's forum," is that plaintiffs can file their cases for a small fee, usually about $6, and usually do not have an attorney. The cases are often settled in less than two months. However, even with the relaxed rules, people representing themselves often do not do well in small claims cases. A Virginia judge said recently that most citizens who represent themselves are at a disadvantage because they do not present adequate evidence and testimony. "People just haven't been to law school and they're facing someone who has and they usually end up losing," said Robert M. Hurst, chief judge of the Fairfax County General District Court.[37]

Opposition to Limiting Access to the Courts

The commitment by Burger and Bell to develop alternatives to litigation has provoked much opposition from consumer and

[35] Junius L. Allison, "Problems in the Delivery of Legal Services," *American Bar Association Journal,* April 1977, p. 519.

[36] American Bar Association, "Report of Pound Conference Follow-Up Task Force," August 1976, p. 12. The task force was headed by Griffin B. Bell, currently the Attorney General.

[37] Quoted in *The Washington Post,* May 15, 1977.

environmental groups, representatives of the poor and public interest lawyers. They argue that the federal courts ought to remain the principal instruments for resolving many of the disputes under discussion. They also fear that Burger's view of access to the federal courts is in reality an attempt to undermine their cases. Shutting down procedural access to the courts is seen by these individuals and groups as a veiled attack on the substantive rights and remedies that they wish to pursue in the federal courts.

"Obviously, certain matters can and should be resolved in forums that are cheaper, quicker, and more informal than the courts," wrote Charles R. Halpern, executive director of the Center for Public Interest Law. "But the effort to identify these matters and to create these forums should not blind us to the importance of opening the courts to a range of significant cases that are too frequently kept out by doctrinal restrictions and high litigation costs."[38]

Sandy DeMent of the National Resource Center for Consumers of Legal Services questioned Burger's selection of minor disputes as the best cases to be funneled into alternative forums. Why not pick on antitrust cases, contract cases or other large issues, she asked? DeMent told Editorial Research Reports that she is not opposed to developing alternatives to litigation, but she said that it was imperative that their use be kept voluntary. She expressed the fear that people would be coerced into using them, and thus effectively denied their day in court.

Public interest lawyers are particularly concerned about the recent Supreme Court decisions that have limited citizen access to the federal courts. Halpern wrote: "The Supreme Court's decisions on standing, class actions, and awards of attorney's fees reflect a trend toward making legal recourse less accessible to ordinary citizens. Such decisions are likely to increase popular dissatisfaction with the administration of justice. It is essential to reverse that trend."

Numerous bills have been introduced in Congress to overturn many of the restrictive Supreme Court decisions and increase citizen access to the courts. Although the bills differ widely in their focus, the one feature common to all is that they run counter to the Supreme Court's effort to reduce the caseload of the federal courts. President Carter placed himself on record April 6 in his consumers' message as favoring "access to justice" legislation. The issues are complex and the debate is certain to continue for some time to come.

---

[38] Charles R. Halpern, "Should Courts Redress Citizen Grievances?" *Judicature*, November 1976, p. 163.

Selected Bibliography

Books

Buckhorn, Robert F., *Nader: The People's Lawyer,* Prentice-Hall, 1972.

Deitch, Lillian and David Weinstein, *Prepaid Legal Services,* Lexington Books, 1976.

Downie, Leonard Jr., *Justice Denied,* Praeger, 1971.

Levitan, Sar A., *The Great Society's Poor Law: A New Approach to Poverty,* Johns Hopkins Press, 1969.

Marks, F. Raymond, *The Lawyer, The Public, and Professional Responsibility,* American Bar Foundation, 1972.

McCarry, Charles, *Citizen Nader,* Saturday Review Press, 1972.

Articles

Allison, Junius L., "Problems in the Delivery of Legal Services," *American Bar Association Journal,* April 1977.

Carter, Luther J., "Public Interest Lawyers: Carter Brings Them Into the Establishment," *Science,* May 27, 1977.

Hager, Barry M., "Access to Justice," *Congressional Quarterly Weekly Report,* June 18, 1977.

Hall, Carlyle W. Jr., "In the Public Interest," *The Center Magazine,* January-February 1977.

Halpern, Charles R., "Should Courts Redress Citizen Grievances?" *Judicature,* November 1976.

"How to Choose a Lawyer (and what to do then)," *Consumer Reports,* May 1977.

"Lower Fees, Better Service—Changes Coming in Law Practice," *U.S. News & World Report,* Sept. 22, 1975.

Rogovin, Mitchell, "Public Interest Law: The Next Horizon," *American Bar Association Journal,* March 1977.

St. Antoine, Theodore J., "Growth Patterns in Legal Services," *AFL-CIO American Federationist,* March 1976.

"The Chilling Impact of Litigation," *Business Week,* June 6, 1977.

"To Advertise or Not to Advertise," *American Bar Association Journal,* March 1977.

Trial magazine, selected issues.

Reports and Studies

American Bar Association, "A Primer of Prepaid Legal Services," April 1976.

——"Report of the Pound Conference Follow-Up Task Force," August 1976.

——"Report on the National Conference on the Causes of Popular Dissatisfaction with the Administration of Justice," April 1976.

"Causes of Popular Dissatisfaction with the Administration of Justice," Hearings Before the Senate Committee on Constitutional Rights, May 19, 1976.

Editorial Research Reports, "Legal Profession in Transition," 1972 Vol. II, p. 581; "Politics and the Federal Courts," 1977 Vol. I, p. 473.

"Reducing the Costs of Legal Services: Possible Approaches by the Federal Government," A Report prepared for the Senate Subcommittee on Representation of Citizens Interests, Oct. 8, 1974.

MEDIA REFORMERS

by

William V. Thomas

Dec. 23
1977

Editor's Note: A new development since the original publication of this report was the Federal Trade Commission's vote on Feb. 22, 1978, to consider restrictions on television advertising aimed at children. The commission stopped short of proposing an outright ban on certain commercials as recommended by an FTC staff report. The proposal under consideration would prohibit any type of TV commercial directed at audiences composed of "a significant proportion" of children "too young to understand" the purpose of the ad.

The proposed rule also would prohibit commercials for sugared products seen by older children. Hearings on the proposed restrictions were held by the FTC in San Francisco in January 1979. Five weeks of additional hearings are scheduled to be held in Washington, D.C., beginning in March 1979.

MEDIA REFORMERS

LIKE MANY AMERICAN institutions in the last decade, the press and broadcast media have come under increasing criticism. The old debate over their rights and responsibilities has been marked recently by the appearance of hundreds of citizen-organized reform groups. Representing a broad cross-section of political and religious leanings, they are drawn together by the common goal of gaining a greater voice in setting media standards. As the number of so-called "watchdog" organizations has grown, so, it seems, has their determination. Network executives and newspaper editors "may not know it yet," said a spokesman for a religious group, "but they're about to be hit by a revolution."[1]

The charge most frequently made by reform groups is that the press and commercial television networks are more concerned with profits than principles of accuracy and fairness. Particular complaints cover a wide range of alleged faults from biased news coverage in daily papers to a distorted depiction of life on television. Yet underlying nearly every aspect of the current protest is a belief that the First Amendment's guarantee of freedom of the press also implies the right of readers and viewers to help in determining how that freedom should be used.[2]

A general dissatisfaction with news ethics, prompted partly by Nixon administration attacks on the press,[3] has been credited with encouraging the appearance of journalistic self-criticism in many of the nation's papers as well as an increase in space allotted to letters to the editor. Under viewer pressure, a few television advertisers have even said they would withdraw their support from shows that depict violence. But, according to Charles B. Seib, ombudsman for *The Washington Post,* media owners "have not faced up to...the fundamental issues" being raised by angry consumers.[4]

Reed Irvine, chairman of Accuracy in Media (AIM), an organization that monitors press and television news reporting, takes the position that the big media corporations have used

[1] Carl Richardson of the Church of God, quoted in *TV Guide,* Oct. 1, 1977. The Church of God, which claims 457,000 members, organized a TV boycott the week of April 10-16, 1977, to protest "televised violence and sex."

[2] See "Access to the Media," *E.R.R.,* 1974 Vol. I, pp. 447-470.

[3] See "First Amendment and Mass Media," *E.R.R.,* 1970 Vol. I, pp. 41-60.

[4] Charles B. Seib, *The Washington Post,* Nov. 5, 1976.

their power in a biased and therefore potentially dangerous fashion. AIM calls itself a watchdog group devoted to promoting "fairness in reporting on critical issues," which it feels are often shaded by the media's liberal perspective. Others, however, have accused AIM of allowing a politically conservative bias of its own to color much of its activity. Speaking last year to a meeting of journalists, Irvine expressed AIM's basic philosophy this way: "No society is truly free without a free press, but the existence of a free press does not necessarily guarantee a free society. Unfortunately, history indicates that a free press may contribute to its own destruction and to the destruction of all other freedoms.... There is some reason to question whether or not we have gone too far for our own good, perhaps creating a monster which may [destroy] many of the freedoms we cherish, including freedom of the press."[5]

While many reform groups agree on the general goal of increasing access to the media, most of them seek to further their own particular interests. Some have been mobilized to challenge a single news story or broadcast, as was the case when various pro-gun groups joined together in 1975 to protest a CBS-TV program, "The Guns of Autumn," that was critical of hunting. Among business corporations, General Motors and the Mobil Oil Co., monitor the media and run aggressive "opinion advertising" to correct what they consider erroneous news coverage of matters relating to their operations.

Campaign Against Violence on Television

The one issue that seems to unite the often disparate factions of the media reform movement is television violence, which, it is claimed, gives young watchers a warped conception of human behavior. That theory received considerable national attention in October when 15-year-old Ronald Zamora of Miami was tried and convicted of murdering an elderly woman. The defense attorney contended that Zamora was innocent of willful homicide because "he was suffering from and acted under the influence of prolonged, intense, involuntary, subliminal television intoxication.... The tube became [the boy's] parents, his school and church." Zamora, he added, had been so conditioned to kill by watching "endless hours" of televised violence that murder itself was no more than the "acting out of a television script."

A Dade County (Fla.) jury found Zamora guilty and sentenced him to 25 years to life in prison. But the trial, which incidentally was televised in Florida as part of a special experiment allowing cameras in court, raised a number of questions about the effects of watching dramatized mayhem on television. A University of Pennsylvania study in 1976 revealed

[5] Speech to the Missouri Press Convention in St. Louis, Oct. 22, 1976.

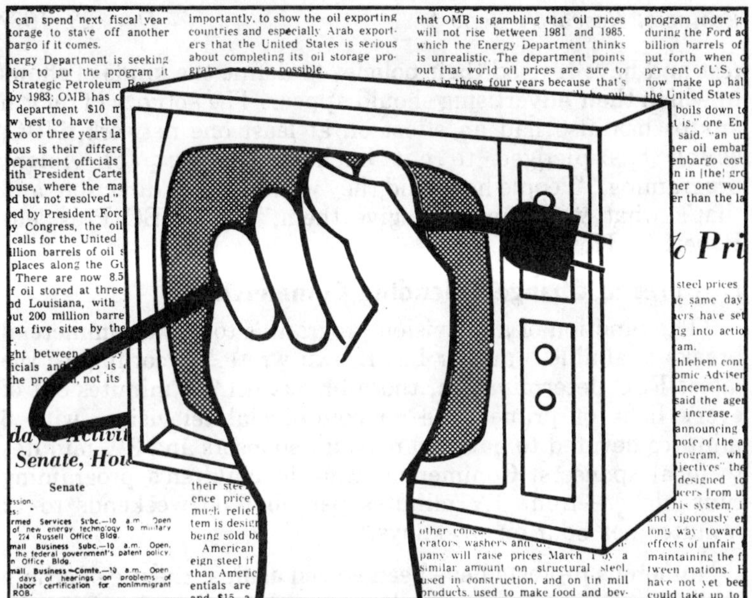

that the index of television violence that year had increased sharply over the previous year—despite a network policy of setting aside a two-hour "family viewing" period free of violence each weekday evening. The most violent shows, the survey found, were those broadcast on Saturday morning and aimed exclusively at children. The study concluded "that while all viewers absorb TV 'lessons' of fear, suspicion and mistrust, children are the most affected by the 'mean world syndrome' of television programing."[6]

Figures cited in July by the National Parent-Teachers Association, which last year began a vigorous campaign against violence on television, indicated that the average child now watches 6 to 6½ hours of television a day, while preschool children view 25 hours of television a week. "We don't think [children] can watch...rape and murder night after night, week after week without being affected by it," said William M. Young, project director of the PTA's current boycott of products that sponsor violent shows. Although some critics of television violence believe that protests should be directed at the networks instead of program sponsors, reform groups have been successful in forcing changes in some programs through the threat of product boycotts.

Media Watch, a monthly newsletter published by the National Citizens Committee for Broadcasting, a Washington-based reform organization, reported in February that a number of companies are concerned about demonstrations of buyer un-

[6] *Violence Profile, No. 8,* 1976.

rest and have revised their policies to define the kinds of shows in which their advertising should appear. The activity of reform groups has also had an effect on at least one network, NBC, which has pledged to cut back its support for violent programing. "People have said they want another direction, and that's what we're going to give them," said NBC President Robert T. Howard.[7]

Pressures to Change Offending Commercials

"The function of a television program is to make commercial breaks available," author Les Brown wrote.[8] According to the latest FCC determination, those breaks fill 9½ minutes out of every hour of prime time on commercial television, with 6 minutes devoted to national network sponsors and 3½ minutes to local sponsors. Commercial time in children's programing runs higher—from 9½ minutes per hour on weekends to 12 minutes per hour on weekdays.[9]

Numerous protests have been voiced against the use of ethnic and sexual stereotypes in television advertising. In 1967, the Mexican-American Anti-Defamation Committee launched a campaign against the "Frito Bandito," a Mexican cartoon character used in television ads for Frito-Lay corn chips. After four years of controversy, during which time protest groups picketed supermarkets and TV stations in the Southwest, the Frito-Lay Co. finally agreed to discontinue "Frito Bandito" commercials.

The National Organization for Women, whose media task force monitors television commercials, has managed to have some ads "offensive to women" changed or canceled. But a recent NOW survey of 1,241 TV commercials concluded that most product advertisers continue to portray women in a bad light, "as dependent, unintelligent, submissive creatures who are the adjuncts of men."[10]

A U.S. Civil Rights Commission study on women in the media reported that women are misrepresented not only in television advertising but also in most network comedy shows where they frequently are seen in demeaning roles. "The women in situation comedies still tend to be subordinate to the men in their lives," the study said. "Mary [in the "Mary Tyler Moore Show"] calls her boss 'Mr. Grant' even though everyone else calls him 'Lou.' Edith [in "All in the Family"] scoots into the kitchen to fetch Archie a beer and rarely fails to have dinner on

---

[7] Quoted in *Media Watch*, January-February 1977.

[8] Les Brown, *Television: The Business Behind the Box* (1971), p. 65.

[9] Federal Communications Commission, "Report and Policy Statement on Children's Television Programs," *Federal Register*, 1974, p. 39400.

[10] NOW survey cited in the U.S. Civil Rights Commission study "Window Dressing on the Set," August 1977, p. 12.

Rating Television Violence

The following rankings were compiled by the National Citizens Committee for Broadcasting over a two-week period during the spring 1977 television season. They were based on the number and length of violent incidents per show compared to the total time and incidents of violence in all prime time programing. NCCB defines violence as "an overt expression of physical force (with or without weapon) against oneself or other.... An action to be considered violent must be plausible and credible and must include human or human-like characters. It may be an intentional or accidental action, humorous or serious or a combination of both...."

10 Least Violent Shows		10 Most Violent Shows	
Program	**Network**	**Program**	**Network**
Alice	CBS	Starsky and Hutch	ABC
All in the Family	CBS	Wonder Woman	ABC
Bob Newhart	CBS	Baa Baa Black Sheep	NBC
Phyllis	CBS	Baretta	ABC
Maude	CBS	Walt Disney	NBC
Good Times	CBS	Rockford Files	NBC
Welcome Back Kotter	ABC	Quincy	NBC
Fish	ABC	Charlie's Angels	ABC
Happy Days	ABC	Police Woman	NBC
M.A.S.H.	CBS	Kojak	CBS

the table by 6 p.m."[11] The commission's appraisal of television programing itself became a target of criticism in the press. Its recommendations for policing the networks were greeted as an exercise in bureaucratic overkill.

The current focus of the campaign to reform television commercials is on advertising directed toward children. Action for Children's Television (ACT), a public-interest group with the goal of improving children's programing, asked the FCC in 1970 to eliminate all advertising from children's shows and to require every television station to broadcast at least 14 hours of commercial-free children's programs a week. In response to the ACT petition and other expressions of citizen concern, the FCC in 1974 created a special unit to study problems related to children's television. Since that time, the commission's policy has been to rely on the sponsors and producers of children's shows to adopt their own standards of self-regulation, governing commercials and program content. Advertising revenue pays for the programs, the FCC reasoned, and banning all ads on children's television "could have a very damaging effect on the amount and quality of the shows."[12]

---

[11] *Ibid.*, p. 23.
[12] "Report and Policy Statement on Children's Television Programs," *op. cit.*, p. 39399.

The commission's approach has not pleased the critics, who say it has tended to place the interests of broadcasters above the public interest. "In view of the FCC's reluctance to force producers to limit advertising," said Maureen Harmonay of ACT, "we have requested permission to air counter-commercials that inform parents and children about the hazards of certain foods and other products advertised on TV." In November, the U.S. Court of Appeals for the District of Columbia upheld an FCC rule exempting most product commercials from the obligations of the "fairness doctrine" *(see p. 95),* which requires stations to broadcast opposing opinions. However, the appeals court ordered the commission to consider requiring stations to set aside one hour a week for the presentation of messages and lengthier programing by members of local communities and public-interest spokesmen.

News Council's Forum for Grievances

Since its founding in 1973, the National News Council has proven to be one of the most respected news monitoring organizations in the country. Set up under the auspices of the Twentieth Century Fund, the independent council, composed of 18 voluntary members, has two main goals: "to examine and report on complaints concerning the accuracy and fairness of news reporting in the United States [and] to initiate studies and report on issues involving freedom of the press."

In judging the alleged misdeeds of the news media, however, it has no legal authority to enforce its decisions. Like the 24-year-old British Press Council, on which it is modeled, its power is derived solely from its ability to influence public opinion. Yet that power, wrote Executive Director William B. Arthur, "is totally dependent on the judgment of editors to publish the council's findings."[13]

Although some major news organizations, including *The New York Times* and the Associated Press, opposed its creation in fear that it would breed an atmosphere of regulation, the National News Council has received considerable praise from many leaders in journalism for its professional standards. But its work remains largely unknown to the public. In its 1975 report on ethics, the American Society of Newspaper Editors said the council's "integrity...is without question.... It has established a record that deserves more attention than either editors or the public have so far given it."

In January 1977, CBS became the first major broadcast network to pledge its cooperation with the council. CBS Chair-

---

[13] William B. Arthur, "The News Council Lives!" *The Bulletin of the American Society of Newspaper Editors,* November-December 1973, p. 6.

Major National Media Reform Groups

Accuracy in Media (AIM), Washington	Corrects alleged errors or omissions in news reporting
Action for Children's Television (ACT), Newtonville, Mass.	Works for improvement of children's television programing
Alternate Media Center, (AMC), New York	Studies the uses of cable television and ways in which citizens can gain access to the medium
Aspen Institute Program on Communication and Society, Washington	Studies communications policy issues and publishes books and research papers
Cable Television Information Center, Washington	Monitors legal developments affecting cable television and assists local governments in establishing cable TV operations
Citizens Communications Center, Washington	A nonprofit public interest law firm specializing in communications cases before FCC and courts
National Association for Better Broadcasting (NABB), Los Angeles	The first national consumer group to promote the public interest in broadcasting, it evaluates network programing and participates in hearings before Congress and FCC
National Black Media Coalition (NBMC), Washington	A coalition of over 70 black media reform groups promoting minority needs in national broadcasting
National Citizens Committee for Broadcasting (NCCB), Washington	Seeks to make broadcasting responsive to public interest
National Federation of Community Broadcasters (NFCB), Washington	Represents the interests of community radio stations before the FCC and other federal agencies
National News Council, New York	Examines complaints of inaccuracy and unethical conduct by news-gathering organizations
National Organization for Women, Media Task Force, Washington	Promotes the positive image of women in the media and monitors the FCC
Office of Communication of the United Church of Christ, New York	Provides assistance in negotiating public grievances with local broadcasting stations
Public Advertising Council, Los Angeles	Produces public service announcements for public interest groups
Reporters Committee for Freedom of the Press, Washington	Offers legal defense and research services for journalists

man William Paley said the council "has furnished an impartial and expert group to which aggrieved parties can appeal for review in the interest of fair treatment by the news media."[14] Paley added that CBS News will report any council findings adverse to the network. In a further effort to publicize the council's proceedings, the *Columbia Journalism Review,* a bimonthly media magazine, recently began carrying reports of its decisions.[15]

More than 450 complaints have been ruled on by the National News Council in its four years of existence. In November, for example, it decided that an NBC News documentary entitled "Danger! Radioactive Waste" was "seriously flawed" in reporting two instances of possible radioactive harm to persons and animals. The council said it could not find evidence for a portion of the program which suggested radioactive waste material caused medical problems for one family and some cattle.

NBC responded that it stands by the facts presented in the show, but promised it would carefully look into the complaints. Among allegations currently under investigation are: (1) charges by the Teamsters Union against *Time* magazine for its reporting last July of mismanagement of a union pension fund; and (2) a grievance filed against WBBM-TV, a CBS affiliate in Chicago, for its broadcast of a news series in March that allegedly gave the impression the drug Laetrile "was effective in combating cancer."

In an attempt to bridge the gap between the public and the press, a small number of regional news councils have been started in this country and Canada. According to the National News Council, there are at present five regional media review organizations in the United States: the Minnesota Newspaper Association, the Iowa Freedom of Information Council, the Delaware News Council, the Honolulu Community-Media Council, and the Riverside, Calif., Press Council. The Ontario Press Council, the only such group in Canada, was created in 1972 when eight Ontario dailies[16] agreed to establish a "self-governing council...to control and discipline the press and other news media."[17]

[14] Quoted in an Associated Press interview, Jan. 25, 1977.

[15] The *Columbia Journalism Review* began its coverage of National News Council activity in its March-April 1977 issue.

[16] *The Brantford Expositor, The Kitchener-Waterloo Record, The London Free Press, The Hamilton Spectator, The Ottawa Citizen, The Owen Sound Sun-Times, The Toronto Star* and *The Windsor Star.*

[17] From a 1968 report of the Royal Commission on civil rights in Ontario, quoted in *The Bulletin of the American Society of Newspaper Editors,* January 1974, p. 13.

Matters of Federal Regulation

TRADITIONALLY, the First Amendment rights to freedom of speech and of the press have been invoked by broadcasters and publishers to defend their operations from government interference. But increasingly, public-interest groups have begun to cite those same rights to justify their demands for access to the media. Pointing to the growing number of communications companies that control newspapers as well as radio and television outlets,[18] reformers contend that today's giant media monopolies pose a dangerous threat to individual freedom of expression.

"Freedom of the press must be something more than a guarantee of the property rights of media owners," wrote law professor Jerome A. Barron, a leading advocate of greater public access to mass communication.[19] Barron argued this theory before the Supreme Court in 1974 in a case in which an unsuccessful candidate for state office in Florida, Pat L. Tornillo, was denied the right to reply to a critical editorial in *The Miami Herald.* Arguing that the concentration of news media ownership was a potential abridgement of rights assured by the First Amendment, Barron maintained the establishment of a federal right-to-reply law was needed to offset the Supreme Court's 1964 decision in *New York Times v. Sullivan.* In the 1964 case, the Supreme Court ruled that in order to win a libel judgment, a public figure or other newsworthy person must prove he was the victim of a deliberate, false accusation published with "actual malice" in mind.

The court decided unanimously against Tornillo's right-to-reply petition, emphasizing that the First Amendment gave editors final authority over what should be published in their papers. However, since then the court has retreated somewhat from its 1964 position on libel. In at least two cases, the court has limited the broad protection of news organizations by drawing a narrow definition of "public figures."[20] In the 1974 case of *Gertz v. Robert Welsh,* the court ruled that Elmer Gertz, a civil-rights activist and author, was not a public figure. In a similar ruling in 1976, *Time* magazine had to pay damages for inaccurately reporting information about a prominent Florida socialite, Mary Alice Firestone, whom the court determined was not a "public figure" because she played no major role "in the affairs of society."

---

[18] See "News Media Ownership," *E.R.R.*, 1977 Vol. I, pp. 183-202.

[19] Jerome A. Barron, *Freedom of the Press for Whom?* (1973), p. iv.

[20] See "The Demise of the Public Figure Doctrine," by John J. Watkins, in *Journal of Communications*, summer 1977.

Unlike the press, broadcasting is already subject to right-to-reply laws. In 1959, the FCC set forth its "fairness doctrine," requiring radio and television stations to air opposing points of view on public issues. The doctrine was extended in 1967 to require broadcasters to notify persons or groups when they were the subject of criticism in on-the-air discussions of controversial issues and to give them an appropriate opportunity for rebuttal.

The Supreme Court upheld the constitutionality of the fairness doctrine in the 1969 *Red Lion Broadcasting* decision,[21] in which the court decided that a radio station that had broadcast a "personal attack" had to provide reply time free of charge. The court declared that the fairness doctrine was necessary "in view of the...scarcity of broadcast frequencies, the government's role in allocating those frequencies, and the legitimate claims of those unable without government assistance to gain access to those frequencies for the expression of their views...."

The need for federal regulation of broadcasting became evident shortly after the invention of radio. While the medium was still in its infancy, Congress passed the Radio Act of 1912, which gave the Department of Commerce the authority to distribute operating licenses. But by the early 1920s, there were so many stations on the air, some of them using the same frequencies, that listeners often had trouble receiving clear, consistent reception. With radio station owners clamoring for the enforcement of power and frequency assignments, Congress created the Federal Radio Commission in 1927, designating the public interest as the most important criterion by which it should regulate the radio industry.

The Federal Communications Commission, established by the Communications Act of 1934, replaced the FRC. Its jurisdiction was expanded to cover both wire and wireless interstate transmissions. Through its license renewal authority, the FCC was empowered to hold local broadcasters accountable for the way in which they used the public airwaves. The Supreme Court affirmed the FCC's charter in a 1940 ruling in which it decided that:

> ...[N]o person is to have anything in the nature of a property right as a result of the granting of a license. Licenses are limited to a maximum of three years' duration, may be revoked, and need not be renewed. Thus the channels presently occupied remain free for a new assignment to another licensee in the interest of the listening public. Plainly it is not the purpose of the FCC to protect the licensee against competition, but to protect the public.[22]

---

[21] *Red Lion Broadcasting v. Federal Communications Commission,* 395 U.S. 369.

[22] *Federal Communications Commission v. Sanders Brothers Radio Station,* 309 U.S. 470, 475.

The coming of television not only increased the number of broadcast stations nationwide but made it necessary for the FCC to adopt regulations suitable to the new medium. In an effort to bring television to as many communities as possible, the commission generally awarded large cities three VHF (very high frequency) channels. By 1945, it had assigned or reserved all available VHF channels, even though channels in some sparsely populated regions went unused for years. As the demand for television grew in the 1950s and 1960s, the FCC opened the UHF (ultra high frequency) range of channels (14 through 83) for use by both commercial and public broadcasting.

Through the years, the stated aim of FCC policy has been to promote local ownership of broadcast outlets. But in the so-called "prime market" cities—cities with the biggest potential audiences—"absentee" media corporations, including the networks, control many of the radio and television stations. Critics of the FCC contend that it has never actively enforced its local ownership policy in a way that would discourage the networks from purchasing choice local stations.

FCC Action on Licensing and Programing

Newton N. Minow, upon being named FCC chairman by President Kennedy in 1961, quickly identified himself as an outspoken critic of commercial television, describing its fare as a "wasteland." He told the National Association of Broadcasters: "...[W]hen television is bad, nothing is worse. I invite you to sit down in front of your television set when [a] station goes on the air...and keep your eyes glued to that set until the station signs off. I can assure you that you will observe a vast wasteland. You will see a procession of game shows, audience participation shows, formula comedies about totally unbelievable families...violence, sadism, murder...private eyes, gangsters, more violence, and cartoons. And endless, commercials—many screaming, cajoling and offending...."[23]

Minow warned that the FCC would use its license renewal power to force broadcasters to upgrade their offerings. "Renewal will not be *pro forma* in the future," he said. "There is nothing permanent or sacred about a broadcast license." His warnings marked the beginning of a period of increased commission activity, particularly in educational or "public" television, which it encouraged as an alternative to commercial TV. The first important backing came in 1962 when Congress authorized the federal government to make grants for the construction of noncommercial television stations. An amendment to the Communications Act of 1952 prohibited the FCC from interfering with the actual purchase of a broadcast facility.

[23] Speech to the National Association of Broadcasters, Washington, D.C., May 9, 1961.

However, Minow, who was determined to increase the number of educational television channels, held up FCC approval of the sale of a New York station to a commercial group until non-commercial buyers could be found. His action, in 1962, drew heated criticism from network officials, who complained to the White House that the commission had overstepped its bounds. But President Kennedy gave Minow his full support. "You keep this up!" the President told him.[24]

Later, Minow virtually assured the future of public television when he persuaded Congress to pass a law requiring all television sets sold in the United States after January 1963 to be equipped with VHF as well as UHF channels. Previously, according to television historian Erik Barnouw, "set manufacturers, many of whom had VHF stations, had been in no hurry to spread the competition."[25]

There was no mistaking the government's anti-monopoly attitude toward the television networks in the Kennedy administration. In 1963, under Minow's leadership, the FCC banned the "option clause" in contracts between commercial networks and their local affiliates. The clauses gave the networks control over large blocs of time on affiliate stations. The elimination of the "option clause," however, had only a minimal effect on commercial programing, since most stations continued to fill their schedules with network shows.

Facilitating Access to the Media

THE FOUNDING FATHERS believed that the free flow of information and ideas was necessary to the function of democracy in America. But that ideal, some observers suggest, is being threatened by mergers and acquisitions in the communications industry. The concern is that the concentration of ownership reduces journalistic competition and, it is feared, the sense of responsibility to the public. As Congress prepares to rewrite the Federal Communications Act fully for the first time since 1934, these matters seem certain to receive legislative attention. The House Interstate and Foreign Commerce Subcommittee on Communications hopes to begin a draft revision of the act in January.

According to the author of a study on "cross-ownership," 60 million Americans live "in areas where at least one newspaper

[24] Quoted in Erik Barnouw, *Tube of Plenty: The Evolution of American Television* (1975), p. 303.

[25] *Ibid.*, p. 303.

Campaign Against Cigarette Advertising

The 1964 Surgeon General's report linking smoking and cancer marked the beginning of a vigorous campaign by anti-smoking groups to have cigarette commercials banned from radio and television. Under pressure from the American Cancer Society and other health and consumer organizations, the Federal Communications Commission ruled in 1967 that broadcasters were required under the fairness doctrine to make air time available for anti-smoking messages, since the pro-smoking messages contained in cigarette ads were judged a controversial matter of legitimate public interest.

As a result, the commission's order opened the way for thousands of messages warning of the dangers of smoking. By 1969, cigarette sales had dropped by more than 12 billion from the 540 billion cigarettes sold the previous year.

In 1970, Congress passed legislation that prohibited all cigarette commercials from radio and television. Subsequently, the FCC ruled broadcasters were no longer required to carry anti-smoking messages, and the spots all but disappeared. The following year, cigarette sales began to increase steadily, reaching a new peak of 620 billion in 1976.

Cigarette ads in newspapers and magazines were unaffected by the ban. They simply did not "generate the same kind of outrage that TV commercials engendered," former Sen. Frank E. Moss (D Utah, 1959-1976) said. However, the tobacco industry agreed in 1971 to disclose the tar and nicotin content of the cigarettes they advertised in print.

and one television station have the same owner."[26] While many owners maintain that joint newspaper-broadcast operations afford customers superior service, media reform groups across the country are almost unanimous in viewing them as a threat to public access and independent news coverage. In January, the Supreme Court is expected to hear arguments on the constitutionality of the cross-ownership question. Over 200 media combinations in 44 states could be affected by the outcome.

At issue in the case, *American Newspaper Publishers Association v. National Citizens Committee for Broadcasting,* is whether newspaper owners may be prohibited from acquiring radio and television stations in the same city in which their papers are published, and whether the FCC or the courts are empowered to order divestiture where newspaper and broadcast facilities are co-owned in a single "market" area. The Department of Justice has long contended that cross-ownership is an

[26] William T. Gormley Jr., "How Cross-Ownership Affects News-Gathering," *Columbia Journalism Review,* May-June 1977, p. 38. Gormley is the author of "The Effects of Newspaper-Television Cross-Ownership on News Homogeneity," a study published in 1975, funded by the John and Mary R. Markle Foundation.

antitrust violation in that it virtually eliminates competition for advertising revenue.

An FCC ruling in 1975 prohibited common control of newspapers and radio and television stations but allowed joint operations to continue in localities having only one daily newspaper and one broadcast outlet. However, the U.S. Court of Appeals for the District of Columbia ordered the commission to apply the rule to all media combinations so long as the public interest is not harmed.

The American Newspaper Publishers Association has contended that the appeals court went beyond its authority in the review of FCC decisions. The publishers association argued that in the licensing of broadcasters—many of whom also happened to own newspapers—the commission had declared they were serving the public interest. In a brief to the Supreme Court, ANPA said: "The prospective rules promulgated by the FCC and the retrospective divestiture required by the court of appeals seriously impair the constitutionally protected right to publish a newspaper.... Moreover, these rules will prevent broadcasters—often the only persons in a community who can combine journalistic expertise with adequate capital—from starting a new daily newspaper or acquiring an existing newspaper which otherwise might cease publication."

Should the appeals court ruling stand, cross-ownership in dozens of cities would be broken up. In early December, *The Washington Post* and *The Detroit News* announced plans to trade company-owned television stations in the two cities. The exchange, which will not become final until it gains FCC approval, is seen as a response to the divestiture decision by the court of appeals.

Udall's Bill to Aid Independent Newspapers

In a related effort aimed at helping independent newspapers survive, Rep. Morris K. Udall (D Ariz.) in October introduced a bill to create a trust fund to finance estate tax liabilities incurred by small weekly or daily papers. The fund would be supported by contributions from individual newspapers that stand to benefit from it and would be open only to papers not owned by a chain[27] or a public corporation. The American Newspaper Publishers Association reports that 1,762 daily newspapers were published in the United States in 1976 and, according to newspaper analyst John Morton, six of every ten were under group—chain—control.[28]

Media critic Ben H. Bagdikian, a professor of journalism at

[27] Udall's bill defines a chain as a company owning two or more newspapers.
[28] Morton is with the Washington office of the New York-based brokerage firm of Colin, Hochstin Co. He issues the *John Morton Newspaper Research* newsletter.

the University of California at Berkeley, said the bill "is a good idea for the remaining papers, mostly small, that are family held...and for people who start up a paper and build it up so it has a great deal of value.... It's medicine applied late, but better late than never."[29] The ANPA, which opposes divestiture, said it supports Udall's bill "as an important first step" in correcting present tax inequities that fall the hardest on small independent newspapers.

Many who favor the dismantling of the giant media corporations contend that diversity is not necessarily synonymous with size. Concentrations of ownership, they add, more often tend to foster a uniformity of judgment rather than a free traffic of varying opinion. Typical of this thought is a comment by Jim Hoge, editor-in-chief of the Chicago *Sun-Times* and *Daily News:* "All the good will in the world by conglomerates...is just not the same as a number of different voices owned by different groups."[30]

The current upsurge in media "empire building" began in the 1960s and is now marked by acquisitions as diverse as film production companies, book publishing enterprises and cable television systems. In contrast to those who look upon this development with misgivings, CBS President John D. Backe argues that only big communication corporations are strong enough to oppose the excesses of big government. "This is an age," he said recently, "when public opinion is the target of every special interest and special pleader. So it is very important that our journalistic and communications institutions be strong enough and diverse enough to resist those who want to foist their particular ideology on the public."[31]

Community Programing on Cable Television

Another "access" issue centers on cable television. The Federal Communications Commission ruled in 1976 that all U.S. cable television systems must provide community access to their facilities. But nurturing public use of cable TV, which transmits video signals by wire rather than over the airwaves, has not been easy. According to David Hoke of the National Federation of Local Cable Programers, "most communities are not aware that public access exists." A National Cable Television Association survey in 1976 reported that only 52 per cent of the operators responding had broadcast community-produced programs.

The idea of participatory television is relatively new. "Community people have long been oriented to the passive role of

[29] Quoted in *The Washington Post,* Oct. 7, 1977.
[30] Quoted in *U.S. News & World Report,* Aug. 15, 1977.
[31] Quoted in *The Washington Post,* Dec. 2, 1977.

broadcast television viewing," Hoke said. "Users do not generally break down the doors of access centers or operator-provided production facilities just because they are available."[32] Communities need to be educated about cable television and the opportunities provided by access, he added.

At present, there are 3,700 cable television systems operating in the United States, serving nearly 12 million households. The industry estimates that the number of subscribers will grow to 20 million by 1980. Under FCC regulations, local governments are responsible for awarding cable franchise privileges, while cable operators themselves have the obligation of alloting time to community groups. But a common complaint, access advocates say, is that many cable owners who hold an unfavorable view of public access rights tend to give little or no assistance to local users. It is further argued that operators who charge exorbitant rental fees for playback and studio facilities are not meeting the FCC goal of providing low-cost community television.

Current federal guidelines permit individual cable systems to carry up to three "distant signal" stations. However, the recent development of so-called "super signal" stations that combine cable television and domestic communications satellites may necessitate a reassessment of FCC policy. Satellites enable a local broadcast outlet to become, in effect, a national station by beaming its signal far greater distances than do conventional broadcast towers. The use of such techniques has been a source of concern to proponents of community access who fear "super signal" cable broadcasts may preclude community-centered programing. One "super signal" station, WTCG in Atlanta, is already in operation. Plans are under way for similar stations in Chicago, San Francisco and Los Angeles.

Carter's Proposals for Public Broadcasting

The Carter administration has underscored its determination to expand community participation in public broadcasting. In October it sent recommendations to Congress that are intended to increase the level of federal subsidy for public radio and television and to encourage more local programing. The White House recommendations, written into the proposed Public Broadcasting Financing Act of 1978, address such problems as public accountability by individual stations, editorializing and minority ownership.

The bill, now before the House Subcommittee on Communications, awaiting action in 1978, proposes raising the funding authorization for public broadcasting from the present

[32] David Hoke, "Cable Access: Myth or Reality?" *Access*, November 1977, pp. 1-4. *Access* is a monthly publication of the National Citizens Committee for Broadcasting.

level of $121-million in fiscal year 1978 to $200-million by 1981. In addition, the amount that stations must raise themselves in order to receive federal money would be lowered slightly. The current ratio is 250 to 100; 225 to 100 is the proposed ratio. Some media reformers have wondered if that ratio will be adequate, but a spokesman for the White House Office of Telecommunications Policy said the figure is not final and could be revised if circumstances warrant. The Carter legislation would also require public broadcast stations to open their meetings and their financial records to public scrutiny. The bill further proposes:

1. Earmarking 25 per cent of the money appropriated to the federal Corporation for Public Broadcasting to be used for program development, including local access programing.

2. Setting aside $30-million annually in grants to aid women and minorities who want to start public stations.

3. Lifting the current ban on editorializing from all stations not licensed to local or state governments. Under the terms of the bill, the ban would still apply, for example, to stations operated by community or state-supported colleges.

The prohibition against editorializing has been in effect since 1967 when Congress established the CPB.[33] But media reform groups as well as Carter administration officials now believe it should be removed so as to allow stations to air editorial comment on issues of public importance. "We cannot see why simply because a station bases its revenues on the sale of commercial products...it has a greater right or takes a greater risk in editorializing than one whose funds are a mixture of individual, foundation and corporate donations, and federal funds," said Frank Lloyd of the Office of Telecommunications.[34]

Media reform groups generally view the new proposals as a boost for public broadcasting. "What's most heartwarming about the Carter action," said Nicholas Johnson, chairman of the National Citizens Committee for Broadcasting, "is that it demonstrates that [the President] has taken the time and interest to grasp the potential and purpose and needs of this alternative broadcast system. It is the first time in 10 years, since President Johnson proposed the Corporation for Public Broadcasting, we could say that about a President...."[35] Yet while the government's change in attitude may be significant, it addresses only a part of the problem of public access to the media. The public demand is for a greater role in shaping broadcast and newspaper policies and practices.

---

[33] See "Financing of Educational Television," *E.R.R.*, 1967 Vol. I, pp. 161-180, and "Public Broadcasting in Britain and America," 1972 Vol. II, pp. 805-824.

[34] Testimony at hearings before the House Subcommittee on Communications, Oct. 19, 1977.

[35] Nicholas Johnson, "Carter Looks at Public Broadcasting," *Access*, November 1977, p. 8. Johnson served as chairman of the FCC from 1966 to 1973.

Selected Bibliography

Books

Barnouw, Erik, *Tube of Plenty: The Evolution of American Television,* Oxford, 1975.

Lazarus, Simon, *The Genteel Populists,* Holt, Rinehart and Winston, 1974.

Paletz, Donald L., Roberta E. Pearson and Donald L. Willis, *Politics in Public Service Advertising on Television,* Praeger, 1977.

Price, Monroe and John Wicklein, *Cable Television: A Guide for Citizen Action,* United Church, 1972.

Schorr, Daniel, *Clearing The Air,* Houghton Mifflin, 1977.

Schwartz, Barry N., ed., *Human Connection in the New Media,* Prentice Hall, 1973.

Smith, Ralph Lee, *The Wired Nation: Cable TV the Electronic Communications Highway,* Harper & Row, 1970.

Winn, Marie, *The Plug-In Drug: Television, Children and the Family,* Viking, 1977.

Articles

"America's Press: Too Much Power for Too Few?" *U.S. News & World Report,* Aug. 15, 1977.

Bagdikian, Ben H., "Woodstein U.: Notes on the Mass Production and Questionable Education of Journalists," *The Atlantic,* March 1977.

——"First Amendment Revisionism," *Columbia Journalism Review,* May-June 1974.

Broadcasting, selected issues.

Columbia Journalism Review, selected issues.

Epstein, Edward J., "Journalism and Truth," *Commentary,* April 1974.

Hamilton, John Maxwell, "Ombudsmen for the Press," *The Nation,* March 16, 1974.

"In-House Press Critics: A Selection of Recent Work by Newspaper Ombudsmen," *Columbia Journalism Review,* July-August 1977.

Mallette, M. F., "Should These News Pictures Have Been Printed?" *Popular Photography,* March 1976.

Mencher, Melvin, "The Arizona Project: An Appraisal," *Columbia Journalism Review,* November-December 1977.

[MORE], selected issues.

Powers, Thomas, "Right-to-Reply Laws," *Commonweal,* May 17, 1974,

Reports and Studies

Davis, Pamela, ed., "Citizens Media Directory," National Citizens Committee for Broadcasting, April 1977.

Editorial Research Reports, "Access to the Media," 1974 Vol. I, p. 447; "News Media Ownership," 1977 Vol. I, p. 183; "First Amendment and Mass Media," 1970 Vol. I, p. 41.

National Cable Television Association, "Guidelines for Access," August 1972.

U.S. Commission on Civil Rights, "Window Dressing on the Set: Women and Minorities in Television," August 1977.

POLITICAL PRISONERS

by

Mary Costello

**Oct. 8
1976**

POLITICAL PRISONERS

THE PLIGHT of political prisoners involves more than the suffering of individual men and women whose only crime was to speak out against the policies of their governments or to be considered a threat to those in power. For the most part, political prisoners remain anonymous, the forgotten victims of regimes that will not tolerate dissent. It is only when politicians, artists, journalists, intellectuals and other well-known persons are imprisoned or when governments declare an amnesty for political prisoners, as Spain did recently, that the problem receives much publicity. In the past year, the United States has sought on several occasions to bring the political prisoner issue to world attention.

The United States last November proposed a worldwide amnesty for political prisoners. Daniel Patrick Moynihan, then the U.S. ambassador to the United Nations, appealed to all governments to release "persons deprived of their liberty primarily because they have...sought peaceful expression of beliefs and opinions at variance with those held by their governments or have sought to provide legal or other forms of non-violent assistance to such persons."[1]

In his plea for universal amnesty, Moynihan complained about the "selective morality of the United Nations in matters of human rights." The General Assembly, he contended, did not hesitate in condemning South Africa, Spain, Chile and Israel—countries "which permit *enough* [Moynihan's emphasis] freedom for internal opposition to make its voice heard when freedoms are violated"—while ignoring worse but less-publicized human rights violations in other nations. The reaction to the American proposal tended to confirm Moynihan's charge of "selective morality."

Cuba insisted that the U.S. record on human rights violations gave Washington no moral authority to pass judgment on other countries. The Soviet press described the amnesty proposal as "a futile attempt to distract the attention of world public opinion from acute and particularly specific questions connected with the violations of human rights in many Western countries, the system of apartheid [racial separation] in South Africa, the

[1] Statement to the U.N. Social, Humanitarian and Cultural Committee, Nov. 12, 1975.

persecution of democrats in Chile and the reprisals against dissidents in Spain." Many Arab and Third World nations accused the United States of submitting the amnesty proposal simply to draw attention away from a U.N. vote that had condemned Zionism as a form of racism.[2]

This country soon withdrew its resolution, complaining that the 15 amendments that had been added had emasculated the intent of the proposal. "It might have become a travesty upon the pain of political prisoners and upon the United Nations itself," said the U.S. Representative, Leonard Garment, on Nov. 21. America asked the U.N. body to show its concern for human rights in every nation, Garment said, "but in response, some could not resist the temptation to use this measure as a weapon in their battle against particular enemies. We spoke of universality; we were given parochialism." The following March 4, the United States asked the U.N. Commission on Human Rights to appeal "on humanitarian grounds to all governments to give serious and continuing consideration to the grant of amnesty to political prisoners." The proposal is expected to be taken up when the commission meets again in February 1977.

The United States has also exerted pressure this year on individual nations accused of violating human rights. During his trip to Africa in April, Secretary of State Henry A. Kissinger was critical of Rhodesian and, to a lesser extent, South African policies toward their black majorities. And at a meeting of the 23-member Organization of American States (OAS) in June at Santiago, Chile, Kissinger warned Chilean leaders that "the condition of human rights has impaired our relationship with Chile and will continue to do so." Shortly before Kissinger's speech, the OAS Inter-American Commission on Human Rights had issued reports condemning both the "arbitrary jailings, persecutions and tortures" in Chile and the "cruel, inhuman and degrading treatment" of political prisoners in Cuba.[3]

Amnesty International, a non-partisan human rights organization working for the release of political prisoners everywhere, reports that no nation has a perfect record on "prisoners of conscience"—"persons who are imprisoned for expressing their religious or political beliefs or because of their ethnic origins, provided they have not used nor advocated the use of violence." The United States, despite a few violations of

---

[2] The General Assembly approved an Arab-inspired resolution defining Zionism as "a form of racism and racial discrimination" on Nov. 10, 1975. Israeli Ambassador Chaim Herzog denounced the resolution, asserting that Zionism was a national and not a racial movement, and was to the Jewish people "what the liberation movements in Africa and Asia have been to their own people."

[3] "Fifth Report of the Inter-American Commission on Human Rights on the Status of Human Rights in Cuba," June 1, 1976, and "Second Report on the Situation of Human Rights in Chile," June 28, 1976.

Adapted from Van Gogh's "Prisoners' Round."

Amnesty International lists 112 countries with political prisoners. The number of prisoners probably runs into the hundreds of thousands. Evidence of torture has been found in 61 countries.

the rights of minorities and Vietnam war resisters, has a better record than most countries.

The United States may, by Amnesty International's calculations, have only a handful of political prisoners of its own, but Washington's stand on human rights can be seen in the larger context. Military and economic aid to repressive regimes has been and is being used to stifle non-violent dissent in these countries. Five years ago, the imprisonment and torture of political prisoners by U.S.-supported regimes in South Vietnam, Greece and Spain received wide publicity. The fall of South Vietnam to the Communists, the restoration of democracy in Greece and the grant of amnesty for political prisoners issued by King Juan Carlos of Spain on July 30, 1976, have shifted attention elsewhere. The U.S.-backed countries most often accused of violating human rights today are Chile, Brazil, Uruguay, Paraguay, Iran, South Korea, Indonesia and the Philippines.

Number of Victims and Reasons for Confinement

Amnesty International's latest annual report on political prisoners indicates how widespread the problem is. Between June 1, 1975, and May 31, 1976, the organization "took action on violations of human rights in 112 countries" *(see listing, opposite).* Such lists tell nothing about the numbers and treatment of political prisoners; they show only that Amnesty International was aware that a specific country held one or more prisoners of conscience.

In the United States, Amnesty "groups are working on eight cases," according to the report. Such numbers can be misleading, however. "It is impossible to estimate the number of political prisoners in the U.S.," Amnesty acknowledged. "People are not officially imprisoned because of their political views or actions, or because of their ethnic origin. But in some cases it is difficult to avoid the suspicion that an individual's imprisonment may be due to his political actions, rather than to the crime which he or she is alleged to have committed."[4] The small number of amnesty International cases in Italy, France, Greece, Sweden, Switzerland and the United Kingdom involved prisoners who had refused to serve in the armed forces or had encouraged others to refuse to serve.

In contrast, the report said that Indonesia had "more than 55,000 prisoners, perhaps as many as 100,000" who had been in prison without trial since 1965. In Iran, "the total number of political prisoners has been reported at times throughout the year [June 1975-May 1976] to be anything from 25,000 to 100,000." Amnesty found it impossible to estimate the number of political prisoners in the Soviet Union, Cuba[5] or several other totalitarian states.

Because repressive regimes are loathe to release information on political prisoners and hesitant to allow outside observers in to study the problem, there are no reliable estimates on the number of political prisoners in the world. "Occasionally, stories of political prisoners receive world attention, as in the cases of Kofi Awooner, the Ghana poet, Mihajlo Mihajlov, the

---

[4] During 1975-76, "three American prisoners adopted by Amnesty International have been released." All three—Freddie Lee Pitts and Wilbert Lee in Florida and Martin Sostre in New York—had been imprisoned for crimes they did not commit.

[5] Estimates from other sources for Cuba vary from 20,000 to 100,000 or more.

Amnesty International's List of Countries With Political Prisoners, 1975-76

Africa. Algeria, Angola, Benin, Botswana, Cameroon, Central African Republic, Chad, Congo, Equatorial Guinea, Ethiopia, Gabon, Ghana, Guinea, Ivory Coast, Kenya, Lesotho, Malagasy Republic, Malawi, Mali, Mauritania, Morocco, Mozambique, Namibia, Niger, Nigeria, Rhodesia, Senegal, Sierra Leone, Somalia, South Africa, Sudan, Swaziland, Tanzania, Togo, Tunisia, Uganda, Zaire, Zambia.

The Americas. Argentina, Bolivia, Brazil, Chile, Colombia, Cuba, Dominica, Dominican Republic, Ecuador, Grenada, Guatemala, Haiti, Honduras, Jamaica, Mexico, Nicaragua, Paraguay, Peru, El Salvador, United States, Uruguay, Venezuela.

Asia. Bangladesh, Bhutan, Brunei, Burma, Cambodia, China, Taiwan, India, Indonesia, South Korea, Laos, Malaysia, Nepal, Pakistan, Philippines, Singapore, Sri Lanka, Thailand, North Vietnam, South Vietnam.

Europe. Albania, Bulgaria, Cyprus, Czechoslovakia, France, East Germany, West Germany, Greece, Hungary, Italy, Poland, Portugal, Romania, Spain, Sweden, Switzerland, Turkey, U.S.S.R., United Kingdom, Yugoslavia.

Middle East. Bahrain, Egypt, Iran, Iraq, Israel, Jordan, Libya, Oman, Saudi Arabia, Syria, Yemen, South Yemen.

Yugoslav writer, or Hector Natalio Sobel, the Argentine labor lawyer," Colman McCarthy wrote in *The Washington Post* on Aug. 7, 1976. "But most of the victims remain unknown beyond their families and friends. Governments that jail and torture usually feign wounded pride when newspapers in America or England run stories about their brutality. Denials are issued. If that doesn't work, the line is taken that the current 'limitations on democracy' are temporary until 'order' is restored."

This was the strategy adopted by Indian Prime Minister Indira Gandhi in declaring a state of emergency on June 26, 1975. In a speech to the nation, Mrs. Gandhi expressed hope that a speedy improvement of "internal conditions" would allow her to revoke the emergency proclamation "as soon as possible." More than a year later, the decree is still in effect. It has permitted the government to detain, without charges or trial, thousands of political prisoners, including Mrs. Gandhi's political opponents, journalists and students.[6]

[6] See "India Under Authoritarian Rule," *E.R.R.*, 1976 Vol. I, p. 425. Some estimates of the number detained in India run as high as 100,000; others as low as 10,000.

The "State of Siege" that went into effect in Chile after President Salvador Allende Gossens was ousted and killed in a military coup, Sept. 11, 1973, gave the new government the power to detain political suspects by administrative order without any form of judicial redress. Decrees issued under the regime's new power led to massive arrests of those who held left-wing views, associates of Allende, political and trade union leaders, students, journalists and artists.

A South African court sentenced Breyten Breytenbach, a black poet, to nine years in prison last November. Breytenbach, who had criticized the government's racial policies, was charged with trying to set up an organization for "the revolutionary transformation of South African society under the leadership of the black liberation movement." And last December, Soviet scientist Sergei Kovalyov was sentenced to seven years in a labor camp, followed by three years of exile in Siberia. Kovalyov, a member of Amnesty International and the Initiative Group for the Defense of Human Rights in the USSR, was found guilty of violating Article 70 of the Criminal Code of the Russian Republic.

The article prohibits "agitation or propaganda carried on for the purpose of subverting or weakening Soviet authority or circulating for the same purpose slanderous fabrications that defame the Soviet state and social system, or circulating or preparing or keeping, for the same purpose, literature of such content." Kovalyov's conviction was hardly surprising. In a November 1975 report entitled "Prisoners of Conscience in the U.S.S.R.," Amnesty International noted that to the best of its knowledge, there had never been an acquittal of a political defendant in Russia.

Torture as Method of Intimidating Opponents

Many political prisoners are subjected to torture. Such torture does not refer primarily to the arbitrary action of certain prison guards. Torture today, Amnesty International said in its January 1975 "Report on Torture," is "essentially a state activity," practiced in at least 61 countries[7]—including the United States *(see box, opposite page)*—over the last 10 years.

Despite differences among countries known to torture political prisoners, there is a marked similarity in the reasons

---

[7] Africa—Burundi, Cameroon, Ethiopia, Ghana, Malawi, Morocco, Rhodesia, South Africa, Namibia, Tanzania, Togo, Uganda, Zambia; Asia—India, South Korea, Indonesia, Pakistan, the Philippines, Sri Lanka (Ceylon), North and South Vietnam; Europe—Albania, Belgium, Czechoslovakia, East Germany, Greece, Hungary, Poland, Portugal, Spain; Russia; the Americas—United States, Argentina, Bolivia, Brazil, Colombia, Chile, Cuba, Dominican Republic, Ecuador, Mexico, Paraguay, Peru, Uruguay, Venezuela, Costa Rica, El Salvador, Honduras, Panama, Guatemala, Haiti, Nicaragua; Middle East—Bahrain, Egypt, Iran, Iraq, Israel, Oman, Syria, Turkey and South Yemen.

U.S. Torture of Political Prisoners?

The Amnesty International "Report on Torture" states: "The Eighth Amendment...provides that 'cruel and unusual punishments (shall not) be inflicted.' The use of torture in any phase of the criminal process is illegal and there is no evidence of any authoritatively sanctioned pattern of violations of this law.

"But allegations of police brutality and harsh treatment of prisoners by prison guards abound. The veracity of some of these allegations must be presumed. Certainly, Amnesty [International] has evidence that some of its own adopted prisoners have been subjected to harsh and brutal treatment by the guards of the prisons where they have been detained....

"Nevertheless, it should be emphasized that judicial remedies exist for complaints against inhuman or degrading treatment, even though their effectiveness may sometimes make them appear illusory to the complaintants. It would be incorrect to suggest that there is an administrative practice of torture by the law enforcement authorities of the United States within their own domestic jurisdiction."

for the practice and the methods used. In a report on Chile, the Geneva-based International Commission of Jurists found: "The object of the torture appears to be threefold: to obtain 'confessions' to serve as the basis for subsequent prosecution; to obtain information about associates and activities; and to intimidate both the victim, his associates and the public in general."[8]

Aleksandr Solzhenitsyn, the Russian author and exile who served in labor camps, has described 31 types of physical and psychological torture used by Soviet authorities. These included continuous use of bright lights or loud sounds, burning with cigarettes, confinement in very small cells which were often filled with vermin, lack of food and water, beatings, damage to internal organs, fingernail extraction and various combinations of these torments.[9] Many of them are still used today, but more sophisticated and often more deadly tortures have been found.

The Soviet Union, for example, is reported to rely heavily on mental hospitals where political prisoners are given heavy doses of painful drugs to destroy their physical and psychological morale. From numerous other countries—among the most prominently mentioned are Chile, Iran, the Philippines, Uruguay, Paraguay, Brazil, Uganda, Indonesia, Haiti and

[8] International Commission of Jurists, "Final Report of the Mission to Chile to Study the Legal System and the Protection of Human Rights," April 1974.

[9] Aleksandr Solzhenitsyn, *The Gulag Archipelago* (1973), pp. 103-117. See also "Dissent in Russia," *E.R.R.*, 1972 Vol. I, pp. 479-498.

Guinea—come reports of the use of electric shocks to sensitive parts of the body, beatings, sexual assaults, near drownings ("the wet submarine"), near suffocation in plastic bags ("the dry submarine"), sharp blows to the ears ("the telephone"), stretching the nerves to cause paralysis ("the hook") and other atrocities. Most of the countries accused of such practices have subscribed to Article 5 of the U.N. Declaration of Human Rights. It states: "No one shall be subjected to torture or to cruel, inhuman or degrading treatment or punishment."

Much has been written about the persons who carry out these tortures. Solzhenitsyn wrote in *The Gulag Archipelago*: "Decades later...we retain this firm impression of low, malicious, impious and possibly muddled people [who are required only to]...carry out orders exactly and be impervious to suffering." Amnesty International has said that "the professional torturer is likely to be a man who achieves a relief of mental stress by aggressive acts, who acts out his own conflicts and fantasies by destroying others." He may also be "subject to considerable pressure and frustration." Seldom of high rank, he is forced "to extract information from unwilling suspects in order to satisfy the demands of superior officers."

Others contend that torturers must convince themselves that they are working for the greater good and that their victims are

Human Rights in Chile

The assassination of a former Chilean cabinet member and ambassador to the United States, Orlando Letelier, has focused new attention on human rights violations in Chile. His death occurred Sept. 21, 1976, in Washington, where he lived in exile. A bomb exploded in Letelier's car, killing him and a passenger and injuring another.

Letelier was imprisoned without trial shortly after the military takeover of the Chilean government in September 1973. His release a year later was attributed to pressure put upon the military junta by the United States and Venezuela. He returned to Washington, Judith Miller wrote in the January 1975 issue of *The Progressive,* to work "to help free the more than 20,000 political prisoners still being held in Chile" and "to write a book about the coup and his personal ordeal." Letelier said he had been subjected to physical and psychological torture for a year.

After his death, Sen. James Abourezk (D S.D.) gave voice to the widely held suspicion that Chile's secret police, the DINA (Direccion de Inteligencia National), was responsible for the bombing. "The tyranny of the dictatorship in Chile has now been extended to the United States," Abourezk said.

dangerous and not quite human. Anthony Storr, a clinical lecturer in psychiatry at Oxford University, believes that torturers may be driven not by malice or sadism but by the need to obey orders. They are likely to be "hierarchical people in that they accept and seek authority structures. They are people who obey orders without question."[10]

Amnesty International finds evidence that the practice of torture is becoming internationalized. Experts and their training, as well as torture equipment, are provided by one government for use in another country. There is also evidence that the United States has contributed to this "internationalization" of torture. The Amnesty International publication "Report on Torture" said that many members of Chile's brutal secret police, the DINA, were trained in Brazil. It said others were apprenticed to Brazilians who had been invited by the ruling junta to give courses in Chile to the military and the police. "Among the Brazilian instructors were those fresh from intelligence schools in the United States and the Panama Canal Zone," the report said. "They were given a free hand in Santiago with their own nationals, 250 of whom lodged complaints of torture."

Organized Efforts to Help Political Prisoners

Those who have been imprisoned and tortured for their beliefs or opinions often tell, when they are free to do so, of their sense of isolation and their fear of being forgotten. For many, their only hope during days, months or years of detention is that groups or individuals will publicize their cases and work for their release. Eliseo Bayo, a Spanish journalist imprisoned by the Franco regime in September 1974 for "illegal association" and freed nine months later, acknowledged the efforts made in his and his wife's behalf by Sen. Edward M. Kennedy (D Mass.), American professors, Amnesty International, the Nobel Peace Prize Committee, feminist groups and Spanish intellectuals and labor leaders. "They made it impossible for the government to simply forget about us," he said.[11]

The most effective and concerted pressure for the release of political prisoners comes from Amnesty International, a private, non-profit organization that works for the release of "prisoners of conscience" and the abolition of torture and the death penalty. It was founded in 1961 by British lawyer Peter Benenson. By mid-1976 the organization had 1,665 groups working in 33 countries and it claimed more than 97,000 members in 78 nations, about 8,000 of them in the United States. The London headquarters researches the cases brought to its attention and,

---

[10] Quoted in "Torture as Policy: The Network of Evil," *Time,* Aug. 16, 1976, p. 33.
[11] Eliseo Bayo, interviewed by David Rosenthal, *The Nation,* Sept. 20, 1975, p. 234.

when satisfied that those detained have neither used nor advocated violence, assigns each group three prisoners from different nations—one Western, one Communist and one neutral. To ensure impartiality, no group may "adopt"—work for the release of—prisoners held by its own country's government.

Amnesty International's claim to impartiality has not gone unchallenged. Some critics say that the organization gives more attention to human rights violations by right-wing dictatorships than by those of the left. If such is the case, Amnesty International argues, it is because the organization is unable to confirm allegations of political imprisonment or torture in such closed societies as North Korea, Albania or China. Another challenge involves Amnesty's efforts to exempt from punishment all non-violent acts of "conscience." Any government which exempted all persons from specific laws merely because they said it was against their consciences to obey these laws would soon dissolve in anarchy, it is asserted. The group has also been criticized for its alleged tendency to idolize prisoners of conscience and, often, their political viewpoints as well.

Amnesty groups work for the release of political prisoners by inundating the governments which hold them with letters and appeals, publicizing their cases and sending aid to victims and their families. These efforts, the organization claims, have been responsible for the release of more than 13,000 prisoners of conscience since 1961. Last year alone, 1,599 were freed. Compared to the number of political prisoners in the world, these figures may seem insignificant. But compared to the results achieved by other human rights organizations—including the International Commission of Jurists, the International League for the Rights of Man, the United Nations, Inter-American and European commissions on human rights and various church and professional groups[12]—Amnesty International must be rated as the most effective and successful of the groups devoted to helping political prisoners.

The U.N. and regional human rights commissions are hampered in carrying out their mandates by the fact that they are composed of a number of sovereign states, each trying to protect its own interests. Whether the United Nations or the regional groups give serious consideration to violations of human rights "often depends on many factors," the House Subcommittee on International Organizations and Movements has

[12] They include the World Council of Churches, the U.S. Catholic Conference, the Roman Catholic Church's Vicarate of Solidarity, the American Friends Service Committee, B'nai Brith, the National Conference on Soviet Jews, the Legal Committee for Human Rights, the Federation of American Scientists, PEN (the international writers' association), the Nobel Peace Prize Committee, the International Press Institute and various labor, artists' and women's organizations.

noted. "Most states are willing to criticize the practices of other states only when it is consistent with the general pattern of relations with the state concerned. They often criticize only states with whom they have unfriendly—or distant—relations, or when the victims of oppression are of the same ethnic, religious or racial background as their own people."[13]

Legal Standards for Non-Violent Dissent

POLITICAL PRISONERS can be viewed as victims of a situation in which the power of the state conflicts with individual rights and beliefs. The Greek philosopher and teacher Socrates (460-399 B.C.), sometimes referred to as the first political prisoner, was tried and imprisoned for corrupting Athenian youth because he dared question the dictates of those who ruled the city. Other notables who opposed the prevailing orthodoxy and were punished for their beliefs include Cicero, Christ, Galileo, Martin Luther and Mahatma Gandhi.

The idea that the individual has basic rights not because of his caste or circumstances but because of his humanity was laid down almost a century before the birth of Christ by the Roman orator Cicero. "True law," Cicero wrote in his *Republic,* "is right reason in agreement with nature; it is of universal application, unchanging and everlasting." Through the centuries, this concept became known as the doctrine of natural law and it was from natural law that the notion of natural or human rights was derived.

The 17th-century English philosopher John Locke was the first to assert that natural law implies natural rights. Man, he said in *Two Treatises on Civil Government* (1690), is entitled to "an uncontrolled enjoyment of all the rights and privileges of the law of Nature," especially the right to "life, liberty and estate." John Stuart Mill, in his *Essay on Liberty* (1859), carried the theory of natural or human rights to its logical conclusion. "If all mankind minus one were of one opinion, mankind would be no more justified in silencing that one person than he, if he had the power, would be justified in silencing mankind."

The 18th-century Enlightenment marked the high point of the rational and humanist philosophy of natural law and natural rights. Malise Ruthven describes the spirit of that age: "When in 1764 a 25-year-old Italian marquis, Casare Beccaria,

[13] "Human Rights in the World Community: A Call for U.S. Leadership," March 27, 1974, p. 18.

published his essay on the criminal law, *On Crimes and Punishments,* which advocated, among other reforms, the abolition of torture as a relic of an ancient and barbarous system of justice incompatible with reason and humanity, he struck such a chord of recognition among Europe's ruling classes that his book became an immediate best-seller and Beccaria himself an international celebrity."[14]

The ideas of the Enlightenment found their first and fullest expression in the American Declaration of Independence. That document held certain "truths to be self-evident"—among them that "all men are created equal"; that they are "endowed by their Creator with certain unalienable rights," including life, liberty and the pursuit of happiness; and that governments derive their just powers "from the consent of the governed." To ensure that the rights of the individual would not be abridged by the state, the first 10 amendments to the Constitution were a Bill of Rights that guaranteed, among other things, freedom of religion, speech, the press and assembly, freedom from unreasonable searches and seizures and from cruel and unusual punishments, and the right to a speedy and public trial.

The natural rights philosophy was equally apparent in the French Declaration of the Rights of Man in 1789. Born in revolution like its American counterpart, the French Declaration cited "ignorance, neglect or contempt of human rights" as the chief cause of public misfortunes. It set out a number of individual rights—freedom of opinion, religion and expression, the right to property, the presumption of innocence, equality before the law and freedom from arrest except in conformity with the law. "The aim of all political association is the protection of the natural and imprescriptible rights of man," the Declaration proclaimed.

Mixed U.S. Record on Protecting Human Rights

Virtually every nation in the world has adopted similar declarations of human rights. And every nation, some much more than others, has violated these guarantees. The United States has one of the best records of any country in protecting the individual rights enumerated in the Constitution. But the United States has, particularly in time of real or imagined emergency, violated the letter or the spirit of its laws on human rights.

"From the Boston Tea Party to the most recent destruction of draft records, lawbreaking by citizens pressing for political change and reform has punctured virtually every important period of American political history," former Sen. Charles

[14] Malise Ruthven, "The Extraordinary Revival of Torture to Make People 'Tell,' " *The Times* of London, Jan. 26, 1976.

Goodell (R N.Y., 1968-71) wrote in 1973. "Those with political power, frightened and confused by dissent and unorthodoxy, have just as frequently tried to use the criminal process to control American political life and to repress dissent. President [John] Adams used the Alien and Sedition Acts of 1798 to imprison his critics; grand juries and the ancient doctrines of conspiracy law have been bent to political purposes to silence critics of President Nixon's Vietnam policy."[15]

The Alien and Sedition Acts were defended on the ground that Republican opponents of President Adams and the Federalist Party were tools of the French government and constituted a danger to the nation's security. The Alien Act allowed the President to deport non-citizens whom he considered dangerous to public peace or whom he suspected of "treasonable or secret" intentions. The Sedition Act prohibited "false, scandalous and malicious" statements about elected officials intended to bring them "into contempt or disrepute," or to encourage opposition to any law. Among those prosecuted, New York assemblyman Jedidiah Peck was charged with sedition for circulating a petition which called for repeal of the Alien and Sedition Acts.

Throughout the 19th century, those who opposed the status quo were often harassed or imprisoned. Workingmen and their leaders who tried to organize for higher wages and better working conditions, minorities who sought to exercise their rights and blacks who, after the Civil War, attempted to make use of the freedom they had won were stymied by laws and the courts. By the beginning of the present century, Charles Goodell noted, there was a "bumper crop of political prisoners." One by one, constitutional guarantees "were sacrificed in attempts to preserve political orthodoxy and to protect the status quo."

Individual rights are frequently abridged in time of war, and the two world wars were no exception. Soon after the United States entered World War I in April 1917, Congress enacted a series of laws to prevent any opposition to the war. The most effective of these was the Espionage Act of June 15, 1917. It provided for penalties of up to 25 years in prison and $10,000 in fines for anyone found guilty of expressing pro-German sentiments, encouraging soldiers to be insubordinate or disloyal or interfering with the government's recruitment drive. Almost 2,000 Americans were prosecuted, most of them for questioning the merits or conduct of the war in speeches or written material.

During World War II, the most blatant abrogation of human rights in the United States was the detention of 112,000

[15] Charles Goodell, *Political Prisoners in America* (1973), p. 9.

Japanese-Americans in concentration camps, euphemistically referred to as "relocation centers." An executive order issued by President Roosevelt in 1942 provided that these men and women could be detained behind barbed wire and forced to swear a loyalty oath to the United States and repudiate Japan even if there was no evidence of sabotage on their part. On Feb. 19, 1976—the 34th anniversary of the executive order—President Ford issued a proclamation declaring the 1942 order null and void. Ford called the wartime internment of Japanese-Americans "a setback to fundamental American principles."

In the early years of the Cold War, Communists and radicals were harassed with the same zeal that had been used earlier against others. According to William Preston Jr., "a sustained offensive took place to eliminate disloyalty and induce 100 per cent Americanism among the population at large. A variety of strategies, some deliberate, others spontaneous, served this end: mobbing, imprisonment, conspiracy trials, exposure through congressional and state investigations and loyalty-security testing. Political considerations played a significant role in all of these cases, so that the victims of...repression were also cast as scapegoats for reasons ulterior to their actual behavior."[16]

International Attempts to Safeguard Dissenters

Beginning early in the 19th century, there were a number of binational and multinational agreements by various European powers to prevent specific abuses of human rights. These agreements were usually limited to the protection of rights of aliens and religious and ethnic minorities, and the suppression of the slave traffic. It was only upon realization of the extent of Nazi atrocities that efforts were made in the international community to safeguard the basic rights of all individuals.

The first of these efforts was the United Nations Charter, signed in San Francisco on June 26, 1945. Articles 55 and 56 of that document pledged all members "to take joint and separate action" to promote "universal respect for, and observance of, human rights for all without distinction as to race, sex, language or religion." The Charter also called for the creation of a Commission on Human Rights within the Economic and Social Council. Under the chairmanship of Mrs. Franklin D. Roosevelt, the newly established commission drafted the Universal Declaration of Human Rights.

The Declaration was adopted by the General Assembly on Dec. 10, 1948, without a dissenting voice (the Soviet bloc, Saudi Arabia and South Africa abstained). It proclaimed the rights of

[16] "Shadows of War and Fear," in Alan Reitman (ed.), *The Pulse of Freedom* (1975), p. 111.

every individual to "life, liberty and security of person" (article 3); to "recognition everywhere as a person before the law" (article 6); to "freedom of thought, conscience and religon" (article 18); to "freedom of opinion and expression" (article 19) and to "freedom of peaceful assembly and association" (article 20). The Declaration also held that "no one shall be subjected to torture or to cruel, inhuman or degrading treatment or punishment" (article 5) and "no one shall be subjected to arbitrary arrest, detention or exile" (article 9).

The Universal Declaration of Human Rights is not binding on individual nations. It is, rather, the General Assembly noted in its resolution, a "common standard of achievement for all peoples and all nations." On the day it was approved, Eleanor Roosevelt declared: "This declaration may well become the international Magna Carta of all men everywhere. We hope its proclamation by the General Assembly will be an event comparable to the proclamation of the Declaration of the Rights of Man by the French people in 1789, the adoption of the Bill of Rights by the people of the United States and the adoption of comparable declarations at different times by other countries."

The Universal Declaration served as an inspiration for scores of national and regional covenants to safeguard human rights. The European Convention for the Protection of Human Rights and Fundamental Freedoms (1953), the Inter-American Commission on Human Rights (1959) and the Arab Regional Commission on Human Rights (1968) embodied, sometimes verbatim, the guarantees set out in the U.N. Declaration. It is for this reason that A. H. Robertson, head of the Directorate of Human Rights at the Council of Europe, contends: "We may therefore safely conclude...that the impact of the Universal Declaration has probably exceeded the most sanguine hopes of its authors."[17] Amnesty International offered a different assessment of the U.N. Commission on Human Rights in its "Report on Torture" in 1975:

> The Commission itself is made up of members representing states; consequently it is a political forum which expresses the political interests of member states. Because states share an interest in upholding the doctrine of non-interference, no effective mechanism for examining human rights violations can be set up. This is not at all surprising •s so very few states live up to the high ideals of the Declaration.

Countervailing Laws to Crush Foes of the State

The "Comparative Survey of Freedom" published in 1976 by Freedom House, a New York-based organization which describes itself as "a national organization dedicated to

[17] A. H. Robertson, *Human Rights in the World* (1972), p. 28.

strengthening democratic institutions," indicates that a nation's adherence to the principles of universal and regional declarations of human rights often has little impact on its internal policies. In its country-by-country survey of the observance of political and civil rights, the organization said 1.8 billion persons in 68 nations were "not free" in 1975, up from 1.6 billion in 59 countries a year earlier.[18]

Many of the countries accused of flagrant violations of human rights deny that they have political prisoners. Persons designated by Amnesty International as "prisoners of conscience" are described as criminals by their national governments. The use of laws, states of emergency and decrees to justify the imprisonment of political opponents is widespread. India's state of emergency allows the government to detain without trial anyone accused of "incitement to mutiny" or subversion. And on Aug. 30, 1976, the government proposed a constitutional amendment to make "anti-national" activities a crime. Anti-national activities include anything that "disclaims, questions, threatens, disrupts, or is intended to disrupt the sovereignty and integrity of India or the security of the state or the unity of the nation."

The Iranian constitution lists numerous individual rights, including the rights to equality under the law, personal security and safety and protection against summary arrest and forcible entry into homes. Each right, however, is qualified by the provision "except in conformity with the law." But with laws prohibiting all activity "detrimental to the public interest," the secret police, the SAVAK, can arrest virtually anyone as a criminal.

Under Chile's "State of Siege," a host of decrees have been promulgated for "crimes against the security of the state." This has allowed the ruling regime to arrest scores of persons for "crimes" no more serious than suspected left-wing tendencies. The South Korean constitution of 1972 permits the president to suspend individual rights "in case the national security or the public safety and order is seriously threatened or is anticipated to be threatened." Under this authority, President Park Chung Hee issued an emergency decree in January 1974 to prohibit criticism of the constitution. This facilitated the conviction in August 1976 of 18 Christian leaders, most of them elderly or infirm, for disseminating a manifesto calling for a restoration of democracy in Korea.

For more than half a century, the Soviet Union has resorted to legal statutes to silence dissidents. Aleksandr Solzhenitsyn

---

[18] Raymond D. Gastil, "The Comparative Survey of Freedom—VI," *Freedom at Issue*, January-February 1976, pp. 11-20.

wrote in *The Gulag Archipelago* of political prisoners being bribed, threatened and tortured to sign confessions implicating themselves and others in illegal "anti-Soviet activities." Forced confessions were not really necessary since any criticism of the state could be construed as "systematically spreading false inventions slandering the Soviet political and social system"—a criminal offense.

Amnesty International has not been deterred by the knowledge that prisoners of conscience may have broken laws. Only those who have used or advocated violence in disobeying laws are ineligible. Ivan Morris, chairman of Amnesty International, USA, has explained: "The fact that someone has broken a law is totally irrelevant from our point of view. I should imagine that almost every single prisoner we've ever worked for has broken some law. Our argument would be that any law which puts people in prison as a result of expressing their opinion is an unjust law and is, in fact, a contravention of the Universal Declaration of Human Rights."[19]

U.S. Role in Human Rights Protection

A WORLDWIDE AMNESTY or the abolition of torture for political prisoners is unlikely to be realized in a world in which a nation's security is often equated with the ruling elite's retention of power. "Political imprisonment would seem to be endemic in human society," Douglas Brown has written. "It is a symptom of many incurable diseases, and the time and place at which it is not found are the exception rather than the rule. Even a world government, supposedly transcending all nationalisms and ideologies, would surely produce its own brand of dissidents whose helplessness would be absolute."[20]

A. H. Robertson looks forward to "an international court with wide competence to deal with questions of humanitarian law." He concedes, however, that the establishment of a legal system whose decisions would be binding on individual states is somewhat "utopian" and "unlikely in the near future." Less grandiose but probably more effective, at least in the short term, will be the continuing efforts by individuals, groups and government leaders to publicize the existence and treatment of political prisoners and embarrass the countries that hold them.

Amnesty International has shown that exposure of human

[19] Quoted by George H. Nash, "The Ordeal of Amnesty International," *National Review*, Dec. 6, 1974, p. 1410.

[20] Douglas Brown, "Political Prisoners," *International Review*, spring 1975, p. 40.

rights violations and pressure on governments guilty of these practices can result in thousands of releases. No country wants publicity about the fact that it holds and tortures persons who have committed no crime. Exposés by Amnesty International and various church and professional groups are credited with putting pressure on a number of countries to release at least some of their political prisoners.

In July, the Iranian government announced a general amnesty for members of terrorist organizations who had not participated in acts of violence and who renounced such activity. Peru's leftist military government said in May that it would release all political prisoners and allow exiles to return home. About the same time, Indonesia agreed to free about 2,500 political prisoners this year, promised that all of the country's political prisoners[21] would be freed or tried by 1978 and agreed to open all political prison camps for inspection by Amnesty International.

The Inter-American Commission on Human Rights found in its 1976 report on Chile that there "had been a quantitative reduction in the infringement of certain human rights," including "a reduced frequency of arbitrary arrests." Under pressure from leaders of the Catholic Church and the United States, the military regime in Santiago released a number of political prisoners when Secretary of the Treasury William E. Simon and Secretary of State Henry A. Kissinger visited the country this year.

It can be argued that announcements about freeing political prisoners are merely a public relations ploy and that even if a handful are released, others have been and will continue to be detained by governments that feel too insecure to tolerate domestic opposition. But it can also be argued that outside pressure has been effective in many cases and that without it governments would be much freer to imprison and torture those who dare oppose them.

Outlook for Tying Foreign Aid to Human Rights

Critics of American foreign policy have argued for years that the United States should exert pressure on the repressive regimes it supports by making economic and military assistance dependent upon their observance of human rights. In its 1974 report on human rights, the House Subcommittee on International Organizations and Movements concluded: "The human rights factor is not accorded the high priority it deserves in our country's foreign policy.... Proponents of pure power

[21] In its 1975-76 annual report, Amnesty International noted that the Indonesian government insists "that there are no political prisoners" in the country. Amnesty and others estimate that there could be as many as 100,000.

politics too often dismiss it as a factor in diplomacy. Unfortunately, the prevailing attitude has led the United States into embracing governments which practice torture and unabashedly violate almost every human rights guarantee pronounced by the world community."

The subcommittee recommended that the State Department use "various measures" to dissuade foreign governments from committing serious violations of human rights. These measures would include: (1) private consultation, (2) public interventions through U.N. agencies, (3) withdrawal of military assistance and sales, and (4) withdrawal of certain economic assistance programs. The subcommittee also proposed that the department "respond to human rights practices of nations in an objective manner without regard to whether the government is considered friendly, neutral or unfriendly."

Congress has acted to reduce or suspend economic and military aid to countries accused of human rights violations, but the executive branch often has found ways of circumventing these restrictions. In approving a two-year foreign economic aid bill on Dec. 9, 1975, Congress specifically prohibited development aid to any country engaging "in a consistent pattern of gross violations of internationally recognized human rights" unless Congress determined that the aid benefited needy people.

A foreign-aid bill Congress passed this year barred arms sales to countries violating human rights. President Ford vetoed the measure on May 7 on the ground that it would make Congress "a virtual co-administrator" of U.S. foreign policy. A revised bill which Ford reluctantly signed July 1 allows the termination of military aid to such countries if Congress so specifies in a joint resolution—a resolution that requires the President's signature to become effective.

Under this law, Congress has the power to ask the State Department for reports on the human rights situation in countries requesting security assistance. In preparation for the 1977 foreign aid legislation, Sen. Hubert H. Humphrey, chairman of the Senate Foreign Relations Subcommittee on Foreign Assistance, requested information on 17 countries which, he said, "have been frequently mentioned as having questionable human rights practices." These countries are Argentina, Brazil, Chile, Uruguay, Paraguay, South Korea, Indonesia, the Philippines, Iran, Ethiopia, Nigeria, Mozambique, Zaire, India, Pakistan, Bangladesh and Spain. In addition, the House Subcommittee on International Organizations and Movements asked for reports on possible human rights violations in Argentina, Haiti and Peru.

A recent congressional investigation of political prisoners in Uruguay and Paraguay made the point that the U.S. government was continuing to provide military and economic aid to regimes that commit gross violations of human rights. Edy Kaufman of Amnesty International told the House subcommittee on July 27 that there were some 5,000 political prisoners in Uruguay. "This is by far the highest prisoner-per-capita ratio in the whole South American continent. Approximately one in 500 Uruguayan citizens is a political prisoner." Torture is commonplace, Kaufman testified, and at least 30 political prisoners have died from torture in the last two years. A week later, Hewson A. Ryan, Deputy Assistant Secretary of State for Inter-American Affairs, acknowledged that "there has been apparent torture in Uruguay." But he defended the continuance of U.S. military aid on the ground that terrorists in Uruguay and Argentina were trying to overthrow the government and establish a Communist state. Nevertheless, in September when Congress approved the foreign aid appropriations bill for fiscal year 1977, it prohibited military assistance, credits or training funds for Uruguay.

Bonnie Potter, writing in *The New Leader,* identified four main arguments used by the State Department "against tying foreign aid to human rights performance": (1) that economic and social underdevelopment breed repression, and these must be dealt with first; (2) that "quiet" diplomatic efforts bring more relief than dramatic denunciations and political gestures; (3) that international law requires "non-interference in the internal affairs of other governments" and, finally, (4) that human rights considerations often conflict with America's political and strategic interest.[22]

In explaining U.S. aid to South Korea, Secretary Kissinger summed up State Department policy toward friendly governments that violate the human rights of their citizens: "The Korean human rights situation is an important element in our policy considerations. We have strongly made known our views to the Korean Government," Kissinger told the House International Relations Committee on March 29, 1976. But, he continued, "at the same time, we cannot lose sight of our basic concerns over the security situation on the Korean peninsula."

Greater Use of Asylum for Political Prisoners

It can be argued that the amount of pressure the United States is able to put on regimes dependent upon American aid is limited and the leverage this country can exert on unfriendly or relatively self-sufficient nations like Cuba or Iran is minuscule.

---

[22] Bonnie Potter, "The Problem of Human Rights," *The New Leader,* Dec. 22, 1975, pp. 4-5.

If Washington cannot make the world safe for peaceful political dissent and if proposals for a worldwide amnesty pose too much of a threat to too many governments, what can be done to aid political prisoners? Amnesty International would argue that under existing conditions the best hope lies in mobilizing public opinion with a constant barrage of written and visual material to overcome what the organization calls "the conspiracy of silence."

As the Cuban exile community in the United States has shown, one way of generating publicity about human rights violations is for the United States and other democracies to grant asylum to victims of repression. Rose Styron, a member of the board of Amnesty International, USA, noted that the Chilean government had offered dissidents "permanent exile as an alternative to permanent imprisonment." This, she wrote, "is clearly unjust punishment for patriots, but those who choose to leave may help free those who cannot, through raising international awareness and marshaling international pressure on the junta."[23]

Stephen S. Rosenfeld, a foreign-affairs writer for *The Washington Post,* proposed last Dec. 5 that "the United States offer itself as a haven for foreign political prisoners...." It would be especially important, Rosenfeld wrote, "to free ourselves from thinking that we only open our doors to people fleeing communism. We've accepted 650,000 Cubans, 30,000 Hungarians and 130,000 Vietnamese for essentially anti-Communist reasons in the last 20 years. By shaming contrast, the number of people we've accepted under the Attorney General's 'parole' authority[24] from one avowedly anti-Communist government, Chile, is 21." Partly as a result of publicity about torture and arbitrary imprisonment in Chile, the number of Chileans who have been accepted under the Attorney General's parole power has risen to about 1,150, according to recent Immigration and Naturalization Service figures.

Neither pressure from individuals, groups or governments nor offers of asylum will eliminate the problem of political prisoners. The world that George Orwell envisioned for 1984, a world in which faceless potentates, aided by technology, crush those who doubt or question the dictates of "group think," often seems alarmingly close. That it is not closer is due in large measure to those persons and organizations who continue to believe in and struggle for a concept that was proclaimed in the Declaration of Independence 200 years ago—that all men are endowed with certain "unalienable rights."

---

[23] "Special Report on Chile," in Amnesty International, *Report on Torture* (1975), p. 281.

[24] Under the 1952 Immigration and Nationality Act, the Attorney General was allowed to admit aliens into the United States for emergency reasons without going through the formal procedures of admittance.

Selected Bibliography

Books

Goodell, Charles, *Political Prisoners in America,* Random House, 1973.
Lea, Henry C., *Torture,* University of Pennsylvania Press, 1973.
Machan, Tibor R., *Human Rights and Human Liberties,* Nelson-Hall, 1975.
Ostro, Ernest A., *Prisoners of Conscience: War Resisters in a Federal Penitentiary,* Holt, Rinehart & Winston, 1975.
Rietman, Alan (ed.), *The Pulse of Freedom: American Liberties, 1920-1970,* W. W. Norton, 1975.
Robertson, A. H., *Human Rights in National and International Law,* Oceana, 1968.
——*Human Rights in the World,* Humanities Press, 1972.

Articles

Amnesty Action (published by Amnesty International, USA), selected issues.
Brown, Douglas, "Political Prisoners," *International Review,* spring 1975.
Freedom at Issue (published by Freedom House), selected issues.
Matchbox (published by Amnesty International, USA), selected issues.
Mower, A. Glenn Jr., "Human Rights in Western Europe," *International Affairs,* April 1976.
Navasky, Victor S., "Art, Politics and Torture Chambers," *The New York Times Magazine,* Aug. 15, 1976.
Sagan, Leonard A. and Albert Jonsen, "Medical Ethics and Torture," *New England Journal of Medicine,* June 24, 1976.
Styron, Rose, "Uruguay: The Oriental Republic," *The Nation,* Aug. 14-21, 1976.
"Torture as Policy: The Network of Evil," *Time,* Aug. 16, 1976.

Reports and Studies

Amnesty International, "The Amnesty International Report, 1975-76," September 1976.
—— "Chile: An Amnesty International Report," September 1974.
—— "Prisoners of Conscience in the U.S.S.R.," November 1975.
—— "Report on Torture," January 1975.
Editorial Research Reports, "Dissent in Russia," 1972 Vol. I, p. 481; "Human Rights Protection," 1968 Vol. I, p. 243.
House Subcommittee on International Organizations and Movements, "Human Rights in the World Community: A Call for U.S. Leadership," March 27, 1974.
International Commission of Jurists, "Final Report of the Mission to Chile to Study the Legal System and the Protection of Human Rights," April 1974.
Inter-American Commission on Human Rights, "Fifth Report of the Inter-American Commission on Human Rights on the Status of Human Rights in Cuba," June 1, 1976.
—— "Second Report on the Situation of Human Rights in Chile," June 28, 1976.
United Nations Economic and Social Council, "Human Rights," 1973.

RIGHT TO DEATH

by

Helen B. Shaffer

Jan. 27
1978

RIGHT TO DEATH

THE RIGHT-TO-DIE movement presents problems peculiar to our time. While the main issue is not new, modern conditions have changed its character in a way that makes it press more insistently on the minds and emotions of people than ever before. To the fear of death has now been added the fear of dying "badly," that is, as a helpless, lonely, possibly comatose inmate of an institution where the patient is subjected to painful or humiliating treatment with no hope of surcease while death is held at bay. The result is that many new adherents have been won to the principle of the right of personal choice, under conditions of extreme illness or infirmity, on the time to depart this life.

Until recently, to die was not generally conceived of as a right. To die was everyone's fate and it was taken for granted that few would seek to hasten their inevitable end. To die "well" was to die with courage, faith, resignation to God's will. For centuries theologians discoursed on the question of suicide, which they believed contrary to God's will, and on the question of one's obligation to accept painful treatment as a means of prolonging life. Ordinary believers rarely studied these arguments but accepted the Christian church's traditional strictures on suicide.

Secular-minded proponents of euthanasia in the modern era won little support of their views, much less acquiescence by the state to their demands for legalization of "mercy killing," deliberately putting to death the suffering, incurable patient. Today, however, in the case of a patient in a terminal stage of illness, who has no awareness of life or prospect of regaining it, and whose meager life processes are being sustained by machines, regardless of whether the individual feels physical pain, public opinion appears to be turning in favor of removing artificial supports and ending what might be considered a synthetic life.

With this turn of opinion, some states are asserting, through their legislatures and courts, a newly articulated principle that the government has the power to protect an individual's right to die under prescribed conditions. While this is not yet a universally accepted rule, legislative and judicial activity in this field has stirred up a new debate on the proper role of the state in dealing with so personal a matter.

Even among those who favor "unplugging the machine" for hopeless cases, there are differences as to the appropriate circumstances for taking this action, and there are also differences over the role of government in establishing those criteria. This debate is particularly acute and painful when it concerns the fate of the newborn with serious uncorrectable defects. Fear of abuse of permissiveness in life-or-death situations is a concern to both those who favor and those who disapprove of letting the hopelessly ill or deformed die without prolongation of life by machine, surgery, or drastic medication.

This new phase of the euthanasia movement is almost certain to grow in its impact on individual lives and on institutions of society that set standards for public and professional policies in law, medicine and human rights. The movement has already forged new principles of legal permissiveness on the termination of life. It has spurred legalization for broader definitions of death. Limited resolutions of conflicts over individual cases in litigation have affected standards of civil rights, criminal liability and regulation of medical practice.

Meanwhile, the need to make a difficult decision in each case puts a tremendous emotional burden on families of the patients—many of whom are unable to speak for themselves—as well as on the medical personnel attending them. The question of who shall take responsibility for the fateful decision in the case of a mentally incompetent or underage patient is one of the most difficult of all.

Perhaps the most profound consequence of these developments has been that people have been made more conscious of human mortality, and the limitations of medical science in overcoming this fact of life. Long pushed out of sight by social taboos and the discomfort of contemplating one's own demise, these new issues have helped create a new era of candor and openness on a subject which no one can ultimately ignore.[1]

Recent State Laws on 'Natural Death'

The most concrete evidence of the rapid proliferation of interest in the right-to-die issue is the recent spurt of activity in state legislatures. Until 1976 no bill introduced on this issue progressed sufficiently to reach the stage of committee hearings. But that year California became the first state in the nation to enact such a law. California's Natural Death Act, signed by Gov. Edmund G. Brown Jr. on Sept. 30, 1976, recognizes the

[1] See "Approaches to Death," *E.R.R.*, 1971 Vol. I, pp. 289-306.

right of an adult to direct his doctor to withdraw life-prolonging treatment if there is no hope of recovery.

To give validity to the patient's demand, instructions must be in writing and it is legally binding only if executed after the patient has been diagnosed as having a terminal condition; if not, the document becomes advisory rather than obligatory. The directive is valid only for five years after it is signed and it may be revoked at any time by the signer. The measure specifically exempts physicians who follow these instructions from civil suit or criminal charges for this action.

Bills patterned on the California model, some with modifications, have been introduced in several other states, and right-to-die statutes already have been enacted in Arkansas, California, Idaho, Nevada, New Mexico, Oregon, North Carolina and Texas. Evidence of interest goes beyond actual enactment. During the 1977 legislative sessions, 60 right-to-die bills, sponsored by 192 legislators, were introduced in lawmaking bodies of 41 states. In South Carolina, Tennessee and Washington, right-to-die bills passed one branch of the legislature but failed in the other house. New Hampshire passed a bill of this kind, but it was vetoed by Gov. Meldrim Thomson Jr. The State House of Representatives voted to override the veto but it was upheld in the Senate.

Currently in the new 1978 sessions, right-to-die bills are being considered in at least 21 states: Delaware, Florida, Georgia, Hawaii, Illinois, Iowa, Kansas, Michigan, Minnesota, Mississippi, Missouri, Nebraska, New York, Ohio, Oklahoma, Pennsylvania, Rhode Island, South Carolina, Tennessee, Washington and Wisconsin. In several states, the measures are carryovers from 1977. This reflects action by some states in 1977 to provide for a study of the issues before taking up the bills in 1978.

Karen Quinlan Case and Other Rulings

Public interest and legislative activity have been stimulated by publicity given to court cases arising over the legality of "pulling the plug" on patients in terminal illness. Moral and religious questions are closely interwoven with the legal in these contests. The most publicized and influential of recent cases was that of Karen Anne Quinlan of Landing, N.J. Miss Quinlan, then age 21, fell into a deep sleep on April 15, 1975, after a party at which she was said to have ingested barbiturates and alcoholic drinks. After a brief period of intermittent awakenings, she subsided into a coma from which she has never recovered.

Placed in a hospital on a life-sustaining regimen, including use of a respirator and forced feeding of food and vitamins, she continued to breathe while her body deteriorated. In time her weight fell by 50 per cent and her body assumed the fetal position with arms and legs rigid against her body. She gave no indication at any time of being aware of herself or her surroundings. Her case was described medically as a "persistent vegetative state" and doctors saw no possibility of recovery.

Some months later, her father, Joseph Quinlan, after gaining approval of his parish priest, asked the doctors to remove the respirator so his daughter could proceed to a natural death. The doctors and hospital administrators refused. The father then asked the New Jersey Superior Court in Morristown to declare his unconscious daughter incompetent and to name him guardian with authority to order termination of the use of the respirator. He also filed suit to enjoin the county prosecutor from bringing criminal charges against him or doctors responsible for cutting off the machine. The suits, in effect, sought legal judgments on the situation *before* rather than *after* the act in question.

Judge Robert Muir Jr. of the Superior Court on Nov. 10, 1975, denied both petitions. He held the state had a compelling interest in preserving life without inquiring into the quality of that life. Furthermore, he denied the legality of giving life-and-death power over an incompetent to anyone, even a parent. There was no constitutional right to die, he said, and "in this age of advanced medical science" he had no intention of resolving "the extensive civil and criminal legal dilemmas" which could "set precedents that would affect future litigation concerning euthanasia." In short, removing the respirator would be homicide under the law.

Quinlan appealed and won a reversal from a unanimous New Jersey Supreme Court. While several of his arguments were dismissed,[2] the opinion handed down by Chief Justice Richard J. Hughes on March 31, 1976, said that Miss Quinlan had the right to request termination of treatment as a "right of privacy" and that, since she was incompetent, that right could be exercised by a guardian. The father was named legal guardian and he was given the right, with the concurrence of family, attending physicians and a hospital "ethics committee," to authorize withdrawal of the breath-sustaining machine. Ironically, Miss Quinlan, after being "weaned" from the respirator, continued to breathe naturally. She is now in a nursing home, receiving conventional care with intravenous feeding, but doctors still see no possibility of recovery from the coma.

---

[2] The court threw out, for example, the claim that to continue the breath-sustaining treatment was "cruel and unusual punishment" and the claim that the lower court's decision was a denial of religious freedom.

In general, decisions in such cases tend to permit termination of extraordinary treatment, especially when the condition of the patient has severely deteriorated. The Massachusetts Supreme Judicial Court ruled on July 9, 1976, that therapy to prolong life could be withheld from a dying person who was unable to make a judgment for himself. The patient was an elderly male resident of a state school for the retarded. Testimony in the case pointed out that the patient, for lack of understanding, would be frightened and resist the painful treatment which at best could only prolong his life for a short time, while without treatment he would die without pain.

> *"We think the State's interest [in the preservation and sanctity of life]...weakens and the individual's right to privacy grows as the degree of bodily invasion increases and the prognosis dims."*
>
> Chief Justice Richard J. Hughes
> of the New Jersey Supreme Court,
> Quinlan case decision

In another case, Essex County (Mass.) Probate Judge Henry R. May ruled on Dec. 23, 1977, that doctors could accede to the wish of the husband of a severely ill, comatose woman that she be disconnected from life-sustaining equipment.

Decisions like these, while indicative of a trend, constitute a kind of *ad hoc* judgment and leave many questions as yet unanswered. This accounts, in part, for the pressure on legislatures to establish basic principles or at least guidelines for determining legal—and morally acceptable—procedures. They have also impelled professional societies and other interested organizations to take positions on the medical, legal, religious, moral, ethical and human implications of the right-to-die question.

No pressure for legal action at the federal level is being brought, even by the most active promoters of right-to-die legislation. Their efforts are confined largely to lobbying in the state legislatures. Congressional interest has been limited to studying the issues. A one-day hearing, Nov. 6, 1975, called by Sen. Edward M. Kennedy (D Mass.), as chairman of a Labor and Public Welfare subcommittee, dealt with "moral, ethical and legal questions of extraordinary health care," but the senator specified that no legislation was contemplated. Dr. Willard

Gaylin, president of the Institute of Society, Ethics and the Life Sciences, told the subcommittee he did not see a "legislative solution."

Medical Reasons Underlying New Interest

Current interest in the right-to-die movement is manifested by the large run of articles in medical and law journals discussing the new implications of legislation and court decisions on practices in their professions. An even larger volume of reporting and commentary has flowed into publications addressed to the general public. As recently as 1968, the publishers of material presented at a symposium on the subject remarked that "the literature on death is far from abundant."[3] A decade later, a book on euthanasia, *Freedom to Die* by O. Ruth Russell, lists in its bibliography more than 600 books, articles, texts and reports on hearings and meetings that pertain to her subject, most of them dating from the late 1960s and the 1970s. In another recent major work, *Death, Dying and the Biological Revolution* by Robert M. Veatch, research director of the Institute of Society, Ethics and the Life Sciences at Hastings-on-Hudson, N.Y., some 120 "general readings" are listed.

The reasons for the recent surge of popular and professional interest are multiple. The great advance in medical science, especially in the application of life-sustaining machinery, is often cited. The development of techniques for organ transplants has added a new dimension to the old debate, for the transplant process is closely related to the near-death situations of both the prospective donor and prospective recipient of a viable organ.

Medicine's improved capability for saving the lives of infants who in the past would have been stillborn or fated to die soon after birth presents new problems in this area. Medical advancement can also be credited in large part for the greater longevity of the population, thus increasing the percentage of old people who are most likely to figure in "right-to-die" cases. The growing number of aged persons has meant that more people approach their final hours in hospitals and nursing homes.

More younger and healthier people undergo the emotionally searing experience of witnessing the suffering or the unhappiness of institutionalized friends and relatives. Many are moved by the horror of watching the decline of a degenerating shell of someone they had known in the past as a sentient

[3] Roger Denniston, in a foreword to the book *Man's Concern With Death* by Arnold Toynbee, et al. This was the American edition published by McGraw-Hill Book Co. in 1969. Denniston represented Hodden and Stoughton, Ltd., London, the original publisher of the book, in 1968.

human being. The enormous expense to the family of extraordinary medical attention is another factor, especially when the ministrations of medical science appear to be futile. Those working for right-to-die legislation in the states have reported that in many cases sponsoring legislators were first drawn to the issue by the experience of watching a beloved friend or relative make the slow descent into death under these painful and sometimes humiliating conditions.

The right-to-die movement, however, goes beyond these concrete factors. In one sense the movement is a phase of the overall push for civil rights in all areas of life. "People today are more demanding of their rights," the director of the Euthanasia Educational Council in New York told Editorial Research Reports. "They want more personal control over their lives. It is happening all over." The tendency to question what was once sacrosanct authority, an aspect of the 1960s and 1970s, also plays a part in daring to question the wisdom of the doctor in treating terminal patients.

Ethical Question in History

THE DEBATE today represents a new and significantly changed phase of a debate on euthanasia that dates back to ancient times. The word euthanasia is from the Greek: "eu" for good and "thanatos" for death, thus a "good death," meaning one free of suffering and with the dying person content or reconciled to his fate. Interest in this subject has risen and fallen over the centuries, but never before has it had so powerful a pertinence in the life of everyone.

In general, the precursors of modern civilizations were more concerned with what happens after death than with the process of dying. Belief in an afterlife was one way of assuaging distress at the inescapable prospect of death. Even today the increased study of dying has led to a resurgence of belief that death is but a passage to another and possibly better state of existence. Elisabeth Kubler-Ross, a pioneer in the modern movement to ease the last days of the dying, has come to give credence to the claims of some patients who, returning to consciousness after having been given up for dead, say they actually experienced a brief stay beyond the curtain of death and found it beautiful.[4]

[4] "There is no total death. Only the body dies. The self or spirit...is eternal," writes Kubler-Ross in *Death: The Final Stages of Growth* (1975). See also her foreword to the book *Life After Life* (1975), by Raymond A. Moody Jr.

Leading philosophers of the ancient Greek and Roman world debated the virtues of suicide and euthanasia for the unfit. Aristotle in *Politics* and Plato in *The Republic* wrote approvingly of putting deformed infants to death. Plato attacked "the invention of lingering death" by treatment of mortal illness; he criticized a sickly man who "could do nothing but attend upon himself and...so dying hard, by the help of science...struggled on to an old age."

He agreed with Socrates that any effort to treat seriously diseased bodies was wrong because it would "lengthen out good-for-nothing lives or...have weak fathers begetting weaker sons." And Seneca the Roman said "mere living is not good, but living well...the wise man will live as long as he ought, not as long as he can."[5] Suicide as an act of political protest or to avoid shame of defeat or failure of duty is a phenomenon familiar to ancient societies, and it has persisted into the present.[6]

Christian opposition to voluntary death,[7] whether by suicide or "mercy killing," received its early impetus from St. Augustine of Hippo, who said suicide is "detestable and damnable wickedness," contrary to the Sixth Commandment, "Thou Shalt Not Kill."[8] Church law sought to discourage suicide by denying rites of Christian burial to suicides; it also encouraged adoption of civil laws that called for confiscation of suicides' properties. Eight centuries later St. Thomas Aquinas reinforced St. Augustine's strictures on suicide; only God, he said, had the right to determine when a person should die.

Enlightenment's Influence on Right to Die

Despite the church's stand, Sir Thomas More, the British statesman-scholar-prelate who opposed Henry VIII's break with Rome, recommended easing into death for those suffering painful terminal illness. In *Utopia,* which describes his concept of an ideal society, More set forth views which have caused him to be called the father of modern euthanasia. He wrote:

> "...[I]f the disease be not only incurable but also full of continual pain and anguish, then the priests and magistrates exhort the man, seeing he is not able to do any duty of life, and by outliving his own death is noisome and irksome to others and grievous to himself.... And seeing his life is to him but a torment, ...he

---

[5] Citations in O. Ruth Russell's *Freedom to Die* (1977), p. 53, and Robert M. Veatch's *Death, Dying, and the Biological Revolution* (1976), pp. 12-15.

[6] See Arnold Toynbee's *Man's Concern with Death* (1968), p. 72.

[7] Toynbee credited "Christian conscience" for failure of Hitler's plan to exterminate all aged, infirm and feeble-minded persons in the German population during the Nazi regime (1933-1945) but added that it failed to keep the Nazis "from murdering millions of Jews." *Ibid,* pp. 73-74.

[8] According to Russell (p. 54), many Christians were committing suicide at the time (fifth century) and St. Augustine's view "may have been based partly on practical considerations since a high birth and survival rate among Christians at this time was crucial to the spread of Christianity."

will...either dispatch himself out of that painful life...or else suffer himself willingly to be rid of it by others.[9]

Support for the right to die grew in the 17th and 18th centuries under the influence of the Enlightenment, which stressed individual rights and freedom of conscience. John Donne and David Hume were among the British and Diderot, Montesquieu and Voltaire among the French philosophers who defended the right to suicide. France in 1790 legalized suicide.

Modern use of the term "euthanasia" is traced to the book *Euthanasy: Or Happy Talk Towards the End of Life,* written by an Englishman, William N. Mountford. The book went into four editions between 1848 and 1852. A new spate of writings on the subject was launched in England with publication in 1872 of an essay, "Euthanasia," by S. D. Williams. Another British philosopher, Lionel A. Tollemache, exerted considerable influence in the late 19th century with writings in which he questioned the right of the state to forbid the severely ill to seek release in death.[10]

In the United States in the early years of this century, Dr. Charles Eliot Norton of Harvard advocated euthanasia. A pro-euthanasia bill, the first in the nation, was introduced in January 1906 in the Ohio legislature. The bill was defeated, but not before it engendered much controversy. Bitter debate in the press also followed the disclosure in 1912 that a New York woman in constant distress from an incurable disease had petitioned the state legislature to allow her doctor to put her painlessly to death.

Another stir was engendered in 1917 when a Des Moines doctor, William A. Guild, addressing a convention of the American Association of Progressive Medicine in Chicago, sought support for legalized euthanasia for the aged, infirm and incurably diseased. In the same year a Chicago doctor, Harry J. Haiselden, was acquitted of charges that he chose not to save the life of a baby girl born with a microcephalic head. Fifteen other doctors supported his defense. On the whole, however, the medical profession remained opposed to legalizing euthanasia.

Notable Topic of Discussion in the 1930s

A resurgence of interest during the 1930s was marked by a proliferation of books, articles, editorials and public discussions. Despite gains in support for euthanasia, efforts to push legislation were unsuccessful. A bill introduced in the British House of

---

[9] Quoted by Russell, *op. cit.*, p. 56. Sir Thomas was canonized in 1935, four centuries after his execution for opposing the monarch.

[10] Other influential works of this period are *Euthanasia: Or Medical Treatment in Aid of an Easy Death* (1887) by Dr. William Munk, a fellow of the Royal College of Surgeons, and *Euthanasia: The Aesthetics of Suicide* (1894) by Baron Harde-Hickey in 1894.

Lords in 1939 was rejected and nothing came of legislation introduced in Nebraska in 1937 and in New York in 1939. It was in this decade, however, that euthanasia societies were founded, first in England in 1935, then in the United States three years later. Among supporters of the movement in England at that time were biologist Julian Huxley, Dr. William R. Inge (former dean of St. Paul's Cathedral), author A. A. Milne, diplomat Harold Nicolson, playwright George Bernard Shaw and novelist H. G. Wells, and in America, Dr. Foster Kennedy (professor of neurology at Cornell Medical College) and Dr. George W. Jacoby (president of the American Neurological Association).

Dr. Kennedy presented his views, favoring euthanasia not only for those in painful terminal illness but for incurably defective infants, not only before professional gatherings but in an article in the May 20, 1939, issue of *Collier's,* a popular weekly of the period. Dr. Jacoby's pro-euthanasia book, *Physician, Pastor and Patient,* published in 1936, was considered the most influential book on the subject since the one by Tollemache a half century earlier. The pro-euthanasia doctors tended to blame religious superstition and conservatism of the church for resistance to euthanasia legislation.

Public interest was further stirred when Charlotte Perkins Gilman, great-granddaughter of Lyman Beecher, the abolitionist minister, committed suicide in 1935, leaving behind a note and the manuscript for an article in which she said she preferred a quick death to a lingering one from cancer. Open debates continued to flourish at professional meetings and in the popular press. The first article in an American medical journal to advocate legalization of euthanasia was published in *Medical Record* in 1939.

Ambiguity of Opinion Over Mercy Killing

Support subsided during World War II. The Nazi regime's disposal of the old, the feeble-minded, the mentally ill—anyone it considered unfit—cooled enthusiasm for euthanasia. Although the ostensible motive of the Nazis was eugenic—to "protect" the genetic stock of the German people—the policy pointed up the potential for government abuse of power in this area. But interest stirred again soon after the war. In New York City in 1947 a group of leading Protestant ministers joined other proponents of voluntary euthanasia to urge the legislature to consider a proposed bill.[11]

---

[11] Among prominent signers of a statement by 54 New York Protestant ministers supporting euthanasia for victims of painful, incurable disease were Dr. Harry Emerson Fosdick and Dr. Henry Sloane Coffin. Dr. Robert Latou Dickenson, former president of the American Gynecological Association, director of the American College of Surgeons and chairman of the obstetrical section of the American Medical Association, was among leading physicians in support.

Two years later a petition signed by 379 Protestant and Jewish religious leaders favoring euthanasia under controlled conditions was sent to every member of the New York legislature. These actions stirred equally vociferous opposition from other doctors and clergymen and their organizations. A Gallup Poll of June 30, 1947, showed that only 37 per cent of the people questioned said they believed doctors should be allowed to terminate the life of a sufferer of an incurable disease even if the patient and family requested it.

Publicity given to sensational cases in which euthanasia had been practiced kept the subject alive but without greatly increasing the movement's support. Indicative of the ambiguity of attitude toward euthanasia and the depth of the dilemma faced by those involved in actual cases was the fact that few of those charged with "mercy killing" were actually convicted, even when there was no doubt the act had occurred. Sympathy for the defendant who killed as an act of love and compassion overcame religious and moral convictions against it as well as laws forbidding it.[12] Juries or judges usually acquitted on the ground of temporary insanity or gave suspended sentences, or else the charges were dropped for inadequacy of evidence.

Typical was the sensational trial of Hermann Sander, a New Hampshire physician who was charged with murder in late 1949 for injecting air into the veins of a 59-year-old patient dying of cancer, an act which he candidly recorded on the patient's hospital chart. He was acquitted in 1950 on the ground that it was not certain whether the woman died before or after the injection. Dr. Sander was supported by a petition signed by 90 per cent of the population in his community, including the widower of the patient.[13]

Euthanasia Society; Its Aims and Work

The generally permissive outcome of "mercy killing" cases contrasted with the rigidity of anti-euthanasia laws. This situation, plus intermittent efforts to push pro-euthanasia legislation, finally drew the legal profession into exploring the underlying issues. A recent historical review of the movement notes that "law journals in the [19]50s began for the first time to publish articles on euthanasia, many of which reflected the reactionary atmosphere during the early part of the decade."[14]

---

[12] A rare case in which a "mercy killer" was convicted and sentenced to death involved John F. Noxon, a Massachusetts attorney who was sentenced in September 1943 for killing his six-month-old mentally deficient son. The sentence was commuted to life imprisonment and five years later Noxon was released on parole.

[13] This case stirred considerable pro and con comment. Billy Graham, the evangelist, told a Boston audience on Jan. 8, 1950, that Dr. Sander should be punished "as an example." The Hillsboro County (N.H.) Medical Society dropped him from membership but later reinstated him. The New Hampshire Registration Board revoked his license to practice medicine but permitted him to apply for reinstatement in two months.

[14] Russell, *op. cit.*, p. 115.

The torch for euthanasia during these years was carried by the Euthanasia Society of America, organized in New York in January 1938, three years after a similar society was founded in England. Its object was to conduct national campaigns of "education" aimed at winning support for proposals to legalize euthanasia. The founder and first president of the U.S. society was Charles Francis Potter, well-known then as author of books on religion and other topics. Among the prominent persons who served on its board of directors were Fosdick, author Sherwood Anderson, author-psychologist Havelock Ellis, birth-control crusader Margaret Sanger and playwright Robert E. Sherwood.

The 1960s brought not only a growth of interest in the subject but a significant shift of emphasis. This was the decade of great advancement in the life-saving powers of the medical profession. While this constituted a great boon for many who were rescued from invalidism or death for a life of reasonable vigor, it also produced the troublesome problem of extending a miserable life for those who would prefer death or lacked any cognizance of their own existence. To the normal fear of death was now added the fear of being trapped by medical science into a protracted period of dying, subject to painful treatment and isolation in an institution, or sustained as a "vegetable" at great expense to the surviving family.

The Euthanasia Society responded to the change of climate in 1967 by dropping its name and reconstituting itself into two separate units: the Euthanasia Educational Council and the Society for the Right to Die. Both are housed in the same suite of offices in New York City. The former circulates a newsletter, *Euthanasia News,* reprints of articles and audio tape transcripts of material on the subject, sponsors or participates in conferences and workshops, promotes the development of courses or seminars on how to deal humanely with the dying. This material is available to laymen and to those whose professions will bring them into contact with the old and the sick. One function is to provide model copies of a "Living Will," a document in which an individual asks not to be subjected to extraordinary means for extending life in the event he or she is in a terminal stage of illness.

The Society for the Right to Die is a lobbying organization whose aim primarily is to encourage and support proposals for right-to-die legislation, evaluate pending bills and recommend model legislation. It serves as a clearinghouse for information, annually circulates a manual analyzing current legislation and provides witnesses to testify at hearings on pending legislation in the states. Both units are nonprofit, dependent for funds on private contributions.

A Living Will

TO MY FAMILY, MY PHYSICIAN, MY LAWYER, MY CLERGYMAN
TO ANY MEDICAL FACILITY IN WHOSE CARE I HAPPEN TO BE
TO ANY INDIVIDUAL WHO MAY BECOME RESPONSIBLE FOR MY HEALTH, WELFARE OR AFFAIRS

Death is as much a reality as birth, growth, maturity and old age—it is the one certainty of life. If the time comes when I, ______________________________ can no longer take part in decisions for my own future, let this statement stand as an expression of my wishes, while I am still of sound mind.

If the situation should arise in which there is no reasonable expectation of my recovery from physical or mental disability, I request that I be allowed to die and not be kept alive by artificial means or "heroic measures". I do not fear death itself as much as the indignities of deterioration, dependence and hopeless pain. I, therefore, ask that medication be mercifully administered to me to alleviate suffering even though this may hasten the moment of death.

This request is made after careful consideration. I hope you who care for me will feel morally bound to follow its mandate. I recognize that this appears to place a heavy responsibility upon you, but it is with the intention of relieving you of such responsibility and of placing it upon myself in accordance with my strong convictions, that this statement is made.

Signed ______________________________

Date ______________________________

Witness ______________________________

Witness ______________________________

EUTHANASIA
derived from the Greek, meaning "good death"

Copies of this request have been given to ______________________________

____

____

____

Prepared by the
EUTHANASIA EDUCATIONAL COUNCIL
250 West 57th Street, New York, N.Y. 10019

The emphasis in the euthanasia movement today is on forswearing the use of extraordinary means of prolonging life in hopeless cases. This is sometimes referred to as "passive euthanasia" as opposed to "active euthanasia" which would require a direct act to cause death in such cases. Polling by Louis Harris Associates in 1973 and again in 1977 indicated that support had developed for both forms of euthanasia. People were asked:

"Do you think a patient with a terminal disease ought to be able to tell his doctor to let him die rather than to extend his life when no cure is in sight...?" The percentage of "yes" responses rose from 66 to 71 in the four years. To another question—"Do you think the patient who is terminally ill, with no cure in sight, ought to have the right to tell his doctor to put him out of his misery"—the negative response dropped from 53 to 38 per cent.

Dilemmas in Law and Medicine

THE RIGHT-TO-DIE movement presents questions which still defy resolution and in some cases its successes have created new dilemmas, especially for the medical profession. For one thing there remains the question of whether an irreversibly comatose patient is actually alive even though the person's breathing and heartbeat are sustained artificially. Another difficulty is how to establish criteria for deciding when further treatment is useless.

Terminology in legislation is often ambigious. Incurable illness may apply to persons who still have the prospect of many months or years of a reasonably active life. How can the doctor be sure that the patient's refusal of treatment is not the result of temporary depression caused by the shock of learning that the illness is incurable? Still another question is how much should the patient be told. The view put forth by most supporters of the right to die is that patients have a right to be told exactly what their illness is and the probable outlook with or without treatment. But many doctors insist that some patients do not want to be told everything and that their will to live may be damaged by learning the gravity of their illness.

Adding to the dilemma is the fact that individuals differ in physical and mental reactions to disease and to medication. Disease itself can be erratic, sometimes moving ahead slowly, sometimes racing explosively through the body, sometimes going mysteriously into remission for considerable lengths of time. Decisions in these cases are particularly difficult when the patient is unable to speak for himself.

Concern that breath-sustaining treatment may be applied to a person who is actually dead rather than merely comatose has helped spur pressure for new definitions of death. From as far back as history records, the standard criterion, rarely questioned, was that death ensued when the heart stopped beating and breathing ceased. Since these functions can now be artificially sustained when the patient has apparently lost forever all sensitivity to surroundings or awareness of life, the drive has been to substitute or add "brain death" as a criterion for total demise of the individual.

To date 18 states[15] have enacted a statutory definition of

[15] Alaska, California, Georgia, Idaho, Illinois, Iowa, Kansas, Louisiana, Maryland, Michigan, Montana, New Mexico, North Carolina, Oklahoma, Oregon, Tennessee, Virginia and West Virginia.

death. Passage of these laws followed the publication in 1968 of new criteria for a definition of death drawn up by the Ad Hoc Committee of the Harvard Medical School. Among the Harvard criteria are: "irreversible coma"; "no spontaneous muscle movement...[or] spontaneous respiration or response to stimuli such as pain, touch, sound or light"; removal from a respirator for three minutes resulting in "no spontaneous breathing"; absence of reflexes indicating no activity in the central nervous system; and a "flat" encephalogram showing no sign of brain wave activity.

Varied Legislation for Redefining Death

The laws, however, are not replicas of the Harvard document. "All 18 states recognize that death may be pronounced on the basis of irreversible cessation of brain function," states a review of brain death legislation published in the *Journal of the American Medical Association.*[16] But the authors of the article say none of the laws "describes in detail the specific criteria for determining brain death." The authors found three major types of laws, all presenting certain problems. One type establishes alternative definitions of death: this is considered a "major flaw" because it seems to indicate that there are two separate kinds of death and could raise suspicion that one type of death might be chosen to facilitate the removal of an organ for transplant by declaring a potential donor dead at an earlier stage in the dying process than a nondonor. This is a touchy problem and one which has caused indignant relatives to sue doctors, charging them with removing the organs prematurely.

A second type of law provides that death ensues if the physician finds respiration and circulatory function have ceased; but if these functions are being supported by artificial means, the doctor may pronounce the patient dead because of an irreversible cessation of brain function. One state, Louisiana, requires that brain death determinations must be made by two physicians and, if organ transplant is contemplated, one of the physicians must not be associated with the transplantation.

Still a third type of law follows the recommendation of the Law and Medicine Committee of the American Bar Association which was approved by the ABA House of Delegates in 1975. It states simply: "For all legal purposes, a human body with irreversible cessation of total brain function, according to usual and customary standards of medical practice, shall be considered dead." No criteria are offered, leaving that to the doctor or, if necessary, the courts on the basis of medical evidence. A major reason for the variations and complexities of death-

---

[16] Frank J. Veith, M.D., et al., "Brain Death," *Journal of the American Medical Association,* Oct. 17, 1977, pp. 1741-1748.

defining laws, according to this review, is "the present climate of public mistrust of the medical profession" which "has prompted legislators to enact more complicated laws in an attempt to protect patients from erroneous...declarations of death."

Question of the Right to Refuse Treatment

In general, competent adults have the legal right to refuse medical treatment. There are exceptions, however. Robert M. Veatch, in his book *Death, Dying and the Biological Revolution,* cites, for example, a case in which Judge J. Skelly Wright of the U.S. Court of Appeals for the District of Columbia ordered blood transfusions for a woman who had refused them. The judge said that he so ruled because, among other reasons, she had a seven-month-old child and thus "a responsibility to the community to care for her infant." Veatch said he found possibly 100 cases in American legal history involving refusal of medical treatment. "Some of the cases and the rulings...have been so complex that legal scholars have stated...that the right to refuse treatment is in doubt," he wrote.

The problem arises chiefly in cases of minors and adults who are incompetent to make their wishes known. In a number of cases, judges have overruled religious objections of parents to having life-saving procedures performed on an afflicted child. In other cases, patients with religious scruples have refused to sign documents giving doctors permission to take life-saving measures but indicated they would submit to a court order. Thus they could have their lives saved, according to their wish, without offense to their religious scruples. There have been other cases in which an adult has refused treatment but a relative has sought to overrule the patient's expressed wish by seeking a legal declaration that the patient has become incompetent to make that decision.

Those with foresight who care about their right to die without futile intervention may write instructions that if they should become incompetent measures should not be taken to prolong their lives needlessly. The most popular form which this request takes is the "Living Will" first devised in 1967 by the Euthanasia Educational Council. On request, the council will mail a copy. It is not legally binding, but the signer hopes "you who care for me will...feel morally bound to follow its mandate." Its legal validity as a mandate has never been tested in court although some of the right-to-die laws provide for a written declaration of desire to refuse treatment under certain conditions.

One of the consequences of the new concern for the right to die is the impact on the medical profession. Traditionally the doctor has been king in determining what to do for the seriously and terminally ill. Throughout training and practice, the emphasis has been on his duty to save lives rather than to terminate them. Accustomed because of his expertise to relative autonomy in the sickroom, many doctors and their organizations do not welcome intervention of the law into an area which they feel should be governed by medical judgments.

Prospect of Change in Treating the Dying

Right-to-die sponsors have brought pressure on the medical profession to take what they consider a more humane as well as a technically expert approach to patient care. They stress treatment of the dying patient in terms of giving comfort, both psychological and physical, rather than merely providing life-extension treatment. The Euthanasia Educational Council, among others, has promoted the development of courses in medical and nursing schools as well as in-service workshops to help doctors, nurses and other hospital attendants overcome their reticence in dealing with the dying in a personal way.

Dr. Christopher Lasch, a University of Rochester historian, believes that doctors are undergoing a change of heart. "There is talk [among doctors] of 'natural' death—letting the patient die at his own speed, without intervention of machines," he writes. "Some hospitals have instituted seminars on 'the dynamics of death and dying' designed to make doctors as well as patients face death without flinching." He considers these "signs of a new humility, in what has become the most arrogant of professions" and possibly "the beginning of an important change in the [medical and scientific] professions in general."[17]

Although withdrawal of "heroic" measures when the outcome is hopeless has received at least some approval by all major church groups, some opposition to right-to-die activity emanates from those who fear legalizing withdrawal may be a first step toward approval of active euthanasia. This view is sometimes presented by "right to life" movement leaders, whose main activities are opposition to permissive abortion.[18]

While there appears to be no disposition in any professional group to press at this time for legalizing active euthanasia, the issue is not entirely dead. *Psychology Today* magazine, for example, has printed an excerpt from a book, *Common Sense Suicide,* to be published in April, which vigorously argues for the right of elderly persons to choose suicide rather than the pain of living "in the near imprisonment of nursing homes or hospitals." Doris Portwood, the author, writes that the subject at least should be reopened to "rational discussion."

---

[17] Christopher Lasch, "Birth, Death and Technology: The Limits of Cultural Laissez-Faire," reprint of essay from The Institute for Society, Ethics and the Life Sciences.

[18] See "Abortion Politics," *E.R.R.*, 1976 Vol. II, pp. 765-784.

Books

Alsop, Stewart, *Stay of Execution,* J. B. Lippincott, 1973.
Becker, Ernest, *The Denial of Death,* Free Press-Macmillan, 1973.
Beneficent Euthanasia, Marvin Kohl, ed., Prometheus Books, 1975.
Dilemmas of Euthanasia, John A. Behnke and Sissela Bok, eds., Anchor Press-Doubleday, 1975.
Kubler-Ross, Elisabeth, *On Death and Dying,* Macmillan, 1969.
——*Death; The Final Stage of Growth,* Prentice-Hall, 1975.
Russell, O. Ruth, *Freedom to Die,* Human Sciences Press, rev. ed., 1977.
Toynbee, Arnold, et al., *Man's Concern With Death,* McGraw-Hill, 1968.
Veatch, Robert M., *Death, Dying, and the Biological Revolution,* Yale University Press, 1976.

Articles

Cantor, Norman L., "Quinlan, Privacy and the Handling of Incompetent Dying Patients," *Rutgers Law Review,* winter 1977, pp. 243-266.
Crowther, C. Edward, "Care Versus Cure in the Treatment of the Terminally Ill," *The Center Report* (Center for the Study of Democratic Institutions), April 1976.
Flannery, Ellen J., "Statutory Recognition of the Right to Die: the California Natural Death Act," *Boston University Law Review,* January 1977.
"Helping the Dying Die: Two Harvard Hospitals Go Public With Policies," *Science,* Sept. 17, 1976.
Jaretski, Alfred II, M.D., "Death with Dignity-Passive Euthanasia," *New York State Journal of Medicine,* April 1976, pp. 539-543.
Portwood, Doris, "A Right to Suicide?" *Psychology Today,* January 1978.
Veatch, Robert M., "Death and Dying: The Legislative Options—An analysis of three types of bills," *The Hastings Center Report,* October 1977.
Veith, Frank K., M.D., et al., "Brain Death," *Journal of the American Medical Association,* Oct. 10 and Oct. 17, 1977 (two parts).

Reports and Studies

Euthanasia Educational Council, "Changing Attitudes Toward Euthanasia," Excerpts from papers at eighth annual euthanasia conference, New York, Dec. 6, 1975.
——A Living Will, revised April 1974.
——*Euthanasia News* issues, case histories, reprints of articles, conference papers and other materials.
Lasch, Dr. Christopher, "Birth, Death and Technology: The Limits of Cultural Laissez-Faire," reprint from The Institute for Society, Ethics, and the Life Sciences (undated).
Society for the Right to Die, *Legislative Manual 1977.*
U.S. Senate Labor and Public Welfare Subcommittee on Health, *Moral, Ethical, and Legal Questions of Extraordinary Health Care,* printed transcript of hearing Nov. 6, 1975, U.S. Government Printing Office, 1976.

REVERSE DISCRIMINATION

by

Sandra Stencel

Aug. 6
1976

Editor's Note: A widely publicized reverse-discrimination lawsuit was decided by the U.S. Supreme Court on June 28, 1978. In the case, *Regents of the University of California v. Allan Bakke,* the court ruled that universities may not set aside a quota of seats in each class for minority group representatives and thus deny white applicants the opportunity to compete for those places. But the court held in the same case that it is constitutionally permissible for officers to consider race as one of the factors that determine which applicants are accepted.

A key question left unresolved in the *Bakke* decision is whether it is permissible for employers and other institutions that have not been found guilty of prior illegal discrimination voluntarily to adopt affirmative action programs, which by their very nature involve some discrimination against majority group members.

This question could be answered by the Supreme Court during its 1978-79 term. The court in December 1978 agreed to hear a case brought by a white worker, Brian Weber, against his employer, Kaiser Aluminum, and his union, the United Steelworkers of America. Weber was refused in-plant training he sought because half of the trainee positions were set aside for blacks and women. Weber went to federal court, contesting his rejection as reverse discrimination. He won in both federal district court and in a court of appeals.

In Weber's case, the court of appeals emphasized — in holding the Kaiser training program illegal — that their had been no showing of prior discrimination by Kaiser. The Justice Department, in asking the Supreme Court to review the case, suggested it be sent back to the appeals court for reconsideration in light of the *Bakke* decision.

Sears, Roebuck & Co., which has been charged by the Equal Employment Opportunity Commission with discriminating in pay and advancement against women and minority-group members, filed a counter suit against 10 federal agencies in January 1979. Sears charged that the federal government's own policies had created an "unbalanced workforce" dominated by white males.

REVERSE DISCRIMINATION

IN TEXAS, two white employees of a Houston trucking firm were fired in 1970 after being charged with stealing 60 one-gallon cans of antifreeze from a customer's shipment. A black worker charged with the same offense was kept on.

In Virginia, 328 men and 57 women applied for two full-time positions in the sociology and anthropology department of Virginia Commonwealth University. No men were interviewed for the jobs; two women were hired.

In Chicago, on Jan. 5, 1976, U.S. District Court Judge Prentice H. Marshall gave the city 90 days to hire 400 new police officers. Of these, 200 were to be black and Spanish-named men and 66 were to be women. The judge also imposed a similar quota on future hiring.

In California, a white student was denied admission to the law school at the University of California's Davis campus in 1975 even though he had better grades and test scores than 74 other applicants admitted under a special minority admissions program.

These incidents and others like them have sparked an increasingly bitter debate over what has come to be known as "reverse discrimination"—giving preferential treatment to women, blacks and persons from other minority groups in such areas as employment and college admissions. The policy is defended as fair and necessary to compensate for past discrimination. It is criticized as "robbing Peter to pay Paul." The critics say that all persons should be judged solely on their personal qualifications.

The furor stems from the government's decade-old policy of requiring educators and employers to take "affirmative action" to prevent racial or sexual discrimination. To make up for alleged past discriminatory hiring practices, the government forced businesses and organizations holding federal contracts to set up goals and timetables for hiring minorities and women. Many employers complain that they are trapped between the government's demands to increase opportunities for women and minorities on the one hand, and, on the other, charges by white males that affirmative action constitutes reverse discrimination.

Growing numbers of white males, charging that they are victims of reverse discrimination, are going to court seeking redress. "The suits present a thorny problem for the courts," said *U.S. News & World Report.* "On the one hand, the preferences being attacked have a legally sanctioned goal—the correction or prevention of racial or sexual bias. But those not covered by such preferences charge it is just as illegal to discriminate against whites and males as against minorities and women."[1]

A recent ruling by the U.S. Supreme Court could result in a significant increase in lawsuits charging reverse discrimination. The Court ruled on June 25, 1976, that the Civil Rights Acts of 1866 and 1964 protect white people as well as blacks against racial discrimination. The ruling was the result of a suit filed by the two white employees of the Houston trucking firm who were fired for stealing company cargo although a black man who participated in the theft was not. With the help of the U.S. Equal Employment Opportunity Commission, the two men sued the company and their union on discrimination charges. The case was dismissed in lower federal court, which held that only minority group members could bring such charges under these laws. But on appeal the Supreme Court ruled the suit valid and held that the two civil rights laws ban discrimination against whites "upon the same standards as would be applicable were they Negroes."

The full meaning of the court's decision is not yet clear. To some observers it appeared to cast doubt on hiring and promotion quotas that favor blacks and women over white males. However, Justice Thurgood Marshall, author of the majority opinion, said the Court was not considering the legality of affirmative action programs.

Suits by White Males Charging Discrimination

The Supreme Court earlier had sidestepped a decision on reverse discrimination in the highly publicized DeFunis case *(see p. 162)*. The plaintiff, Marco DeFunis, charged that he had been turned down by the University of Washington Law School while minority applicants with lower grades and test scores were admitted. When the Court in 1974 refused to decide the case on its merits, four justices dissented. One of the four, William J. Brennan, said: "Few constitutional questions in recent years have stirred as much debate, and they will not disappear. They must inevitably return to the federal courts and ultimately again to this court."

Several cases alleging reverse discrimination are expected to come before the Supreme Court in the near future. A definitive

[1] " 'Reverse Discrimination'—Has It Gone Too Far?" *U.S. News & World Report,* March 29, 1976, p. 26.

AT&T Cases

The legal complexities involved in reverse discrimination are perhaps best illustrated by a recent court ruling against American Telephone and Telegraph Co. In 1973, after more than two years of litigation, AT&T agreed to hire and promote thousands of women and minority group members. Following the guidelines laid out in their court-approved affirmative action plan, AT&T promoted a woman service representative over a male employee who had more experience and seniority. The man sued, contending that he was a victim of sex discrimination.

On June 9, 1976, U.S. District Court Judge Gerhard Gesell of Washington, D.C., ordered AT&T to pay the man an undetermined sum in damages. Although Judge Gesell held that the company had acted correctly in promoting the woman, he went on to say that the impact of its past discriminatory policies should fall on the company, not on "an innocent employee who had earned promotion." On the other hand, Gesell ruled that the man was entitled only to damages. To award him the promotion he was denied "might well perpetuate and prolong the effects of the discrimination [the 1973 agreement] was designed to eliminate."

If Judge Gesell's opinion is upheld by the higher courts, employers will face yet another expensive cost in complying with court orders to correct past discriminatory employment practices.

ruling would provide welcome guidance to the lower courts which have handed down contradictory rulings. In several recent cases the courts have ruled in favor of men who charged that employers were giving preferential treatment to women and minorities. For example, on June 9, U.S. District Court Judge Gerhard Gesell of Washington, D.C., ordered the American Telephone & Telegraph Co. to pay damages to a male employee passed over for promotion in favor of a less-experienced woman *(see box above)*.

Another federal judge in the District of Columbia, Oliver Gasch, ruled on July 28 that Georgetown University's policy of setting aside 60 per cent of its first-year law school scholarships for minority students constituted reverse discrimination and therefore violated the 1964 Civil Rights Act. The ruling came in a suit filed by a white student, J. Michael Flanagan, who claimed he was discriminated against because no more scholarships were available for white students by the time he had been admitted to the law school, although scholarship funds still were available for minority students.

In the case involving Virginia Commonwealth University, U.S. District Court Judge D. Dortch Warriner of Richmond ruled on May 28 that the school had acted illegally when it gave hiring preferences to women over equally qualified male applicants. The suit was filed by Dr. James Albert Cramer, a professor with temporary status in the school's sociology department and one of the 328 men to apply for full-time positions. Cramer contended that the university, in denying him a job because he was male, violated the Fourteenth Amendment's guarantee of equal protection under the law and the Civil Rights Act which bans discrimination on the basis of race, color, religion, sex or national origin. The university argued that under state and federal guidelines it was required to take affirmative action to hire women and minorities to "eliminate the effects of past discrimination" against them.

Judge Warriner held that under the equal-protection clause, "where sex is the sole factor upon which differential treatment is determined, there is no constitutional justification for treating the sexes differently." He said that even if the university was guilty of past discrimination, its preferential policies were unconstitutional because the civil rights law prohibits employment practices that "predicate hiring and promotion decisions on gender-based criteria."

In contrast, some other recent court rulings have upheld preferential treatment as a legal way of overcoming the effects of past discrimination. For example, the New York State Court of Appeals on April 8 held that the Brooklyn Downstate Medical Center had acted properly when it gave certain admissions preferences to minority applicants. The court said that reverse discrimination was constitutional "in proper circumstances." The test of constitutionality, the court held, should be "whether preferential treatment satisfies a substantial state interest.... It need be found that, on balance, the gain to be derived from the preferential policy outweighs its possible detrimental effects."

Case For and Against Preferential Treatment

Many of those who advocate preferential hiring and admissions policies deny that it amounts to reverse discrimination. "There is no such thing as reverse discrimination," said Herbert Hill, national labor director for the National Association for the Advancement of Colored People. "Those who complain of it are engaging in a deliberate attempt to perpetuate the racial status quo by drawing attention away from racial discrimination to make the remedy the issue. The real issue remains racial discrimination."[2]

Others, while acknowledging the dilemmas posed by preferential treatment, insist that such policies are necessary to wipe out the effects of past discrimination. "While there may be an element of unfairness in preferential treatment," said the authors of a law journal article, "some price must be paid to overcome

[2] Quoted in " 'Reverse Discrimination'—Has It Gone Too Far?" *U.S. News & World Report*, March 29, 1976, p. 29.

Preferential Treatment: Two Views

"Preferential remedies to end employment discrimination may be likened to starting one controlled forest fire in order to bring a raging one under control. At first the idea may seem illogical, but the remedial principle is sound."

—Professors Harry T. Edwards
and Barry L. Zaretsky
Michigan Law Review

"There is no constitutional right for any race to be preferred."

—Supreme Court Justice
William O. Douglas in
DeFunis v. Odegaard

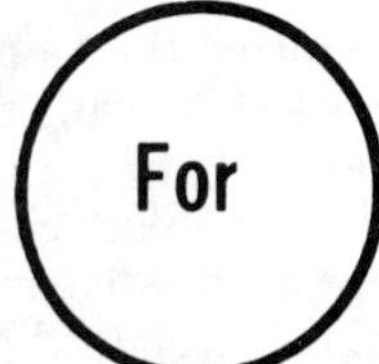

"...[A] preference which aids minorities is perfectly consistent with the purpose of the Fourteenth Amendment."

—Brief submitted to Supreme Court
De Funis v. Odegaard

"Where individuals have overcome individual hardship, they should be favored, but what offends me deeply is the shorthand we us, which is race."

—Professor Alan Dershowitz of
Harvard Law School quoted
in ***The New Republic***

"The reverse discrimination aspect of affirmative action is, in reality, the removal of that benefit which American society has so long bestowed, without question, upon its privileged classes."

—Shirley E. Stewart,
Cleveland State Law Review

the longstanding pervasive patterns of race and sex bias in this nation. The minor injustice that may result...is, on balance, outweighed by the fact that temporary preferential remedies appear to be the only way to effectively break the cycle of employment discrimination and open all levels of the job market to all qualified applicants."[3]

Affirmative action, it is pointed out, is not the first government program to prescribe differential treatment as a social policy. The Veterans Preference Act of 1944 stipulated that veterans should be given special consideration when seeking employment with the federal government. This statute granted persons extra points on competitive civil service examinations solely because they were veterans.

Economic statistics also provide an argument for the preferential treatment of minorities and women. According to the Census Bureau's latest findings, for 1974, black families had a median income of $7,808—half of the families earned more and half earned less. That was only 58 per cent of the white families' median income ($13,356), a drop of three percentage points since 1969.[4] There is a similar—and widening—gap between the earnings of men and women. The Department of Labor reported the median income of full-time women workers in 1975 was $6,975 while that of men was $12,152; women's earnings thus were only 57 per cent as high as men's, down from 64 per cent in 1955. *The Wall Street Journal* observed: "The average female college graduate earned less last year than the average male high-school dropout."[5]

Critics of affirmative action charge that the original purpose of that policy—the achievement of full and equal employment and educational opportunities—has been perverted. This theme dominates a controversial new book, *Affirmative Discrimination: Ethnic Inequality and Public Policy* (1975) by Harvard sociologist Nathan Glazer. He wrote: "In the early 1970s, affirmative action came to mean much more than advertising opportunities actively, seeking out those who might not know of them, and preparing those who might not yet be qualified. It came to mean the setting of statistical requirements based on race, color and national origin...." As a consequence of this shift in policy, Glazer said, "Those groups that are not considered eligible for special benefits become resentful."

[3] Harry T. Edwards and Barry L. Zaretsky, "Preferential Remedies for Employment Discrimination," *Michigan Law Review*, November 1975, p. 7. Edwards is a professor of law at the University of Michigan and Zaretsky is an assistant professor of law at Wayne State University.

[4] See U.S. Bureau of the Census, Current Population Reports, Special Studies, Series P-23 No. 54, "The Social and Economic Status of Black Population in the United States, 1974."

[5] *The Wall Street Journal*, July 6, 1976. See also U.S. Department of Labor, "1975 Handbook on Women Workers," and Lester C. Thurow's "The Economic Status of Minorities and Women," *Civil Rights Digest*, winter-spring 1976, pp. 3-9.

Glazer also raised the question of which groups should qualify for special treatment.

> The statistical basis for redress makes one great error: All "whites" are consigned to the same category, deserving of no special consideration. That is not the way "whites" see themselves, or indeed are, in social reality. Some may be "whites," pure and simple. But almost all have some specific ethnic or religious identification, which, to the individual involved, may mean a distinctive history of past—or perhaps some present—discrimination.

"Compensation for the past is a dangerous principle," Glazer went on to say. "It can be extended indefinitely and make for endless trouble."

Disputes Over Hiring and Admissions in Academia

The backlash against affirmative action and preferential treatment has been particularly strong in the academic community. "By using statistics to determine the presence of discrimination and ignoring differences in qualifications, the federal government is undermining the integrity and scholarly function of the university," Professor Allan C. Ornstein of Loyola University of Chicago has written.[6] Government intrusion into more and more aspects of university life was the theme of the 1974-1975 annual report issued recently by Harvard President Derek Bok.

> In a few short years [he said], universities have been encumbered with a formidable body of regulations, some of which seem unnecessary and most of which cause needless confusion, administrative expense and red tape. If this process continues, higher education will almost certainly lose some of the independence, the flexibility and the diversity that have helped it to flourish in the past.

Bok was particularly concerned about the mounting costs of complying with federal regulations.[7] It has been reported elsewhere, for example, that when Reed College in Portland, Ore., sought to hire some new faculty members recently, it was told by the Department of Health, Education and Welfare—which is responsible for administering affirmative action programs in educational institutions—to advertise nationally instead of going through normal academic channels. As a result, the small private college was flooded with some 6,000 applications. In addition, HEW demanded that Reed keep records on all the applicants not hired and make detailed reports on prime candidates who reached the finals, including their race, sex, qualifications, prior experience, and why Reed did not hire

---

[6] Allan C. Ornstein, "Quality, Not Quotas," *Society*, January-February 1976, p. 10.
[7] See "Future of Private Colleges," *E.R.R.*, 1976 Vol. I, pp. 305-322.

them.[8] The University of California at Berkeley has estimated that it will spend some $400,000 to implement an affirmative action plan.

Some educators charge that the government is forcing colleges to hire underqualified and unqualified persons merely because they are women or members of a minority group. Colleges that fail to comply face the loss of federal funds which can amount to millions of dollars. In 1971, for example, HEW froze $13-million in federal research contracts with Columbia University when the school failed to come up with an acceptable affirmative action plan. Educators often tell the story of the HEW representative who, when informed that there were no black teachers in the religion department of Brown University because none who applied met the requirements for ancient languages, replied: "Then end these old-fashioned programs that require irrelevant languages."[9]

HEW has shown some sensitivity to the special characteristics of academic employment. In December 1974 it reviewed the existing codes applying to affirmative action. This "memorandum to college and university presidents," signed by Peter E. Holmes, director of the department's Office of Civil Rights, stated that under existing law, colleges and universities could hire the "best qualified" person for a position. The memo concluded that the legal commitment to affirmative action merely required a school to show "good faith attempts" to recruit women and minorities.

What disturbs some eduators more than reverse discrimination are signs that preferential admissions to professional schools have brought in students who cannot do the work. Dr. Bernard D. Davis, a professor of bacterial physiology at Harvard Medical School, suggested recently that academic standards in the nation's medical schools have fallen in recent years because of the rise in the number of students with "substandard academic qualifications."

"It would be a rare person today," he wrote in *The New England Journal of Medicine,* "who would question the value of stretching the criteria for admission, and of trying to make up for earlier educational disadvantages...." But in their eagerness to help disadvantaged students, he charged, some medical schools are graduating students who may not be qualified to be doctors. He cited the example of one unidentified student who had been awarded a degree although he failed to pass a mandatory examination in five attempts. "It would be cruel," Dr. Davis wrote, "to admit students who have a very low probability of measuring up to reasonable standards. It is even crueler to abandon those

[8] See Ralph Kinney Bennett's "Colleges Under the Federal Gun," *Readers Digest,* May 1976, p. 126.

[9] The university later received an apology from HEW for the representative's remarks.

standards and allow the trusting patients to pay for our irresponsibility."[10]

The number of black students in American medical schools has increased greatly in recent years, from 783 in 1968 to 3,456 in 1976, in part because of special-admission efforts. There is also evidence of a higher failure rate among black students. At the University of Michigan Medical School, for example, the failure rate is 20 per cent for blacks and 4 per cent for whites. Recent medical school graduates of predominantly black Howard University, *The Washington Post* has reported, have failed their national board examinations—the final tests most medical school graduates take to become doctors—at a rate three and a half times above the national average.

Those who support preferential admissions to medical schools say that grades and test scores are not always a good indication of who will make good doctors. Said Dr. Alvin Poussaint, dean of student affairs at Harvard Medical School, "We need caring doctors, doctors with concerns and abilities not disclosed on the standards tests."[11]

Development of Affirmative Action

WHEN CONGRESS passed the Civil Rights Act in 1964, it was generally believed that discrimination took place primarily through conscious, overt actions against individuals. But it quickly became apparent that the processes of discrimination were much more subtle and complex than originally envisioned. It was discovered that normal, seemingly neutral policies such as seniority, aptitude and personnel tests, high school diploma requirements and college admission tests could perpetuate the effects of past discrimination. This led to the development of the affirmative action concept.

The need for affirmative action was spelled out by President Johnson in a commencement address at Howard University on June 4, 1965.

> Freedom is not enough [Johnson said]. You do not wipe out scars of centuries by saying "now you're free to go where you want and do as you desire." You do not take a person who for years has been hobbled by chains and liberate him, bringing him up to the

[10] Bernard D. Davis, "Academic Standards in Medical Schools," *The New England Journal of Medicine*, May 13, 1976. His article drew widespread criticism, including charges of racism, and he subsequently said it had been misrepresented in the press.

[11] Quoted in *The Washington Post*, June 1, 1976.

starting line of a race and then say "you're free to compete" and justly believe that you have been completely fair.

The following Sept. 24 Johnson issued Executive Order 11246 requiring federal contractors "to take affirmative action to ensure that applicants are employed, and that employees are treated during employment, without regard to their race, creed, color or national origin."[12] Every major contractor—one having more than 50 employees and a contract of $50,000 or more with the federal government—was required to submit a "written affirmative action compliance program" which would be monitored by the Department of Labor's Office of Federal Contract Compliance.

In January 1970, Secretary of Labor George P. Schulz issued guidelines for the affirmative action plans required by the executive order. The guidelines, which were revised in December 1971, stated that affirmative action was "results oriented." A contractor who was considered to have too few women or minority employees had to establish goals for each job classification, by sex and race, and timetables specifying the date when the situation would be corrected.

Philadelphia Plan Controversy Over Job Quotas

The Department of Labor had already—on June 29, 1969—announced a plan to increase minority employment in the construction trades in Philadelphia. The "Philadelphia Plan" set goals for the number of blacks and other minority workers to be hired on construction projects financed by federal funds. Secretary Schulz stressed that contractors who could not meet the hiring goals would not be penalized if they showed a "good faith effort" to fulfill them.

Controversy over the plan arose on Aug. 5 when Comptroller General Elmer B. Staats[13] issued a ruling that the Philadelphia Plan violated the 1964 Civil Rights Act by requiring racial hiring quotas. Staats dismissed the plan's distinction between a quota system and a goal system as "largely a matter of semantics." The purpose of either, he said, was to have contractors commit themselves to considering race or national origin in hiring new employees.

The Nixon administration continued to defend the plan. It pointed out that Congress had given the Attorney General, not the Comptroller General, authority to interpret the 1964 Civil Rights Act and that Attorney General John Mitchell had approved the Philadelphia Plan. It was incorrect, Mitchell said in a statement issued Sept. 22, 1969, to say that the 1964 act forbade

---

[12] Executive Order 11246 was amended in 1967 to apply to sexual discrimination.

[13] The Comptroller General of the United States works for Congress, not the executive branch.

employers to make race a factor in hiring employees. "The legal definition of discrimination is an evolving one," he said, "but it is now well recognized in judicial opinions that the obligation of non-discrimination, whether imposed by statute or by the Constitution, does not require, and, in some circumstances, may not permit obliviousness or indifference to the racial consequences of alternative courses of action...."

The Department of Labor put the Philadelphia Plan into effect the next day and soon afterward announced that similar plans would become effective in New York, Seattle, Boston, Los Angeles, San Francisco, St. Louis, Detroit, Pittsburgh and Chicago. The AFL-CIO and the building trades unions actively opposed such plans and lobbied for the inclusion of a provision in a 1970 appropriations bill to give the Comptroller General authority to block funds for any federal programs he considered to be illegal. Congress narrowly defeated this provision after President Nixon threatened to veto the appropriations bill if it was included. Critics of the Philadelphia Plan then turned to the courts, but in 1971 the plan was upheld in federal appeals court.[14]

Extension of Rules to Education; DeFunis Case

Educational institutions originally were not covered by the fair-employment section of the 1964 Civil Rights Act. This oversight was amended by the Equal Employment Act of 1972. "Discrimination against minorities and women in the field of education is as pervasive as discrimination in any other area of employment," said the House Committee on Education and Labor at the time. Similar views were expressed by the Senate Committee on Labor and Public Welfare: "As in other areas of employment, statistics for educational institutions indicate that minorities and women are precluded from the most prestigious and higher-paying positions, and are relegated to the more menial and lower-paying jobs."

According to Howard Glickstein, director of the Center for Civil Rights at the University of Notre Dame, the need for the inclusion of colleges and universities within the coverage of the Equal Employment Act was illustrated by the extent to which charges of discrimination have been filed with the EEOC. In 1973, he said, approximately one out of four EEOC charges involved higher education. "While a charge is not proof..., I believe that the large number of charges filed against educational institutions in the short time they have been covered by the act is indicative of a widespread and pervasive problem."[15]

---

[14] *Contractors Association of Eastern Pennsylvania* v. *Secretary of Labor*, 442 F 2d 159 (3d Cir. 1971).

[15] "Discrimination in Higher Education: A Debate on Faculty Employment," *Civil Rights Digest*, spring 1975, p. 12.

In addition to coping with charges of discrimination in employment, colleges and universities also were under heavy pressure to increase the number of women and minority students, particularly in graduate and professional schools.[16] To meet these demands most schools adopted preferential admissions programs, favoring minority group members.

Among the schools adopting a preferential admissions policy was the University of Washington. In 1971 its law school received 1,600 applications for 150 openings that September. Among the applicants rejected was Marco DeFunis, a white Phi Beta Kappa graduate of the university's undergraduate program. Among those admitted were 36 minority-group students whose grades and law school admission test scores were lower than those of DeFunis. The law school acknowedged that minority applicants had been judged separately. DeFunis sued, charging that he had been deprived of his constitutional right to equal protection under the law.

A trial court in Seattle agreed and ordered the school to enroll him. The university complied but appealed and the state supreme court, in 1973, ruled in favor of the school. DeFunis then appealed to the U.S. Supreme Court, and Justice William O. Douglas granted a stay that permitted him to remain in school pending a Supreme Court decision. But the Court, by a 5-4 vote on April 23, 1974, refused to decide the case—on the ground that the question was moot because DeFunis had been attending school and was expected to graduate within two months.

The Court's action was anti-climactic in a case which had produced substantial advance publicity. Some 64 organizations spoke up on the issue in 26 "friend of the court" briefs submitted to the Court. Among those submitting briefs supporting DeFunis were the Anti-Defamation League of B'nai B'rith, the Joint Civic Action Committee of Italian Americans, the Advocate Society (a Polish-American lawyers' association), the AFL-CIO, the National Association of Manufacturers and the U.S. Chamber of Commerce. Briefs defending the university were submitted by the former deans of the Yale and Harvard law schools, Louis Pollak and Erwin Griswold, the American Bar Association, the National Urban Coalition and a number of educational institutions, including the national associations of both law schools and medical schools.

Justice Douglas, one of the four dissenting justices, submitted a separate 29-page opinion in which he sharply criticized preferential admissions policies. Each application should be considered in a racially neutral way, Douglas emphasized: "A

---

[16] See "Blacks on Campus," *E.R.R.*, 1972 Vol. II, pp. 667-684.

DeFunis who is white is entitled to no advantage by reason of that fact; nor is he subject to any disability.... Whatever his race he had a constitutional right to have his application considered on its individual merits in a racially neutral manner."

But Douglas went on to say that schools should not have to judge applicants solely on the basis of their grades or test scores. A black applicant "who pulled himself out of the ghetto into a junior college...," Douglas wrote, "may thereby demonstrate a level of motivation, perseverance and ability that would lead a fair-minded admissions committee to conclude that he shows more promise for law study than the son of a rich alumnus who received better grades at Harvard."

Complaint Investigations and Leading Decisions

The Equal Employment Opportunity Commission was created by the 1964 Civil Rights Act to investigate employment discrimination complaints. In 1972, upon passage of the Equal Opportunity Act, the commission gained authority to bring civil suits directly against employers it found to be engaging in discriminatory practices. The EEOC's impact on American business has been characterized in a law journal in the following way:

> The period from 1964 to 1974 marked a major change not only in the composition of the national work force, but, perhaps more importantly, in the attitudes and personnel policies of those involved in the labor market. It was a decade in which employment expectations and opportunities of...blacks and women were expanded greatly. Employers and unions were forced to reconsider carefully their standards for hiring, promotion and membership.[17]

In most instances, change did not come easily or voluntarily. Most cases required court action. Some of the leading cases were these:

> Anaconda Aluminum Co. in 1971 was ordered to pay $190,000 in back wages and court costs to 276 women who alleged that the company maintained sex-segregated job classifications.
>
> Virginia Electric Power Co. in 1971 was ordered to pay $250,000 to compensate black workers for wages they would have earned if they had not been denied promotion by a discriminatory system. The company also was told that one-fourth of the new employees in union jobs should be non-white.
>
> Black employees of the Lorillard Corp. were awarded $500,000 in back pay in 1971 by a court that found contracts between the company and its union limited access of blacks to most jobs. The company and union were ordered to assure that blacks had equal opportunity for assignment and promotion in all jobs.

---

[17] "The Second Decade of Title VII: Refinement of the Remedies," *William and Mary Law Review*, spring 1975, p. 436.

The Household Finance Corp. was ordered in 1972 to pay more than $125,000 to women employees who charged that they were denied promotions because of their sex. HFC also agreed to train women and minority employees for better jobs.

The American Telephone & Telegraph Co., in one of the most important of all affirmative action settlements, agreed in January 1973 to open thousands of jobs to women and minority groups, and to pay $15-million in back wages for past discrimination *(see box, p. 565)*.

The government won a significant victory in June 1974 when the Supreme Court ruled[18] that employers must pay men and women equal pay for what is essentially equal work. Under the ruling, Corning Glass Works of New York was ordered to pay approximately $500,000 in back pay to women who had been receiving a lower base salary for daytime work than men who did similar jobs at night. That same month the Bank of America reached an out-of-court settlement of a class-action suit filed on behalf of its women employees. Bank of America agreed (1) to pay an estimated $10-million in compensatory salary increases for its women employees, (2) to set up a $3.75-million trust fund for education and "self-development" programs for women employees, and (3) to increase the over-all proportion of women officers to 40 per cent by 1978, up from 18 per cent.

Merrill Lynch, Pierce, Fenner & Smith, the country's biggest securities firm, settled two separate but related bias suits on June 4, 1976, when it agreed to pay $1.9-million in back pay awards to women and minorities affected by alleged discriminatory hiring and promotion practices. Merrill Lynch also agreed to spend $1.3-million on a five-year affirmation action plan designed to recruit more women and minority employees.

Controversy Over Seniority Rights

EMPLOYMENT OPPORTUNITIES for women and minorities expanded rapidly between 1964 and 1973. By 1974, however, the situation had begun to change. The United States entered an economic recession and employers, both public and private, began to lay off workers, often using the long-accepted principle of "last hired, first-fired," whereby workers who lacked seniority were laid off first.

Fearing that this practice would erode the improvements in minority and female employment of the preceding years, civil rights advocates tried to outlaw the use of straight seniority

[18] *Corning Glass Works v. Brennan,* 427 U.S. 188.

systems, arguing that they perpetuated the effects of past discrimination. If women and minorities had not previously been discriminated against, it was said, they would have have an opportunity to build up more seniority. Minorities "are being penalized twice," said Herbert Hill of the NAACP, "once by not being hired, and now once they are hired, by being laid off first."[19] To remedy this situation and protect the job gains of women and minorities, some persons suggested a system of "artificial" or "retroactive" seniority dating from the time the employee originally was turned down for a job.[20]

Defenders of the "last in—first out" principle argued that it was a non-discriminatory way of dealing with job losses. Moreover, they said, granting seniority to someone who had not earned it amounted to reverse discrimination. The concept of "fictional" seniority is alien to American jurisprudence, said William Kilberg, a Department of Justice attorney.[21] Union officials said that seniority was too important to the daily lives of workers to be compromised. It affects not only layoff and rehiring policies, but promotions, vacations, transfers, overtime distribution, job assignments and even parking space. Often eligibility for pensions or profit sharing is related to length of service. Finally, pro-seniority forces pointed out, the 1964 Civil Rights Act upholds a "bona fide" seniority system.

> Title VII, section 703 (h) states: "[I]t shall not be an unlawful employment practice for an employer to apply different standards of compensation, or different terms, conditions or privileges of employment pursuant to a bona fide seniority or merit system...provided that such differences are not the result of an intention to discriminate because of race, color, religion, sex or national origin..."
>
> Title VII, section 703 (j) states: "Nothing contained in this title shall be interpreted to require any employer...to grant preferential treatment to any individual or to any group because of the race, color, religion, sex or national origin of such individual or group on account of an imbalance which may exist with respect to the total number or percentage of persons of any race, color, religion, sex or national origin employed by any employer..."

Supreme Court Ruling on Retroactive Seniority

Though the lower courts have split on the question of fictional seniority, the Supreme Court offered some clarification of the issue on March 24, 1976. It upheld the right to award seniority

---

[19] Quoted in "Last Hired, First Fired—Latest Recession Headache," *U.S. News & World Report*, April 7, 1975, p. 74.

[20] See Michael J. Hogan, "Artificial Seniority for Minorities As a Remedy for Past Bias vs. Seniority Rights of Nonminorities," *University of San Francisco Law Review*, fall 1974, pp. 344-359; Michael Joseph, "Retroactive Seniority—The Courts as Personnel Director," *Oklahoma Law Review*, winter 1976, pp. 215-223; and Donald R. Stacy, "Title VII Seniority Remedies in a Time of Economic Downturn" *Vanderbilt Law Review*, April 1975, pp. 487-520.

[21] Quoted by Bertrand B. Pogrebin, "Who Shall Work?" *Ms.*, December 1975, p. 71.

rights retroactively to persons who could prove they would have been hired earlier had they not suffered from illegal racial or sexual discrimination. Thus if a woman or a black had been rejected for a job in, say, 1970, and was finally hired in 1973, he or she today would be entitled to six years seniority instead of three.

The ruling came in a case brought by two black men—Harold Franks and Johnnie Lee—against Bowman Transportation Co. in Atlanta. Franks, a Bowman employee, had been denied a promotion because of his race. Lee was refused a driver's job on the same basis. Lower courts found clear evidence of illegal discrimination, and ordered the company to remedy its actions—but refused to go as far as to order the company to award Franks and Lee retroactive seniority.

The Supreme Court disagreed. Justice William J. Brennan, author of the majority opinion, asserted that if the person merely was awarded a job he should have had, he "will never obtain his rightful place in the hierarchy of seniority...He will perpetually remain subordinate to persons who, but for the illegal discrimination, would have been...his inferiors." Chief Justice Warren E. Burger, one of the three dissenting justices, said awards of retroactive seniority at the expense of other employees were rarely fair. "I cannot join in judicial approval of 'robbing Peter to pay Paul,' " he said. Burger suggested that victims of such discrimination be given a monetary award in lieu of the seniority grant. AFL-CIO Special Counsel Larry Gold said the ruling provided "full remedy to employees who have actually suffered from discrimination."[22] But at the same time labor spokesmen reiterated their opposition to any effort to undermine the basic principles of seniority systems.

Layoffs or Worksharing: A Search for Alternatives

The Franks case still leaves a number of questions unanswered. The ruling applies only to applicants who can prove they were victims of discrimination. What about persons who never bothered to apply for jobs because they were aware of a company's long history of discrimination? Are they entitled to fictional seniority also? Nor did the ruling resolve the "last hired—first fired" controversy. The Court currently is reviewing several petitions to hear cases seeking to abolish seniority systems that would affect a disproportionate number of minority and female workers in a layoff situation. Pro-seniority forces hope the Court follows the example of U.S. Appeals Court Judge Leonard I. Garth of Philadelphia who, in a case involving Jersey Central Power and Light Co., ruled in February 1975 that anti-discrimination goals cannot take precedence over workers'

[22] Quoted in *Time*, April 5, 1976, p. 65.

seniority rights in layoffs without a specific mandate from Congress.

Some companies are searching for alternatives to seniority-based layoffs. Some possibilities were discussed in February 1975 at a conference sponsored by the New York City Commission on Human Rights. One suggestion was to reduce the hours worked by all employees. This could be accomplished in several ways: shutting down the plant or office for a specified time per month, adopting a shorter workweek or workday, eliminating overtime, encouraging voluntary leaves of absence or early retirement. Employees also could be encouraged to accept voluntary wage cuts and deferral of raises, bonuses and cost-of-living increases. Furthermore, employers should determine if they could cut costs, other than wages, without interfering with plant operations or harming the position of minorities and women.

If layoffs were unavoidable, they could be made on a rotating basis so that each employee could work part of the time. This would spread the layoff burden among all employees rather than concentrating it among the newly hired. Another plan discussed at the New York conference was that of laying off newly hired women and minorities in the same proportion as the over-all layoff. For instance, if 10 per cent of the work force must be dismissed, just 10 per cent of the low-seniority women and minorities would lose their jobs. A few companies are even experimenting with "inverse seniority," which requires older employees who have accumulated high unemployment benefits—such as union-negotiated supplemental unemployment payments—to bear the brunt of layoffs.

Most people agree that the best solution to the layoff problem is full employment. But until that goal is reached the courts will have to determine where the rights of women and minorities end and where those of whites and males begin.

Selected Bibliography

Books

Glazer, Nathan, *Affirmative Discrimination: Ethnic Inequality and Public Policy,* Basic Books, 1975.

O'Neil, Robert M., *Discriminating Against Discrimination: Preferential Admissions and the DeFunis Case,* Indiana University Press, 1975.

Articles

Bennett, Ralph Kinney, "Colleges Under the Federal Gun," *Readers Digest,* May 1976.

Civil Rights Digest, spring 1975 issue.

Davis, Bernard D., "Academic Standards in Medical Schools," *The New England Journal of Medicine,* May 13, 1976.

Edwards, Harry T. and Barry L. Zaretsky, "Preferential Remedies for Employment Discrimination," *Michigan Law Review,* November 1975.

Egan, Richard, "Atonement Hiring," *The National Observer,* July 3, 1976.

Foster, J.W., "Race and Truth at Harvard," *The New Republic,* July 17, 1976.

Hechinger, Fred M., "Justice Douglas's Dissent in the DeFunis Case," *Saturday Review/World,* July 27, 1974.

Hook, Sidney and Miro Todorovich, "The Tyranny of Reverse Discrimination," *Change,* winter 1975-1976.

Joseph, Michael, "Retroactive Seniority—The Court as Personnel Director," *Oklahoma Law Review,* winter 1976.

Pogrebin, Bertrand B., "Who Shall Work?" *Ms.,* December 1975.

Society, January-February 1976 issue.

Stewart, Shirley E., "The Myth of Reverse Race Discrimination," *Cleveland State Law Review,* Vol. 23, 1974.

Thurow, Lester C., "The Economic Status of Minorities and Women," *Civil Rights Digest,* winter/spring 1976.

Virginia Law Review, October 1974 issue.

William and Mary Law Review, spring 1975 issue.

"Court Turning Against Reverse Discrimination," *U.S. News & World Report,* July 12, 1976.

"More Seniority for the Victims," *Time,* April 5, 1976.

"Racism in Reverse," *Newsweek,* March 11, 1974.

"Reverse Discrimination—Has It Gone Too Far?" *U.S. News & World Report,* March 29, 1976.

Reports and Studies

Editorial Research Reports, "Black Americans, 1963-1973," 1973 Vol. II, p. 623; "Blacks on Campus," 1972 Vol. II, p. 667; "Future of Private Colleges," 1976 Vol. I, p. 305.

U.S. Bureau of the Census, "The Social and Economic Status of the Black Population in the United States, 1974."

U.S. Department of Labor, "1975 Handbook on Women Workers."

U.S. Equal Employment Opportunity Commission, "Affirmative Action and Equal Employment: A Guidebook for Employers," January 1974.

ANTI-SMOKING CAMPAIGN

by

Sandra Stencel

page

Feb. 17
1978

Editor's Note: The anti-smoking campaign was given new ammunition early in 1979. The U.S. surgeon general, Dr. Julius B. Richmond, released a report in January reaffirming and expanding earlier warnings about the health dangers of cigarettes. The report emphasized the risks to women who smoke. It stated that women who smoke while pregnant are likely to give birth to smaller, less-healthy babies than non-smokers.

The report avoided taking a stand on one controversial issue — discussed on p. 174 — whether a non-smoker can be seriously harmed by inhaling the smoke from someone else's cigarette. The evidence is too new and limited to allow a solid conclusion, the report said.

The report's release on Jan. 11, 1979, was timed to coincide with the 15th anniversary of the 1964 surgeon general's report on smoking. It also was the first anniverary of a federal anti-smoking program launched on Jan. 11, 1978, by the Secretary of Health, Education and Welfare Joseph A. Califano Jr. Among other things, Califano asked the Federal Trade Commission to set maximum levels of tar, nicotine and carbon monoxide in cigarettes, and for the Treasury Department to recommend increases in the federal excise tax on cigarettes with high tar and nicotine content.

ANTI-SMOKING CAMPAIGN

IN LOS ANGELES, a school district employee quit his job because he was bothered by smoke from co-workers' cigars and cigarettes. The California Unemployment Insurance Appeals Board refused to pay the man unemployment benefits on the ground that he did not have "good cause" for resigning. However, a state court judge overturned the board's decision last July 22 and awarded the man $990 in unemployment benefits.

In Atlantic City, a state court judge ruled last April that an employee of the New Jersey Bell Telephone Co. had a right to work in a smoke-free environment. The employee presented medical documentation of an allergic reaction to cigarette smoke and the judge ordered the company to provide "safe working conditions...by restricting the smoking of employees to non-work areas."

In Chicago, dozens of persons have had to spend the night in jail because they were unable to post a $25 bond after being arrested for smoking on Chicago Transit Authority buses or trains. Since July 1975, hundreds of Chicagoans have been fined up to $300 for violating the city's anti-smoking law.

The battle between smokers and non-smokers is on and will probably get much hotter in 1977, spurred by the increasing activism of anti-smoking groups such as GASP (Group Against Smokers' Pollution) and ASH (Action on Smoking and Health). Buoyed by the success of their four-year-old campaign to ban smoking in public places, militant non-smokers are pressing for more stringent action. "A growing number of smokers now understand that their smoke is annoying to other people," ASH Executive Director John F. Banzhaf has said. "We're finding more and more that they are willing to live with reasonable restrictions."[1]

But according to the tobacco industry, the ultimate goal of the movement is to prohibit the use of tobacco and cripple the industry. To prevent this from happening and to fight the growing number of anti-smoking laws, the Tobacco Institute, the

---

[1] Quoted in *The Christian Science Monitor*, July 7, 1976. Banzhaf is professor of law at George Washington University, Washington, D.C.

lobbying and public relations arm of the industry, has opened a counter campaign aimed at protecting the rights of smokers. Passions run high on both sides. There have been reports of fistfights and even more serious assaults occurring over demands for smoke-free air. *Washington Post* columnist William Raspberry wrote recently that a column on the no-smoking question had elicited more reader response than to "such presumably weightier matters as capital punishment [and] affirmative action...."[2]

Many of the nation's 53 million[3] smokers claim that laws banning smoking in public places are an infringement of their civil rights. Anti-smoking groups respond by quoting health authorities who say tobacco smoke is hazardous to the health of everyone who breathes it. In fact, according to some findings, smoke from the burning end of a cigarette, cigar or pipe is potentially more dangerous than the smoke inhaled by the smoker. "The time has come when our goal can no longer be simply to protect the smoker from himself," Jesse L. Steinfeld, a former U.S. Surgen General, told the third World Congress on Smoking and Health in June 1975. "The time has come to protect ourselves from the smoker."[4]

Decrease in Percentage of Adult Smokers

A nationwide survey released last June by the U.S. Public Health Service indicated that the proportion of American adults who smoke cigarettes has decreased in recent years. Of the 12,000 persons surveyed, only one-third smoked cigarettes, as the following figures show:

Cigarette Smokers*	**1975**	**1970** (*in percentages*)	**1964**
Men	39.2	42.2	52.8
Women	28.9	30.5	31.5
Total	33.5	36.3	42.5

*Ages 21 and older

The survey also provided other evidence that the public's attitude toward smoking had turned increasingly negative *(see table, p.184)* However, the picture is not crystal clear. There is evidence of an upsurge in smoking among teenagers *(see box, p. 175)* and, despite the percentage decline in cigarette smoking among adults, the nation's population increase has resulted in record sales of cigarettes year after year. Americans smoked 620 billion cigarettes in 1976, the Department of Agriculture

[2] *The Washington Post*, Dec. 13, 1976.
[3] Figure used by U.S. Public Health Service.
[4] The congress, held in New York City, was sponsored jointly by the American Cancer Society and the National Cancer Institute.

reported at the year's end. That was 13 billion more than in 1975 and 84 billion more than in 1970.

Paradoxically, more than half of the smokers interviewed in the Public Health Service survey said they would like to see smoking allowed in fewer places than it is now, and more than one-third of the smokers said it was annoying to be near a person smoking a cigarette. Among non-smokers these feelings were shared by even greater numbers. The nation's smokers are on the defensive, according to Dr. David J. Sencer, director of the U.S. Center for Disease Control. "The American who smokes today is finding his world narrowing," Sencer has said. "He is becoming increasingly beleaguered and is usually ambivalent about smoking."[5]

Movement to Ban Smoking in Public Places

Since 1973, at least 30 states[6] and the District of Columbia have enacted laws that ban smoking in certain public places. Moreover, anti-smoking restrictions have been imposed in hundreds of local communities across the nation. These restrictions may in some instances apply only to elevators or public transportation or theaters but, often, also to hospitals, libraries, museums, auditoriums, restaurants and supermarkets.

Arizona in May 1973 became the first state to enact a statewide anti-smoking law. As amended in April 1974, it prohibits smoking in elevators, indoor theaters, libraries, art galleries, museums, concert halls, physicians' waiting rooms and school buildings, and on all buses. Minnesota's anti-smoking law, which took effect Aug. 1, 1975, is considered the toughest in the nation. Known as the Indoor Clean Air Act, it bans smoking in all public places and public meetings except in designated smoking areas. Restaurants must set aside at least 25 per cent of their tables for non-smoking patrons,[7] hospitals must offer wards and offices must provide desks for non-smokers. Violators are subject to fines of up to $100. One of the newest anti-smoking laws in the nation is California's Indoor Clean Air Act, signed by Gov. Edmund G. Brown Jr. on Aug. 30, 1976. It requires that at least half of the space in public meeting rooms be set aside for non-smokers.

Even in states and localities without anti-smoking laws, some businesses ban smoking in their establishments or restrict it to designated areas. At Merle Norman Cosmetics Co. in Los

[5] News conference in Washington, D.C., June 15, 1976.

[6] Alaska, Arizona, Arkansas, California, Connecticut, Florida, Georgia, Hawaii, Kansas, Maine, Maryland, Massachusetts, Michigan, Minnesota, Nebraska, Nevada, New Hampshire, New Jersey, New York, North Dakota, Oklahoma, Oregon, Pennsylvania, South Dakota, Texas, Utah, Vermont, Virginia, Washington and Wyoming.

[7] Members of Minnesota's Association for Non-smokers Rights are unhappy about a loophole in the law. Because bars and taverns are exempted from the smoking restrictions, many restaurants in the state now label themselves bars.

Angeles, for example, smoking is forbidden in the offices, rest rooms and production lines. Smokers must wait for their coffee breaks and lunch hour to light up—and then only in a special section of the company cafeteria. Controller Mike Hayes estimates that the company saves about $33,000 a year in reduced housekeeping costs, lower absenteeism and improved productivity. The savings are passed on to the employees.

Some companies offer cash bonuses to non-smoking workers. In Birmingham, Ala., non-smoking employees at a savings bank receive a $20 bonus each month. At the Leslie Manufacturing and Supply Co. in Bloomington, Minn., employees who quit smoking are paid $7 a week. Standard Glass Co. of Phoenix, Ariz., offers its employees $360 if they can kick the habit for a year. The president of Intermatic, a heater manufacturing company in Spring Grove, Ill., permits workers to bet up to $100 that they can quit smoking for a year. If they quit, he pays them the money; if they don't, their bets go to the American Cancer Society.

At the federal level, the Civil Aeronautics Board proposed on Oct. 5 to prohibit pipe and cigar smoking aboard commercial passenger aircraft. In addition, the board solicited public comment on the question of whether all smoking should be banned aboard these planes. A decision is expected early this year. Numerous scientific and medical studies have found that cigar and pipe smoke can be more irritating and harmful than cigarette smoke. "Since pipe and cigar smokers don't inhale as frequently or as deeply as cigarette smokers, they pollute the air with even greater concentrations of toxic substances," said John F. Banzhaf of ASH in a petition asking for the proposed ban. The Tobacco Institute has told the board that the ban is not warranted. Since 1973 the CAB has required separate seating for passengers who want to smoke.

Rep. Robert F. Drinan (D Mass.) sought unsuccessfully in the last Congress to place restrictions on smoking at federal and federally controlled property, including military bases, post offices, courtrooms, federal office buildings, and Congress itself. He wanted to require all federal agencies to separate smokers from non-smokers in work, recreation and eating areas, and to forbid smoking in confined public places.

Evidence of Health Hazard for Non-Smokers

Since 1964, the American public has been bombarded with information concerning the health hazards of smoking. Most of this information pertains to the dangers for the smoker. But in the last five years, public health authorities have grown increasingly concerned about the effects of tobacco smoke on non-smokers. The American Medical Association estimates that at

Increased Smoking by Girls and Young Women

The American Cancer Society is particularly concerned about increases in smoking among teenage girls. A study it released in February 1976 indicated that 27 per cent of the American girls of ages 13 to 17 were smokers—in contrast to 22 per cent in 1969. For boys of the same ages, the figure had remained virtually constant at 30 per cent during that time. Moreover, heavy smoking was increasing among the girls; four of every ten smoked a pack a day or more, whereas in 1969 only one in ten smoked that much.

Young women were also more likely to be smokers than they were a decade earlier, the survey further indicated. Some 36 per cent in the 18-34 age group who were surveyed said they smoked, and of these six of every ten smoked heavily. Comparable figures in 1965 were 34 per cent and five out of ten. Dr. Benjamin F. Byrd Jr., president of the American Cancer Society, called the figures "alarming." The Cancer Society reported that among women the death rate from lung cancer had doubled in the past ten years.

least 34 million Americans are sensitive to cigarette smoke. These include people with emphysema, asthma, bronchitis, sinusitis, hay fever and chronic heart disease. Even the average non-smoker can suffer reactions to tobacco smoke. These reactions include eye irritation, nasal symptoms, headache, cough, wheezing, sore throat, sneezing, nausea, hoarseness and dizziness.

Tobacco smoke is a complex mixture of gases, liquids and particles. There are hundreds of chemical compounds in tobacco and hundreds more are created when tobacco burns. Among the most hazardous compounds are tar, nicotine, carbon monoxide, cadmium, nitrogen dioxide, ammonia, benzene, formaldehyde and hydrogen sulphide. Whenever anyone lights a cigarette, cigar or pipe, tobacco smoke enters the atmosphere from two sources: (1) directly from the burning tobacco (sidestream smoke) and (2) from the smoke the smoker sucks in (mainstream smoke) and then exhales.

According to the American Lung Association, sidestream smoke contains twice as much tar and nicotine, three times as much benzpyrene (suspected of being a cancer-causing agent), five times as much carbon monoxide, and 50 times as much ammonia as mainstream smoke. There also is evidence that there is more cadmium in sidestream smoke.[8] Public health officials are investigating the possibility that cadmium is one of the compounds in cigarette smoke that damages the air sacs of the lungs and causes emphysema.

---

[8] American Lung Association booklet, "Second-Hand Smoke: Take a Look at the Facts," 1974

Physicians are particularly concerned about the high levels of carbon monoxide in sidestream smoke. "There is no question that non-smokers can develop toxic levels [of carbon monoxide] in smoke-filled rooms," said Dr. Raymond Slavin of St. Louis University and the American Academy of Allergy.[9] When inhaled, carbon monoxide bumps oxygen molecules out of the red-blood cells and forms a new compound called carboxyhemoglobin. As the amount of this compound increases in the blood, the cells of the body become starved for oxygen.

The hazards posed by high concentrations of carbon monoxide in sidestream smoke first were reported in the Surgeon General's 1972 annual report to Congress on the health consequences of smoking. The report cited studies showing that carbon monoxide levels in a smoke-filled room or automobile could rise to almost twice the federal occupational safety guideline of 50 parts per million. Individuals exposed to such high levels of carbon monoxide, Public Health Service investigators found, cannot distinguish relative degrees of brightness, lose some ability to judge time intervals, and show impaired performance on other psychomotor tests. Exposure to high levels of carbon monoxide is particularly dangerous for persons suffering from chronic heart and lung diseases.

The contention that tobacco smoke poses a serious health hazard to non-smokers has been questioned by the tobacco industry. "When all of the major evidence is considered, the claim of hazard to non-smokers withstands neither a scientific nor 'common sense' evaluation," the Tobacco Institute said in a paper released in July 1973.[10] A recent publication prepared by the R. J. Reynolds Tobacco Co. cites several studies which support the claim that there is no conclusive evidence that cigarette smoke is harmful to non-smokers.[11]

The publication called attention to the work of Drs. Irwin Schmeltz, Dietrich Hoffmann and Ernest L. Wynder of the American Health Foundation. They reviewed 65 studies concerning tobacco smoke in indoor settings and published their appraisal of these studies in the magazine *Preventive Medicine* in 1975. They concluded: "Little has been done to show whether an individual is adversely affected by exposure to room air contaminated by cigarette smoke. Several authors have considered the problem, but in our view no definite conclusions have been arrived at." They went on to say, "On the basis of available epidemiological evidence, it appears that passive inhalation of tobacco smoke by non-smokers or smokers does not increase

---

[9] Quoted in the *Los Angeles Times*, Aug. 29, 1976.

[10] "Smoking and Non-Smoking: What is the Issue?"

[11] R. J. Reynolds Tobacco Co., "The Facts About Public Smoking," 1976.

their risk for chronic illness such as cancer of the respiratory tract, emphysema, or cardiovascular disease." They also said that they found "no data suggesting that passive inhalation of cigarette smoke increases the risk of developing lung cancer."

The R. J. Reynolds Co. also cited an article by Drs. William C. Hinds and Melvin W. First of the Harvard School of Public Health in the April 17, 1975, issue of the *New England Journal of Medicine.* The authors had measured concentrations of tobacco smoke in public places to evaluate the health implications for non-smokers. They sampled the air in restaurants, cocktail lounges, commuter trains, buses and waiting rooms in the Boston area. They reported that even where they detected the highest concentration of smoke, in a cocktail lounge, a non-smoker would not inhale the equivalent of one filter cigarette even after long exposure.

The federal Occupational Safety and Health Administration last year rejected a proposal from the California Health Department to impose a standard requiring employers either to prohibit smoking or to segregate smokers from non-smokers. "The testimony we received did not conclusively prove what the occupational hazard was to a non-smoker from sidestream smoke," said Mark Ashcraft, staff services analyst for OSHA's health standards board.[12]

Question About Infringement of Civil Rights

The debate over non-smokers' rights goes beyond the question of health. It also has become a civil rights issue. "The idea of legislating an area of personal choice...threatens the very foundation of individual freedom on which this country was built," contends Bill Dwyer of the Tobacco Institute.[13] Similar thoughts were expressed by William D. Hobbs, chairman of the R. J. Reynolds Co. "Of course there are those who are annoyed by cigarette smoke," he said, "just as there are those who object to heavy perfumes, garlic on the breath, barking dogs or any of a thousand other things. But there is no issue between smoker and non-smoker which cannot be solved through mutual common courtesy and respect for the rights of others. If the issues of public smoking cannot be handled in this way, we as a people are opening ourselves to ever-increasing governmental restriction in every area of our lives."

Tobacco industry spokesmen are not the only ones who question the legality, morality and necessity of laws banning smoking in public places. U.S. District Court Judge Jack M. Gordon, in a decision last September dismissing a lawsuit seeking to prohibit smoking and the sale of cigarettes at the New Orleans

[12] Quoted in the *Los Angeles Times,* Aug. 29, 1976.
[13] Quoted by Ruth Rosenbaum in *New Times,* Dec. 10, 1976, p. 48.

Superdome, wrote: "For the Constitution to be read to protect non-smokers from inhaling tobacco smoke would be to broaden the rights of the Constitution to limits heretofore unheard of." Defenders of the anti-smoking bans answer with the slogan "Your right to smoke ends where my nose begins." Columnist William Raspberry wrote: "It's well enough to talk about balancing the rights of smokers and non-smokers, but the fact is that non-smoking doesn't hurt anybody. Smoking does, and if the habit is to be an inconvenience to anybody, it ought to be to those who have it."

Some police officials say that they do not have the manpower to enforce the smoking bans. Tobacco Institute President Horace R. Kornegay, in a recent letter to 3,200 police chiefs across the country, said that "it doesn't make sense to enact laws which will divert law-enforcement manpower from the task of apprehending real criminals." But Banzhaf, the ASH director, maintains that "Most people are law-abiding citizens...and they will obey the law if it is properly posted."[14]

History of Anti-Smoking Efforts

SMOKING has been under attack almost continuously since tobacco was introduced to the civilized world over 400 years ago. James I of England, in an essay[15] published in 1604, described smoking as "a custome lothsome to the Eye, hateful to the Nose, harmful to the Braine, dangerous to the Lungs, and, in the black stinking Fume thereof, nearest resembling the horrible Stygian Smoke of the Pit that is bottomless." The monarch threatened to banish doctors who smoked to the "land of the red Indians."

Opposition to smoking in 17th century England was mild compared to measures adopted in other countries. In Turkey, where smoking was thought fit only for the "Christian dog," offenders were led through the streets of Istanbul with pipes thrust through their noses. A Chinese decree of 1638 threatened decapitation to anyone who trafficked in tobacco. Several Popes forbade the use of tobacco on pain of excommunication. In 17th century Russia, where the sale and use of tobacco was banned by Czar Michael, offenders might have their noses cut off.

In the American colonies, the General Court of Massachusetts, beginning in 1629, prohibited the cultivation and use of tobacco both for reasons of morality and practicality;

[14] Quoted in *The Washington Star*, Jan. 25, 1976.

[15] "A Counterblaste to Tobacco."

it wanted to prevent fires. An early anti-tobacco tract in America was published in 1798 by a signer of the Declaration of Independence, the Philadelphia physician Benjamin Rush.

The tobacco habit prevailed nonetheless. Official bans on the use of tobacco gradually were supplanted by taxes on the tobacco trade. By the 19th century, the attack on smoking had become largely a matter of crusading by reformist groups. Late in the century it became entwined with the temperance movement. Children were mobilized to sing songs, carry banners, parade and preach sermons to their elders. Clergymen, educators and some businessmen applauded these efforts. Boxing champion John L. Sullivan denounced cigarettes as unmanly. Henry Ford and popular writer Elbert Hubbard spoke against the cigarette. Thomas Edison refused to hire cigarette smokers. A nationwide "Committee to Study the Tobacco Problem" attracted distinguished persons in every field.

Anti-tobacco groups became so influential in the early 20th century that at least 11 states and numerous cities enacted restrictive laws of one sort or another. New Hampshire in 1901 made it illegal for any person, firm or corporation to make, sell or keep for sale any form of cigarette. Under an Illinois statute enacted in 1907, the manufacture, sale or gift of a cigarette was made punishable by a fine of up to $100 or a jail term of up to 30 days. In New York, women and anyone "actually or apparently under 16 years of age" were forbidden to smoke in public. Anti-cigarette laws also were passed in Arkansas, Idaho, Iowa, Kansas, North Dakota, Oklahoma, Tennessee and Utah.

These restrictions did not seem to affect cigarette sales. In 1909, when the last of the state laws was passed, national sales were twice what they had been five years earlier, according to author Susan Wagner.[16] Cigarette consumption increased still further in World War I. The anti-smoking movement enjoyed a brief revival in the 1920s, after the Eighteenth Amendment to the Constitution was adopted outlawing alcoholic beverages. But gradually cigarettes gained general public acceptance. By 1927, all of the state anti-cigarette laws had been repealed. "Spurred by increased advertising, the political emancipation of women, and the widespread use of liquor during Prohibition," Wagner wrote, "the tide turned in favor of smoking."

Controversy Over Health and Cigarettes

Recent controversy over tobacco use has centered on the health consequences of smoking. The contention that smoking causes disease is almost as old as the use of tobacco itself. But it was not until the 1950s that medical evidence of the link between lung cancer and cigarette smoking became so

[16] Susan Wagner, *Cigarette Country* (1971), p. 44.

Early Cigarette Promotion

The cigarette industry has been described as a house that advertising built. The chief architect of "hard-sell" cigarette advertising was George Washington Hill, president of American Tobacco from 1925 to 1946. Hill promoted his Lucky Strike brand to sales leadership with such slogans as "It's Toasted" and "Reach For a Lucky Instead of a Sweet."

The latter slogan, Hill openly admitted, was designed to make smoking socially acceptable to women. An alluring series of ads was prepared to point out how much healthier it was to smoke Lucky Strikes than to eat sweets. And figure-conscious women responded by the thousands. By 1931, according to Susan Wagner, in her book *Cigarette Country,* Lucky Strike led all cigarettes in sales and alternated with Camels for the No. 1 spot in brand preference between 1930 and 1950.

During the 1930s and 1940s the cigarette industry was confronted with early intimations of the potential harm of smoking. The industry responded with an ad campaign with a medicinal flavor. Magazine pages and radio air waves were filled with such slogans as "Not a cough in a car load" (Old Gold), "Not one single case of throat irritation due to smoking Camels" and "The throat-tested cigarette" (Philip Morris).

Today cigarette manufacturers insist that advertising's only function is to induce the confirmed smoker to abandon his present brand for a new one, not to recruit new smokers. Early promoters such as Hill were more generous in crediting advertising with profound influence upon the overall consumption of cigarettes. "The impetus of those great advertising campaigns...built the cigarette industry," Hill said.*

* Quoted by Maurine B. Neuberger in *Smoke Screen: Tobacco and the Public Welfare* (1963).

pronounced that health groups spoke out to the public on the health danger. The American Cancer Society resolved on Oct. 22, 1954, to "emphasize to the American people that the...available evidence indicates an association between smoking, particularly cigarette smoking, and lung cancer." Earlier that year the Cancer Society and the British Medical Research Council reported independently, following separate three-year statistical studies, that death rates were higher for cigarette smokers than non-smokers.

In 1962 the Royal College of Physicians of London summarized the evidence on the disease-tobacco relationship and called cigarette smoking a serious health hazard. In a report issued March 7, the society concluded: "The strong statistical association between smoking, especially of cigarettes, and lung cancer is most simply explained on a causal basis." The report went on to say: "The conclusion that smoking is an important cause of lung cancer implies that if the habit ceased, the death rate from lung cancer would eventually fall to a fraction, perhaps to one-fifth, or even, among men, to one-tenth of the present level."

The British government soon instituted an intensive anti-smoking campaign. Pressure for similar efforts in this country by the American Cancer Society and others led President Kennedy to direct the Surgeon General to set up an advisory committee to undertake a comprehensive review of all data on smoking and health.

Publication of the committee's report on Jan. 11, 1964,[17] constituted a turning point in the smoking-health controversy. In his foreword, Surgeon General Luther L. Terry noted: "Few medical questions have stirred such public interest or created more scientific debate than the tobacco-health controversy.... The subject does not lend itself to easy answers. Nevertheless, it has been increasingly apparent that answers must be found."

The central conclusion was that "cigarette smoking is a health hazard of sufficient importance in the United States to warrant appropriate remedial action." The committee based its conclusion on statistical studies which found that "cigarette smoking is causally related to lung cancer in men" and that "the magnitude of the effect of cigarette smoking far outweighs all other factors." Data for women was less extensive but pointed in the same direction.

This report also found that cigarette smoking was associated with coronary artery disease, chronic bronchitis and emphysema. The committee recognized that "no simple cause-and-effect relationship is likely to exist between a complex product like tobacco smoke and a specific disease in the variable human organism." But "the continuing and mounting evidence from many sources" led it to decide that "cigarette smoking contributes substantially to mortality from certain specific diseases and to the overall death rate."

Reaction to 1964 Surgeon General's Report

The American Cancer Society hailed the Surgeon General's report as "a landmark in the history of man's fight against disease." Many Americans were shocked by the report's findings. Cigarette sales dropped sharply. During the first six months of 1964, cigarette sales were 11 billion less than during the same 1963 period, according to the Internal Revenue Service. However, as the shock of the Surgeon General's report wore off, cigarette sales recovered. Approximately 540 billion cigarettes were sold in 1968, about 35 billion more than in 1964.

---

[17] Report of the Advisory Committee to the Surgeon General of the Public Health Service, *Smoking and Health* (1964).

The Federal Cigarette Labeling and Advertising Act went into effect on Jan. 1, 1966, requiring all cigarette packages to carry the statement, "Caution—Cigarette Smoking May Be Hazardous To Your Health." However, the law barred, until July 1, 1969, any requirement of a health warning in cigarette advertising.

On June 2, 1967, the Federal Communications Commission ruled that, under the fairness doctrine, broadcasters were required to make available free air time for anti-smoking messages, since the pro-smoking messages of cigarette commercials were judged a controversial matter of legitimate public importance. As a result of the commission's ruling, thousands of messages warning of the health hazards of smoking appeared on radio and television over the next three and a half years. The anti-smoking spots seemed to have had at least a short-term effect. In 1969 cigarette sales declined by more than 12 billion—a greater drop than immediately after the release of the Surgeon General's report.

Congress, however, on March 19, 1970, approved legislation banning all cigarette commercials on radio and television as of Jan. 2, 1971.[18] Subsequently the Federal Communications Commission ruled that broadcasters need not continue running anti-smoking messages. "As a result, the anti-smoking campaign on television shriveled to a relative handful of 'public service' messages."[19] Cigarette sales have increased substantially each year since 1971, reaching a new peak of 620 billion in 1976.

Faced with the possibility of regulation by the Federal Trade Commission, U.S. tobacco companies agreed in February 1971 to disclose the tar and nicotine content of the cigarettes they advertised in print. The following November, the Interstate Commerce Commission imposed a rule restricting smoking to the rear five rows of seats on interstate buses and strengthening ICC regulations regarding non-smoking areas on trains. In making the rule, the commission declared "second-hand" smoke to be an "extreme irritant to humans, particularly with respect to its effect upon eyes and breathing" and judged it "capable of adversely affecting the adequacy and availability" of interstate passenger carrier service. Based on similar reasoning, the CAB in July 1973 required all commercial airlines to provide separate non-smoking sections.

---

[18] The law also changed the health warning on cigarette packages to read "Warning: The Surgeon General Has Determined That Cigarette Smoking Is Dangerous To Your Health." But at the same time it prohibited the Federal Trade Commission from requiring any health warning on printed cigarette advertising before July 1, 1971.

[19] "New Medium For The Message," *Consumer Reports*, May 1976, p. 278.

Pressures on the Cigarette Industry

AFTER CIGARETTE commercials were removed from radio and television in 1971, relatively little attention was given to the issue of cigarette advertising. "Ads in magazines and newspapers simply do not generate the same kind of outrage that TV commercials engendered," Sen. Frank E. Moss (D Utah, 1959-76) said last year.[20] However, pressure to place further restrictions on cigarette advertising has been building. The American Cancer Society, in opening a new five-year campaign against cigarette smoking last October, called on Congress to ban cigarette advertising within five years except for brands with a tar and nicotine content at least 50 per cent below averages for the previous year.

A total ban on tobacco advertising and promotion, including the sponsorship of sporting and other public events, was recommended by the World Conference on Smoking and Health in June 1975. The consumer-products testing group Consumers Union has come out strongly in favor of a total ban on cigarette advertising. "It is uncertain whether an advertising ban would by itself, without an extensive anti-cigarette campaign, significantly reduce the number of new recruits to cigarette smoking," the testing group said in the May 1976 issue of *Consumer Reports*. "But the main argument is an ethical one: It is immoral to permit the advertising of an addictive product that causes lung cancer and contributes to heart disease, emphysema, bronchitis and vascular disease." The Public Health Service survey of adult smoking habits found that a majority of adults it polled (56 per cent), including 42 per cent of the smokers, wanted to stop all cigarette advertising *(see p. 184)*

Many anti-smoking advocates contend that magazines and newspapers should be encouraged to turn down cigarette advertising. Author James Fallows, who advocates such a policy, concedes that "a few publications rely so heavily on cigarette ads that they might not survive a boycott." But, he goes on to say, "For the majority of the publications, this is hardly a question of economic survival.... For most of them taking cigarette ads is not a matter of making a profit, but only of maximizing it."[21] Among the publications that already refuse cigarette ads are *Reader's Digest, National Geographic, Good Housekeeping, The New Yorker* and *The Christian Science Monitor*.

---

[20] Quoted in *Consumer Reports*, May 1976, p. 279.

[21] James Fallows, "The Cigarette Scandal," *The Washington Monthly*, February 1976, p. 13.

Public Attitudes Toward Cigarette Smoking

	Smokers Agree		Non-Smokers Agree	
	1970	1975	1970	1975
Smoking should be allowed in fewer places than it is now.	41.6%	51.0%	65.6%	80.1%
Smoking is enough of a health hazard for something to be done.	79.1	71.8	90.0	90.0
Cigarette advertising should be stopped completely.	49.9	42.6	66.6	62.5
The public knows all it needs to know about the effects of smoking.	49.0	43.4	40.1	38.2
Teachers should set an example by not smoking.	58.1	62.3	79.0	84.1
It is annoying to be near a person smoking cigarettes.	34.1	34.8	72.5	77.0

SOURCE: U.S. Public Health Service, "Adult Use of Tobacco, 1975," June 1976

Katharine Graham, publisher of *The Washington Post,* defended her newspaper's policy of accepting cigarette advertising. "Once a product is admitted to public sale in this country, I see no reason its producers should not be permitted to advertise in the *Post* or elsewhere," she said. Similar thoughts were expressed by John J. McCabe, senior vice president of *The New York Times:* "It seems to us, particularly in this tendentious time, that the advertising columns of *The New York Times* should be available for any legitimate message that our advertisers wish to deliver. This does not mean that we abrogate our responsibility for good taste or fairness. It does mean, however, that we accept advertising [which] may be in conflict with the editorial opinion of the paper."[22]

Inquiry Into Charges of Unfair Advertising

The Federal Trade Commission on July 28, 1976, accused the six major cigarette companies—R.J. Reynolds, Philip Morris, Lorillard, Liggett & Myers, Brown & Williamson, and American Brands—of not living up to a 1972 agreement to make health warnings on cigarette ads "clear and conspicuous." In new amendments to a lawsuit originally filed in U.S. District Court in New York City in October 1975, the commission said the manufacturers had failed to place easily readable health warnings on cigarette ads ranging from billboards to transit posters. The original suit alleged a failure to include proper warnings in

[22] Letters to the editor by Graham and McCabe, *The Washington Monthly,* April 1976, p. 3.

newspaper and magazine advertisements and in promotional displays for vending machines and store counter racks.

Two months earlier, on May 17, 1976, the FTC announced that it would investigate whether the tobacco industry was using deceptive or unfair advertising that would overly influence young people to start smoking. The commission said it would pay special attention to the various promotional activities of the tobacco companies. After cigarette commercials were removed from radio and television, the companies redirected large chunks of their promotion budgets to the sponsorship of such public affairs as music festivals and sports events. Cigarette manufacturers insist that they are not trying to induce nonsmokers to start, but merely are competing with one another for larger shares of a market that already exists.

The outcome of the investigation "is likely to bring a series of new recommendations for laws to regulate the advertising of cigarettes," *Business Week* magazine reported July 5, 1976. In requesting the investigation, the anti-smoking group Action on Smoking and Health had asked the commission to:

> Limit illustrations in cigarette advertising to the product and package themselves, thus eliminating photos that imply smoking is a healthy habit engaged in by handsome, vigorous people.
>
> Prohibit misrepresentations that cigarettes with comparatively lower tar and nicotine contents are not dangerous to the smoker.
>
> Require that every ad discloses the specific tar and nicotine contents of the product in milligram multiples of the lowest ranked brands.
>
> Require full disclosure of the amount of carbon monoxide generated by a cigarette of that brand.
>
> Prohibit the promotional use of any merchandise, premiums, coupons, discounts, contests or other programs designed to induce the purchase and consumption of cigarettes.
>
> Prohibit billboard advertising of cigarettes.
>
> Require that every ad carry this message as prominently as the current warning: "NOTICE: Many people find it very difficult, if not impossible, to quit smoking once they start."
>
> Require that every ad also carry this prominent warning: "NOTICE: Your cigarette smoke may bother, discomfort, and endanger the health of those around you."

Popularity of Brands Low in Tar, Nicotine

Some members of Congress have been pushing the idea of limiting tar and nicotine content in cigarettes. Sens. Gary Hart (D Colo.) and Edward M. Kennedy (D Mass.) say they plan to reintroduce a bill to tax cigarettes on the basis of their tar and nicotine content—the higher the content, the heavier the tax. The bill did not come to a vote in the Senate during the last

Congress. Hart and Kennedy call their bill a reasonable response to persistent evidence linking cigarette smoking to cancer and heart disease. "On the one hand, we want to preserve the option and freedom of individuals to select whatever brand of cigarette they want," Kennedy said. "But we also want to provide an important incentive to the industry itself to come up with lower tar and nicotine cigarettes."[23]

Opponents of the bill contend that it singles out cigarettes unfairly for punitive tax treatment, threatens economic hardship for tobacco-producing areas and ignores the tobacco industry's voluntary shift to the production of cigarettes with less tar and nicotine. The National Cancer Institute noted last year that the average tar content of American cigarettes had dropped to 18 milligrams from 43 milligrams in 1955. During the same period, the average nicotine content dropped to 1.2 milligrams from 2.8 milligrams. Tests conducted by the Federal Trade Commission, announced Dec. 11, 1976, gave the best rating to Carlton 70s, an unusually short, filter cigarette not widely sold, with 0.5 milligrams of tar and .05 milligrams of nicotine. Next were the more popular Carlton king-size cigarettes and a new brand called Now, both with 1.0 milligram of tar and 0.1 milligram of nicotine. At the opposite end of the scale was Players, a brand made by Philip Morris for the American market, with 64 times more tar and 44 times more nicotine than Carlton 70s.

James C. Bowling, vice president of Philip Morris, the second-largest cigarette manufacturer in the United States, contends that there is no medical evidence that links tar and nicotine with disease. "It is all supposition," he said.[24] A study published in September 1976 by Dr. E. Cuyler Hammond, chief of epidemiology and statistics for the American Cancer Society, contradicts that view. The study reported the death rate among smokers of cigarettes high in tar and nicotine was 16 per cent higher than among comparable smokers of cigarettes with low levels of those substances. According to the study, the mortality from lung cancer was 26 per cent lower among the low-tar-and-nicotine smokers than among those who smoked stronger brands. For heart disease, the mortality rate was 14 per cent lower.

On the basis of his findings, Hammond suggested that high-tar-and-nicotine cigarettes should be taken off the market. He also warned that new brands of low-tar-and-nicotine cigarettes that contain additives to enhance flavor should be fully tested to make sure that the chemicals themselves do not pose a cancer risk.

---

[23] Quoted in *Congressional Quarterly Weekly Report,* April 10, 1976, p. 845.

[24] Quoted in *Business Week,* July 5, 1976, p. 51.

Any hope of turning the United States into a non-smoking society in the near future is unrealistic, according to Dr. Gio B. Gori, deputy director of the National Cancer Institute's Division of Cancer Cause and Prevention. Therefore, he insists, more attention should be paid to the development and use of less-hazardous cigarettes. "It is important that we protect those people who continue to smoke despite all warnings," Dr. Gori said. "Leaving them to their fate is neither humane nor economical...."[25]

Issue of Abstinence Vs. Safer Cigarettes

"It may be possible to remove toxic smoke components selectively and thus reduce specific hazards," he said, adding that evidence indicates that there may be "critical" amounts of such hazardous components of smoke as tar, nicotine and carbon monoxide. These amounts could be calculated, Gordi said, and cigarettes could be designed to stay below these critical levels. Gordi also said that the incidence of cigarette-related disease would be lowered if the smoke yield of cigarettes was reduced.

There are others who say that encouraging smokers to quit is the only answer to the smoking problem. Jesse Steinfeld, the former Surgeon General, told the World Congress on Smoking and Health: "Until research can provide a cigarette which is truly harmless and from which the toxic components are removed, society's goal must remain the cessation of smoking...." The Public Health Service's survey of adult smoking habits showed that 61 per cent of the smokers interviewed had made at least one serious effort to quit. Nine out of 10 smokers said they probably would stop smoking if there was an easy way to quit. However, 57 per cent said they expected to be smoking five years from now.

There are all kinds of drugs and devices on the market to help smokers quit. Some smokers turn to commercial clinics such as Smokenders, Smoke Watchers and the Schick Corporation Clinics. Others try methods offered by non-profit organizations such as the American Cancer Society, the American Lung Association or the Seventh Day Adventist Church. "At this time it is virtually impossible to say that one approach is better than another," according to Dr. Donald T. Frederickson, associate professor of public health at New York University School of Medicine.[26] Some smokers may not want to kick the habit. But if the non-smokers' rights movement has its way, they may eventually have to restrict their smoking to the privacy of their homes and a few specifically designated public places.

---

[25] Gio B. Gordi, "Low-Risk Cigarettes: A Prescription," *Science*, Dec. 17, 1976, p. 1243.

[26] Quoted in *Medical World News*, Nov. 1, 1976, p. 53.

Selected Bibliography

Books

Neuberger, Maurine B., *Smoke Screen: Tobacco and the Public Welfare,* Prentice-Hall, 1963.

Trop, Jack Dunn, *Please Don't Smoke in Our House,* Natural Hygiene Press, 1976.

Wagner, Susan, *Cigarette Country: Tobacco in American History and Politics,* Praeger, 1971.

Articles

Action on Smoking and Health (ASH) Newsletter, selected issues.

Banzhaf, John, "Please Put Your Cigarette Out; the Smoke is Killing Me!" *Today's Health,* April 1972.

Dampier, William, "Smoke If You Must—But Not Here!" *Maclean's,* June 28, 1976.

Demarest, Michael, "Smoking: Fighting Fire With Ire," *Time,* Jan. 12, 1976.

Fallows, James, "The Cigarette Scandal," *The Washington Monthly,* February 1976.

"Giving Up Smoking: How the Various Programs Work," *Medical World News,* Nov. 1, 1976.

Gori, Gio B., "Low-Risk Cigarettes: A Prescription," *Science,* Dec. 17, 1976.

Hay, D.R., "Smokers—A Gloomy Prospect for the Neglected Addicts," *Modern Medicine,* Nov. 15, 1976.

"Less Tar, Less Nicotine: Is That Good?" *Consumer Reports,* May 1976.

"New Medium For The Message," *Consumer Reports,* May 1976.

"No Smoking—Some States Mean It," *U.S. News & World Report,* Oct. 20, 1975.

Rosenbaum, Ruth, "Skirmish Over Smokers' Rights," *New Times,* Dec. 10, 1976.

The Tobacco Observer, selected issues.

Reports and Studies

Action on Smoking and Health, "Digest of Non-smokers' Rights Legislation," Nov. 3, 1976.

American Cancer Society, "Report to the Board of Directors from the Task Force on Tobacco and Cancer," 1976.

Hammond, E. Cuyler, "Some Recent Findings Concerning Cigarette Smoking," American Cancer Society, September 1976.

Editorial Research Reports, "Advertising in A Consumer Society," 1969 Vol. I, p. 371; "Regulation of the Cigarette Industry," 1967 Vol. II, p. 863; "Smoking and Health," 1962 Vol. II, p. 813.

R.J. Reynolds Co., "The Facts About Public Smoking," 1976.

Tobacco Institute, "Smoking and Non-Smokers: What Is The Issue?" July 1973.

U.S. Public Health Service, "Adult Use of Tobacco, 1975," June 1976.

—"State Legislation on Smoking and Health, 1975," December 1975.

—"The Health Consequences of Smoking, 1975," June 1975.

REAPPRAISAL OF PRISON POLICY

by

Suzanne de Lesseps

page

Mar. 12
1976

Editor's Note: The Criminal Code Reform Act, discussed on p. 70, was approved by the Senate on Jan. 30, 1978. The bill established fixed rather than indeterminate prison terms, virtually eliminating parole and time off for good behavior from the sentencing process. For a discussion of House action this year on criminal code reform see the editor's note preceding "Crime Reduction: Reality or Illusion."

The trend toward rising crime rates, discussed on p. 73, was reversed starting in 1976. Updated crime statistics are contained in the report on "Crime Reduction."

On the question of prisoners' legal rights, discussed on p. 78, the U.S. Supreme Court ruled April 27, 1977, that prisoners have a constitutional right of access to the courts, and states are required to furnish prisoners with law libraries or alternative sources of legal knowledge in order to protect this right *(Bounds v. Smith).* In another case *(Jones v. North Carolina Prisoners' Labor Union Inc.),* the Supreme Court ruled June 23, 1977, that the First Amendment does not preclude state prison officials from forbidding inmates who are members of prisoners' labor union to solicit other inmates to join or to otherwise take an active part in the operation of the union.

According to the annual *Corrections Magazine* survey of prisons populations, the number of individuals in state and federal prisons increased by 5 per cent during 1977. In numerical terms, the increase was from 281,439 on Jan. 1, 1977, to 294,896 on Jan. 1, 1978.

REAPPRAISAL OF PRISON POLICY

GOVERNMENT officials across the country are currently reevaluating the purpose of the prison. Many of the basic assumptions about prisoner rehabilitation are being questioned. After extensive interviews with leading opinion makers in the field of criminal justice, *Corrections Magazine,* a journal of prison affairs supported by the American Bar Association, has reported that substantial agreement exists on several points:

> There is little or no evidence that correctional "treatment" programs work.
>
> The gradual restructuring of the American correctional system over the last 50 years around the notion of individualized and enforced treatment for all offenders was a mistake.
>
> A radically new approach is needed that will provide both better protection for the public and incorporate a more realistic view of what can and cannot be done to reduce recidivism.[1]

It is often said that the primary purposes for sentencing a criminal to prison are retribution, rehabilitation and deterrence. Before the 19th century, society placed greater emphasis on the first and last goals. Then came successive waves of penal reform that stressed reforming the offender rather than punishing him. The philosophy behind prison corrections became "let the sentence fit the individual" instead of "let the sentence fit the crime." Now, there appears to be a movement back in the other direction.

One of the reasons for the swing toward retribution is the growing body of opinion that rehabilitation has failed to reform criminals and reduce crime. The nation's prison populations are currently at an all-time high, and states are grappling with the problem of how to ease dangerous overcrowding. "The correctional institutions of the United States are on the threshold of a population explosion," U.S. Bureau of Prisons Director Norman A. Carlson said last fall. "The most important reason why the number of inmates is rising is that crime itself is on the increase."[2]

---

[1] Michael S. Serrill, "Is Rehabilitation Dead?" *Corrections Magazine,* May-June, 1975, p. 29.

[2] Speech delivered Oct. 28, 1975, to the Kiwanis Club in Birmingham, Ala.

One prison official who believes that rehabilitation has been ineffective is Allen Ault of the Georgia state prison system. "Rehabilitation, as currently applied, is a myth," he has said. "The responsibility to rehabilitate is placed on the state rather than the offender. We have assumed that all offenders are 'sick' and we have tried to force treatment on them. This has not worked...."[3] Those who believe that efforts to rehabilitate criminals have been futile, have found support in a study by sociologist Robert Martinson of the City University of New York. After examining the results of 231 rehabilitation programs conducted around the country from 1945 to 1967, Martinson concluded: "With few and isolated exceptions, the rehabilitative efforts that have been supported so far have had no appreciable effect on recidivism."[4]

Support for Punitive Theory of Criminal Justice

James Q. Wilson in his well-publicized book *Thinking About Crime* has argued against the standard liberal notion that society should fight crime by getting at its root causes—poverty, unemployment, poor family relationships, and so forth. He said society should concentrate on more practical ways of reducing the crime rate. Government, he suggested, should accept the idea that the main purpose of prisons is not to rehabilitate but rather to isolate and punish. "It is a measure of our confusion," he wrote, "that such a statement will strike many enlightened readers today as cruel, even barbaric. It is not. It is merely a recognition that society at a minimum must be able to protect itself from dangerous offenders and to impose some costs...on criminal acts; it is also a frank admission that society really does not know how to do much else."[5] Wilson wants probation abolished so that anyone convicted of committing a serious crime would have to spend some time in prison. He contends that the certainty of prison would deter many would-be offenders.

Several studies support this thesis. According to Gordon Tullock, a crime-research analyst at Virginia Polytechnic Institute: "There is no question any longer. Economists in the U.S., Canada and England have shown conclusively that punishment does cut down on crime."[6] One of the most comprehensive studies was done by economist Isaac Ehrlich of the University of Chicago. He calculated the effect of imprisonment and length of imprisonment on the rates of seven major types of crimes in 1940, 1950, and 1960. Ehrlich concluded that the prospect of go-

---

[3] Quoted in *The Atlanta Constitution*, Oct. 28, 1975.
[4] Robert Martinson, "What Works?—Questions and Answers About Prison Reform," *The Public Interest*, spring 1974, p. 23.
[5] James Q. Wilson, *Thinking About Crime* (1975), pp. 172-173.
[6] Quoted in *Business Week*, Sept. 15, 1975, p. 92.

ing to prison and longer sentences both reduced crime.[7] Ehrlich, in a separate study, has also indicated that capital punishment serves as a deterrent against murder.[8]

Surprisingly, support for stricter methods of sentencing is also coming from the prisoners themselves. "Criminals should be punished," said Willie Holder, a former convict who heads the "Prisoners' Union," a San Francisco-based organization representing prisoner interests. "Society ought to admit that punishment is a form of retribution and not pretend that prisons are for any other purpose. I've heard many prisoners say they'd rather be beat in the head with a shovel than have their brain constantly examined like they do."[9] Holder has supported voluntary rehabilitation programs and the abolition of probation, parole and indeterminate sentencing. It is ironic that parole and indeterminate sentencing were two of the most important practices arising from 19th-century prison reform.

Dissatisfaction With the Indeterminate Sentence

The reformers advanced the belief that sentences should not be fixed when the offenders entered prison but should be based on how well they "progressed" while in confinement. Gradually, most states adopted the concept of "indeterminate sentencing." This is a general term used to describe a system in which an offender's specific term of imprisonment is left to the discretion of administrative authorities, based on the offender's behavior and performance in prison. The basic philosophy behind the indeterminate sentence is that no two prisoners are alike, and some may take more time to achieve rehabilitation than others.

Indeterminate sentencing became the watchword of prison reformers. As late as 1970, Ramsey Clark, the former Attorney General, wrote: "If rehabilitation is the goal, only the indeterminate sentence will be used.... The sentence contemplates a rehabilitation program specifically designed for each individual convicted. Professionally trained correctional authorities can then carefully observe a prisoner and release him at the earliest time within the limits fixed...."[10] Today, however, the concept of indeterminate sentencing has fallen out of favor with many leading criminologists. They assert that it (1) results in longer sentences than most judges would give, (2) gives correctional officials too much control over a prisoner's life, (3) permits disparity in sentencing, and (4) is psychologically damaging to the prisoners because they can never be sure when they will be released.

---

[7] See "The Deterrent Effect of Criminal Law Enforcement," *Journal of Legal Studies*, Vol. I, 1972.

[8] "The Deterrent Effect of Capital Punishment: A Question of Life and Death," *The American Economic Review*, June 1975.

[9] Quoted by Leroy Aarons, *The Washington Post*, Aug. 17, 1975.

[10] Ramsey Clark, *Crime in America* (1970), p. 222.

Some criminologists also argue that indeterminate sentencing weakens the effect of rehabilitation programs. They say many prisoners volunteer only to improve their chances of being paroled. The prisoners, in effect, are forced to play games with the system. The author Jessica Mitford quoted a convict as saying: "From the vindictive guard who sets out to build a record against some individual to the parole board, the indeterminate sentence grants corrections the power to play God with the lives of prisoners."[11] According to federal Judge Marvin E. Frankel, "indeterminate sentencing, as thus far employed and justified, has produced more cruelty and injustice than the benefits its supporters envisage."[12]

The concept of equal punishment imposed by inflexible sentences has already received support from the Ford administration. In his message to Congress on crime, June 19, 1975, President Ford said: "I propose that incarceration be made mandatory for (1) offenders who commit offenses under federal jurisdiction using a dangerous weapon; (2) persons committing such extraordinarily serious crimes as aircraft hijacking, kidnapping, and trafficking in hard drugs; and (3) repeat offenders who commit federal crimes—with or without a weapon—that cause or have a potential to cause personal injury." He went on to say, "There should be no doubt in the minds of those who commit violent crimes...that they will be sent to prison if convicted...."

In a speech to Wisconsin correctional officials in Milwaukee on Feb. 2, 1976, Attorney General Edward H. Levi proposed that the federal parole system be abolished and the sentencing power of federal judges be reduced. In addition, Levi suggested the creation of a permanent federal commission to set sentencing guidelines for judges in cases not covered by Ford's proposals. "If a judge decided to impose a sentence inconsistent with the guidelines," Levi said, "he would have to accompany the decision with specific reasons for the exception, and the decision would be subject to appellate review." In November 1975, Sen. Edward M. Kennedy (D Mass.) introduced a bill to create a federal sentencing commission. The Kennedy bill is expected to be incorporated in an omnibus Senate bill (S 1) to reform and revise the federal criminal code. S 1 is being considered by the Senate Judiciary Committee.

Problems Caused by Overcrowding of Facilities

Ironically, the "get tough" policy of the Ford administration has come at a time when prison officials around the country are being forced to release minor offenders because of overcrowd-

[11] Jessica Mitford, *Kind and Usual Punishment* (1970), p. 83.
[12] Marvin E. Frankel, *Criminal Sentences* (1972), p. 88.

American Prison Population

State	Number of Inmates Jan. 1, 1975	Jan. 1, 1976	Per Cent Change
Alabama	4,260	4,420	4
Alaska	322	349	9
Arizona	2,072	2,534	22
Arkansas	2,007	2,338	17
California	24,780	20,007	–20
Colorado	1,968	2,104	7
Connecticut	2,805	3,060	9
Delaware	555	701	27
District of Columbia	1,321	1,538	16
Florida	11,420	15,709	38
Georgia	9,772	11,067	13
Hawaii	310	366	18
Idaho	536	593	11
Illinois	6,672	8,110	22
Indiana	4,360	4,392	1
Iowa	1,520	1,857	22
Kansas	1,421	1,696	19
Kentucky	2,958	3,257	10
Louisiana	4,759	4,774	0.3
Maine	527	643	22
Maryland	6,128	6,606	8
Massachusetts	2,047	2,278	11
Michigan	8,702	10,882	25
Minnesota	1,370	1,724	26
Mississippi	2,117	2,429	15
Missouri	3,754	4,150	11
Montana	344	377	10
Nebraska	1,254	1,259	0.4
Nevada	854	893	5
New Hampshire	285	302	6
New Jersey	4,824	5,277	9
New Mexico	979	1,118	14
New York	14,387	16,056	12
North Carolina	11,997	12,486	4
North Dakota	173	205	19
Ohio	9,326	11,451	23
Oklahoma	2,867	3,435	20
Oregon	2,001	2,442	22
Pennsylvania	6,768	7,054	4
Rhode Island	550	594	8
South Carolina	4,422	6,100	38
South Dakota	277	372	34
Tennessee	3,779	4,569	21
Texas	16,833	18,934	12
Utah	575	696	21
Vermont	387	393	2
Virginia	5,635	6,092	8
Washington	2,698	3,063	14
West Virginia	940	1,213	29
Wisconsin	2,591	3,055	18
Wyoming	222	384	73
States and D.C.	203,431	225,404	
U.S. Bureau of Prisons	22,361	24,134	8
Total	**225,792**	**249,538**	**11***

* Average state and federal

SOURCE: *Corrections Magazine*

Parole and Probation Defined

Parole and probation are probably two of the best known but least understood concepts in the correctional system. *Parole* is the release of a prisoner to serve the remainder of his sentence in the community, under certain restrictions and requirements. *Probation* is a substitute for prison custody. A person granted probation does not have to serve any part of his sentence, but is returned to the community immediately after conviction.

Although the same agency usually supervises both parolees and probationers, the two processes have different origins. Parole is the administrative act of an executive agency, while probation is a function of the courts.

ing. In October 1975, the Georgia Board of Pardons ordered the immediate release of 427 prisoners convicted of simple theft or burglary and moved up the release dates of over 4,000. Georgia prisons have been so crowded that some inmates have had to sleep on mattresses on the floor. In South Carolina, another state suffering from prisoner overpopulation, officials have had to make greater use of early parole for young offenders. And in North Carolina, the legislature has acted to ease overcrowding by allowing the early release of prisoners serving less than a one-year sentence.

The worst crowding problems have occurred in southern states. Arkansas has had to house prisoners in house trailers. Virginia plans to convert a warehouse into a prison facility, and South Carolina is considering the use of abandoned schools and factories. For a while, Louisiana corrections officials thought of buying a mothballed Navy ship to house inmates. However, according to Richard Crane, an attorney for the Louisiana Department of Corrections, the state has abandoned the idea. Instead, state officials are planning to renovate a mental hospital and construct two new prisons. The new prisons are scheduled to be completed in about one year.

Several court rulings in the South have focused attention on the seriousness of prison overcrowding. In May 1975, Judge Charles R. Scott of the U.S. District Court in Jacksonville, Fla., ordered Florida officials to reduce the state's prison population to normal levels within one year. In 1965, Florida's prison population was less than 7,000. By December 1975 it had reached almost 16,000. Prisoners have been housed in tents and converted warehouses. "A free domocratic society cannot cage inmates like animals or stack them like chattels in a warehouse and expect them to emerge as decent, law-abiding, contributing members of the community," Scott said. Louisiana and Mississippi are also under federal court order to relieve overcrowding and improve prison living conditions.

On Jan. 13, 1976, U.S. District Judge Frank M. Johnson Jr. declared Alabama's state prison system "barbaric and inhumane" and ordered state officials to implement 44 major changes. These included giving every prisoner at least 60 square feet of living space and "three wholesome and nutritious meals per day." Alabama Gov. George C. Wallace said the state would appeal the federal ruling. The governor indicated that $50 million to $100 million would be necessary to implement the order, and that the state legislature would probably have to increase taxes. "Federal judges are very good about telling you how to spend money, but they don't tell you how to raise the money," Wallace said. The governor also accused the federal government of trying to create a "resort like" atmosphere in the Alabama prison system—a charge Judge Johnson denied.

Similar court orders have been issued to city officials in charge of municipal jails. In Washington, D.C., U.S. District Court Judge William B. Bryant has repeatedly urged authorities to ease overcrowding at the 100-year-old District of Columbia Jail, where teams of inspectors have found over 1,000 housing violations. In November 1975, Judge Bryant ordered the appointment of a compliance officer to implement a reduction in the inmate population and upgrade the physical facilities. In New York City, a series of rulings by U.S. District Court Judge Morris E. Lasker led to the closing of the Manhattan House of Detention, popularly known as the Tombs, in December 1974. On Jan. 6, 1976, Judge Lasker ordered an end to the practice of confining two inmates in one-man cells for more than 30 days at the House of Detention for Men on Rikers Island. In November 1975, the prisoners at Rikers Island had staged a 17-hour riot in protest of living conditions there.

Rise in Crime and the Demand for Punishment

Carlson, the U.S. Bureau of Prisons director, said in his Birmingham speech, that until recently, penal experts had expected the prison population decline of the late 1960s and early 1970s to continue. But, he said, the prison population is climbing and is expected to go even higher in the immediate future. The nation's leading barometer of serious crime, the Crime Index[13] compiled by the Federal Bureau of Investigation from local police reports, rose 38 per cent from 1969 through 1974. The trend continued upward during the first nine months of 1975, the latest period for which crime statistics have been compiled. Crime was 11 per cent higher than in the same nine months a year earlier.

According to a recent survey by *Corrections Magazine*, the

[13] The index takes into account what the FBI considers "serious" crimes—murder, rape, robbery, aggravated assault, burglary, larceny, and motor vehicle theft.

combined population of state and federal prisons reached a record high of 249,538 at the beginning of 1976, an 11 per cent increase over a year earlier *(see table, page 195).* The only state that did not report an increase was California. Its decrease was caused by new, more liberal parole guidelines. The magazine attributed the overall increase in prison population to public demand for harsher sentencing. Commenting on the survey, Lloyd Ohlin, professor of criminology at Harvard Law School, said that "what we're seeing is a massive counterattack" against programs, like probation, that allow offenders to remain in the community. "The climate has shifted in favor of punishment," he added.

In an article written for the *American Journal of Correction,* John J. Flanagan, professor in the School of Social Work at the University of Wisconsin, listed several reasons why he thought the prison population would continue to increase. They included hardening public attitudes and rising crime caused by unemployment and inflation. Flanagan also noted that the number of persons in the 20 to 30 age bracket, which includes a disproportionately high share of criminal offenders, is expected to peak in 1985.[14]

Changing Philosophy of Corrections

HISTORICALLY, the idea of imprisonment as a form of punishment is fairly new. Before the 19th century, floggings, brandings and executions were much more common than incarceration. In early Roman law, imprisonment as a form of punishment was forbidden. The Roman jurist Ulpian wrote: "Prison ought to be used for detention only, but not for punishment." During the Middle Ages, this legal principle was accepted throughout Europe, although it was violated in some instances. By the late 16th century, governments began placing juveniles, beggars and vagabonds in workhouses and houses of correction.

The word "penitentiary" is derived from the word "penitent" and reflects the 18th century notion that solitary confinement, rather than corporal punishment, would cure offenders of their criminal tendencies. The enlightened reformers professed the belief that mankind possessed the ability to change for the better and could be reformed through religious meditation. The

[14] "Imminent Crisis in Prison Populations," *American Journal of Correction,* November-December 1975, p. 20.

tenets of this philosophy were outlined in America in 1787 when Dr. Benjamin Rush delivered a paper on the modern prison system to a small group gathered in the Philadelphia home of Benjamin Franklin.

Rush proposed: (1) that prisoners be classified according to housing assignments and treatment plans, (2) that the prison be supported by inmate labor, and (3) that prisoners be confined for an indeterminate period and released upon showing evidence of their progress toward rehabilitation.[15] In 1790, the Philadelphia Society for Alleviating the Miseries of Public Prisons, now known as the Pennsylvania Prison Society, was instrumental in obtaining passage of state legislation to reorganize the Walnut Street Jail in Philadelphia on the basis of hard labor and isolation. The Walnut Street Jail became the first penitentiary in the United States.

> *"...The degree of civilization in a society can be judged by entering its prisons."*
>
> —Dostoyevsky, 1862.

The principle of solitary confinement was emphasized even more strongly by the creators of the Eastern State Penitentiary which opened on Cherry Hill in Philadelphia in 1829. Here, prisoners were detained in small cells and completely isolated except for an occasional visit. Prisoners were allowed to work in their cells on weaving, carpentry, shoemaking or other crafts.

In New York, state officials formulated a different philosophy of prison management, and allowed the prisoners to work with each other during the daytime. Under this Auburn system—named for the prison where it went into effect—the inmates were still required to remain silent at all times. The Boston Prison Discipline Society endorsed the Auburn Prison system by noting, "The unremitted industry, the entire subordination and subdued feeling of the convicts, has probably no parallel among any equal number of criminals." The report continued: "In their solitary cells, they spend the night, with no other book but the Bible; and at sunrise they proceed in military order, under the eye of turnkeys, in solid columns, with the lock

---

[15] Alan M. Dershowitz, "Criminal Sentencing in the United States: An Historical and Conceptual Overview," *The Annals*, January 1976, p. 125.

march, to their workshops; thence in the same order, at the hour of breakfast, to the common hall...."[16] Although the Pennsylvania and Auburn systems of prison management ultimately failed because of high operational costs and a high rate of insanity among the prisoners, both systems had wide influence.

Emergence of Modern Concept of Rehabilitation

One of the earliest forerunners of the modern parole system was developed at Norfolk Island, an English penal colony off the east coast of Australia, between 1840 and 1844. This "mark" system emphasized training and study rather than solitude. Prisoners worked toward their release by earning marks or credits through good behavior and hard work. The system was refined later in the 1800s by Sir Walter Crofton, director of prisons in Ireland. Irish prisoners served the first part of their sentence in isolation and then were given the opportunity to work with other prisoners. Six months before their scheduled release, inmates spent time in smaller institutions with unarmed guards and were given more freedom and responsibility. A prisoner who misbehaved during this period could be sent back to confinement. The Irish system was imitated in many ways by the reformatories that emerged in the United States during the late 19th century for juveniles and first offenders.

One of the leaders of this reformatory movement was Zebulon Brockway, superintendent of the Elmira Reformatory in New York and a staunch advocate of the indeterminate sentence. In an address to the first Congress of the National Prison Association[17] in 1870, titled "The Ideal of a True Prison System," Brockway rejected the punitive purposes of prisons in favor of reformation and rehabilitation. If prisons were to concentrate on these goals, he said, society would be better protected from crime. In accordance with his thinking, the congress adopted a Declaration of Principles calling for a variety of reforms. Reformatory "cures" were to be tailored to the individual criminal, who was not to be released until rehabilitated.

A year earlier, in 1869, Brockway had succeeded in persuading Michigan to enact the nation's first indeterminate sentencing law, although it applied only to prostitutes. New York followed in 1877 with a broader law, and by 1922 a total of 37 states had adopted indeterminate sentencing. The rehabilitative ideal, as expressed by the 1870 congress, formed the basis of prison management in the 20th century until now. Training and education for employment, not penitence in solitary confinement, were to be the means of reform. Whereas

---

[16] Quoted by Kenneth Lamott, "Is Prison Obsolete?" *Horizon*, summer 1975, p. 44.
[17] Now the American Correctional Association.

before, criminals were viewed as evil sinners who chose a life of crime of their own free will, after 1870 they came to be seen as individuals lacking certain qualities, opportunities and advantages.

Gradually, prisons began to develop what is now often referred to as the "medical model." Crime became associated with disease and inmates were viewed as patients. Psychiatrists, psychologists and social workers were added to prison staffs. Prison administrators began to use medical terminology, implying that criminals could be cured with the proper diagnosis and treatment. Criminologists Norval Morris and James Jacobs have written:

> The search for a "cure" for the criminal has sometimes even taken us beyond the bounds of civilized treatment. Drugs, electroshock therapy, sterilization, and even psychosurgery have all been used to "reform" the prisoner's behavior. What little evidence there is has shown that behavior is seldom changed for the better and that the prisoner's hostility and aggression are often increased when subjected to such treatments. In addition, such techniques have often been misused for purposes of punishment in order to reinforce prison rules, rather than for genuine rehabilitative purposes.[18]

Inmate Protests in Past Decade; Attica Uprising

In the 1960s and early 1970s, the rehabilitative approach to criminal corrections began to show obvious signs of breaking down; riots in protest of prison life erupted across the country.[19] The most famous occurred at the Attica (N.Y.) Correctional Facility on Sept. 9, 1971, when about 1,200 out of 2,245 prisoners overwhelmed 39 guards and held them as hostages. The rebelling inmates demanded 28 specific reforms of prison conditions, all of which the correction commissioner agreed to seek or implement. But the negotiations bogged down on three demands. They were the ouster of the warden, a guarantee of legal amnesty for the rebellious inmates and their free passage to a "non-imperialistic" country.

The negotiations reached an impasse on these points Sept. 12, and those involved in the talks, warning that bloodshed was likely, urged Gov. Nelson A. Rockefeller to come to the scene. The governor refused, saying his appearance at the prison would do no good. Early the next morning, an assault force of 200 state troopers with helicopter support and National Guardsmen in reserve, stormed the facility and quelled the rebellion.

This action brought death, either immediately or later, to 43 persons. It was the highest death toll in an American prison riot

[18] Public Affairs Committee, "Proposals for Prison Reform," Public Affairs Pamphlet No. 510, 1974, p. 13. The Public Affairs Committee is a non-profit educational organization.

[19] See "Racial Tensions in Prisons," *E.R.R.*, 1971 Vol. II, pp. 801-820.

since 1930, when 317 inmates who were locked in their cells at the Ohio State Penitentiary perished in a fire set by other rioting inmates. The Ohio State Penitentiary was again the scene of disorder in 1968. Five convicts were shot to death there when 500 National Guardsmen and policemen charged the prison to quell a riot by 500 prisoners.

One result of the prison riots during this period was that prison officials began to pay more attention to the importance of individual prisoner rights. Pennsylvania, for example, in 1971 issued a "bill of rights" for prisoners, insuring their right to be treated with fairness and dignity. Patterned after the Standard Minimum Rules for the Treatment of Prisoners adopted by the United Nations in 1955, the administrative directive provided for the separation of tried and untried prisoners, and the prohibition of corporal punishment.

Judicial Expansion of Prisoners' Legal Rights

The idea that prisoners have rights has found legal expression only in recent years. A Virginia court ruled in 1871 that a prisoner was a "slave of the state" who "not only forfeited his liberty, but all his personal rights except those which the law in its humanity accords to him." As late as 1948, the Supreme Court held that "lawful incarceration brings about the necessary withdrawal or limitation of many privileges and rights, a reaction justified by the considerations underlying our penal system."[20]

In contrast, the Supreme Court during its 1971-72 term ruled that (1) formal proceedings must be followed in revoking parole, (2) inmates are entitled to be given legal materials, (3) prison administrators must provide inmates with opportunities for religious worship, and (4) a person who is not mentally competent to stand trial for a criminal offense cannot be confined indefinitely. In 1974 the Court ruled that although a prisoner's rights "may be diminished by the needs and exigencies of the institutional environment, [he] is not wholly stripped of constitutional protections.... There is no iron curtain drawn between the Constitution and the prisons of this country."[21]

The National Advisory Commission on Criminal Justice Standards and Goals reported in 1973 that most judicial action expanding the rights of prisoners has come in the lower courts, particularly in federal district courts. "[I]t is in these courts that the 'hands off' doctrine has been either modified or abandoned altogether."[22] Several prisons have been held in violation of the

---

[20] *Price v. Johnston* (1948), 334 U.S. 266.

[21] *Wolff v. McDonnell* (1974), 418 U.S. 539.

[22] *Corrections*, National Advisory Commission on Criminal Justice Standards and Goals, Jan. 23, 1973, p. 19.

Major Prison Disturbances in the 1970s

Site	Date	Action
Soledad Prison (Salinas, Calif.)	Jan. 13, 1970	3 black convicts shot to death in racial fight between prisoners; white guard killed Jan. 16
Essex County Jail (Newark, N.J.)	April 27, 1970	200 inmates riot to protest prison conditions; about 90 rioted again on Nov. 27, 1970
Holmesburg Prison (Philadelphia)	July 4, 1970	29 guards and 84 inmates injured in riot with racial overtones
Tombs (New York City)	Oct. 2-5, 1970	Prisoners hold 26 hostages to protest overcrowding
Cummins Prison Farm (Grady, Ark.)	Nov. 20-22, 1970	Some 500 inmates riot, demanding separate quarters for black and white prisoners
San Quentin (near San Rafael, Calif.)	Aug. 21, 1971	6 persons, including black militant George Jackson and 3 guards, killed in alleged escape attempt
Attica Correctional Facility (Attica, N.Y.)	Sept. 9-13, 1971	43 persons, including 11 prison employees, killed in riot over prison conditions
Rahway State Prison (Woodbridge, N.J.)	Nov. 24-25, 1971	Inmates take six hostages in rebellion over prison conditions

Eighth Amendment ban on "cruel and unusual punishment," as were the overcrowded prisons in Alabama. In December 1975, for example, U.S. District Court Judge Alfonso J. Zirpoli ruled in San Francisco that the conditions and practices in San Quentin Prison's maximum security adjustment section amounted to cruel and unusual punishment.

Zirpoli ordered that the use of tear gas and neck chains be stopped unless the prisoner presented a "clear and immediate danger" of escaping or inflicting bodily harm. The judge also ordered that the outdoor exercise periods for the inmates be expanded. The federal ruling came as the result of a civil suit filed by six San Quentin inmates accused of murdering three guards and two inmates in the 1971 escape attempt at San Quentin in which black militant George Jackson was killed.

Critical Issues Facing Penologists

THE ACTIVE interest and involvement of prisoners in inmates-rights issues is a notable development. Today, prisoners are alerting the public to prison conditions through newspaper stories, books and lawsuits. One of the most revolutionary concepts to emerge is that of a prisoners' union. According to C. Ronald Huff, a social scientist at the University of California at Irvine, the most extensive union type of activity inside a prison was the "Ohio Prisoners' Labor Union." At its peak in 1973 and 1974, the union has since ceased to exist. Huff said this was partly because of conflicts between staff members outside the prison and union members inside.

The California Department of Corrections refused in early 1976 to let inmates organize "Inmate Representing Organizations," staffed by persons outside of prisons who would help prisoners prepare complaints and legal papers. The California Correctional Officers Association, an organization of prison guards, warned that they might strike if the plan was approved. California corrections officials had spent several months discussing the idea of an inmates union with "Prisoners' Union," the San Francisco organization which claims to represent approximately 20,000 convicts and ex-convicts around the country. Staff members perform a lobbying service for inmates by testifying on criminal legislative matters and acting as spokesmen for prisoners' rights. The organization supports three major goals: (1) an end to indeterminate sentencing, (2) establishment of labor rights for working prisoners, including the right to organize and bargain collectively, and (3) recognition of civil and human rights for all prisoners.[23]

The first goal—abolition of indeterminate sentencing—appears to be one on which most penologists agree. "The era of the indeterminate sentence...is quickly drawing to a close," wrote Alan M. Dershowitz, professor at Harvard Law School, in January 1976. "Reaction is beginning to set in."[24] Dershowitz served on the Committee for the Study of Incarceration, composed of liberal lawyers, scholars and social scientists, and funded by the Field Foundation and the New World Foundation.

After four years of study, the committee concluded that rehabilitation was no longer a realistic goal of sentencing. In its

[23] John Irwin and Willie Holder, "History of the Prisoners' Union," *The Outlaw: Journal of the Prisoners' Union*, January-February, 1973, p. 1. Reprinted by C. Ronald Huff, "The Prisoners' Union: A Challenge for State Corrections," *State Government*, summer 1975, p. 147.

[24] Dershowitz, *op. cit*, p. 130.

Arkansas Prison Scandal

One of the nation's most disturbing prison scandals erupted in January 1968 when three human skeletons buried in crude coffins were unearthed at the Cummins Prison in Arkansas. A prison inmate, Reuben Johnson, identified one of the skeletons as that of Jake Jackson, a prisoner who had been listed in prison records as a 1946 escapee. Johnson told news reporters that he had helped bury Jackson and that he had witnessed the murders of 12 prisoners during his term at Cummins. Other Cummins inmates also reported they had witnessed beatings and killings.

A few weeks before the three bodies were discovered, Arkansas Gov. Winthrop Rockefeller had appointed Thomas O. Murton, a professor of criminology, state prison superintendent with instructions to reform the Arkansas penitentiaries. Murton publicly reported that political corruption existed in the state prison system, and that whips and an electrical torture device had been used to subjugate prisoners. Following the discovery of the skeletons, the governor dismissed the new superintendent and charged him with staging a publicity stunt.

A federal grand jury in 1969 indicted 15 former Arkansas prison officials on charges of torturing inmates. The former superintendent of the state's Tucker Intermediate Reformatory, Jim Bruton, was acquitted on eight counts of brutality but in 1970 pleaded no contest to the charge that he tortured inmates with electrical shocks. That same year, a federal district court in Arkansas declared that conditions in the state's penitentiary system were "so bad as to be shocking to the conscience of reasonably civilized people."

final report, published in February 1976 under the title *Doing Justice,* the committee recommended that instead of sentencing an offender according to his need for treatment, he should be sentenced according to the severity of his crime. The parole system would be abolished and the offender would be required to serve the full sentence. In this respect, the committee's plan echoes President Ford's proposal for mandatory sentencing in his 1975 message to Congress on crime.

The committee proposed that only those who commit serious crimes be sent to prison, and then only a few for more than three years. Most first offenders and petty thieves would be let go with only a warning from the judge. "We do not have inflated hopes about working wonders on the crime rate," said Charles Goodell, the chairman, a former member of Congress from New York. "If we're lucky, we may succeed in a modest reduction, but the main advantage of our proposals is that they produce a fairer system of punishment." Goodell said he believed that increasing the certainty of punishment is a greater deterrent to crime than increasing the severity.[25]

[25] Interview with Philip Nobile, *Midwest,* Chicago *Sun-Times* magazine, Jan. 11, 1976.

Not everyone in government or corrections work has given up on the idea of prisoner rehabilitation. The Task Force Committee on Correctional Problems, composed of prison officials from southern states, reported to the Southern Governors' Conference on Jan. 23, 1976:

> We acknowledge that the advocates of a "correctional," as contrasted with a "punitive," approach to offenders, often have oversold the case in the past; but we continue to be firmly of the conviction that the essential validity of a rehabilitative approach remains applicable.

In a survey of 84 of the nation's top correctional administrators, conducted by *Corrections Magazine*, 63 per cent of those responding said that some rehabilitation programs do have a positive effect on inmate behavior. Seventy-two per cent were opposed to eliminating indeterminate sentences.

It is generally agreed that correctional programs achieve their immediate objective; that is, they do teach illiterate inmates how to read and write, and they do turn out competent mechanics, welders, plumbers, electricians and other skilled workers. According to tests given to inmates after they underwent counseling and therapy, some offenders showed less hostility and more constructive attitudes. None of this has been disputed. The controversy is whether rehabilitation programs reduce recidivism.

Several corrections administrators have criticized Robert Martinson's conclusion *(see p. 192)* that rehabilitation has not reduced the rate at which released offenders return to criminal activity. They point out, for example, that his study includes only those programs conducted before 1967—before many rehabilitation projects were properly staffed and administered. They have noted that the Law Enforcement Assistance Administration, a federal agency that allocates money for rehabilitatiion programs of law enforcement and criminal justice, was not created until 1968. Martinson has acknowledged that his information was limited.

Testing of Revised Ideas in New Federal Prison

Regardless of whether rehabilitation reduces recidivism, most penal experts agree that correction officials should abandon the idea that prisoners are sick individuals who can be cured with proper treatment. Norman A. Carlson, the federal prisons director, has written: "Corrections remains primarily an art and only partially a science. Consequently, we cannot prescribe with precision the treatment, and it is painfully obvious that we cannot guarantee a cure."[26]

[26] "The Federal Prison System: Forty-five Years of Change," *Federal Probation*, June 1975.

David Fogel, director of the Illinois Law Enforcement Commission, argues in his book *We Are the Living Proof* that release dates should not be contingent upon behavior in prison. He recommends short, fixed sentences and elimination of parole boards. And he stresses that the participation of prisoners in rehabilitation programs be placed on a voluntary basis. Another criminologist who contends that "choice" should be an integral part of prisoner rehabilitation is Norval Morris of the University of Chicago. Morris believes that the "medical model" should be discarded for two reasons: (1) how a criminal behaves while in prison is not indicative of how he will behave if released to the community, and (2) psychological change cannot be coerced. On May 14, 1976, the U.S. Bureau of Prisons is scheduled to dedicate a new correctional institution at Butner, N.C., that will be administered along the lines prescribed by Morris in his book *The Future of Imprisonment.*

Once at Butner, inmates will be allowed to choose which, if any, psychological treatment projects they want to participate in. All prisoners will be required to work, but they will be given the freedom to choose what they do and when they will do it. Training programs will include optical lens grinding, television production and even police science. To eliminate any uncertainty over release dates, Butner inmates will have definite parole dates set in advance. The new federal prison, with its white concrete buildings, has the look of a modern college *(see above)*. It is divided into seven single-story living units, each housing 50 inmates. There will be no bars on the windows. In fact, prisoners will have keys to their private rooms.

The U.S. Bureau of Prisons is optimistic about the new approach and hopes it can be adopted elsewhere. At the same time, prison officials realize there is no panacea for solving the nation's prison problem. Caught between the public's call for longer sentencing and the explosive potential of overcrowded prisons, they are still searching for answers.

Selected Bibliography

Books

Clark, Ramsey, *Crime in America*, Simon and Schuster, 1970.
Frankel, Marvin E., *Criminal Sentences*, Hill and Wang, 1972.
Mitford, Jessica, *Kind and Usual Punishment*, Alfred A. Knopf, 1973.
Morris, Norval, *The Future of Imprisonment*, The University of Chicago Press, 1974.
Wicker, Tom, *A Time To Die*, Ballantine Books, 1975.
Wilson, James Q., *Thinking About Crime*, Basic Books, 1975.

Articles

Anderson, George M., "Jails, Lockups and Houses of Detention," *America*, Jan. 10, 1976.
Conrad, John P., "The Need for Prison Reform," *Current History*, August 1971.
"Crime: A Case for More Punishment," *Business Week*, Sept. 15, 1975.
Dershowitz, Alan M., "Criminal Sentencing in the United States," *The Annals* of the American Academy of Political and Social Science, January 1976.
——"Let the Punishment Fit the Crime," *The New York Times Magazine*, Dec. 28, 1975.
Fersch, Ellsworth, "When to Punish, When to Rehabilitate," *American Bar Association Journal*, October 1975.
Flanagan, John J. "Imminent Crisis in Prison Populations," *American Journal of Correction*, November-December 1975.
Glaser, Daniel, "Achieving Better Questions: A Half Century's Progress in Correctional Research," *Federal Probation*, September 1975.
Huff, C. Ronald, "The Prisoners' Union: A Challenge for State Corrections," *State Government*, summer 1975.
Lamott, Kenneth, "Is Prison Obsolete?" *Horizon*, summer 1975.
Serrill, Michael S., "Is Rehabilitation Dead?" *Corrections Magazine*, May-June 1975.
Trial: The National Legal Newsmagazine, March 1975 entire issue.

Studies and Reports

Advisory Task Force to Study Local Jails for Virginia State Crime Commission, "Report," December 15, 1975.
Editorial Research Reports, "Racial Tensions in Prisons," 1971 Vol. II, p. 799; "Rehabilitation of Prisoners," 1965 Vol. II, p. 741.
National Advisory Commission on Criminal Justice Standards and Goals, *Corrections*, Jan. 23, 1973.
Robinson, William H., et al., "Prison Population and Costs," Congressional Research Service, Library of Congress, April 24, 1974.
United States General Accounting Office, "Department of Labor's Past and Future Role in Offender Rehabilitation," Aug. 7, 1975.

INDEX

C

D

E

J

K

L

M

N

O

P

Q, R

S

T